Raue/Specht

Act on Copyright Content Sharing Service Providers
Urheberrechts-Diensteanbieter-Gesetz (UrhDaG)

# Act on Copyright Content Sharing Service Providers

Urheberrechts-Diensteanbieter-Gesetz (UrhDaG)

Article-by-Article Commentary

by

Benjamin Raue
Louisa Specht-Riemenschneider

2024

C.H.BECK

Suggested citation:
Raue/Specht/Author, *Act on Copyright Content Sharing Service Providers*, 2024, § [#] mn. [#]

**beck.de**

ISBN 978 3 406 81236 1


Wilhelmstr. 9, 80801 München
Printed in Germany by
Beltz Grafische Betriebe GmbH
Am Fliegerhorst 8, 99947 Bad Langensalza

Typeset by
Reemers Publishing Services GmbH, Krefeld
Cover: Druckerei C.H.Beck Nördlingen

myclimate shape our future

chbeck.de/nachhaltig

# Preface

Art. 17 of the Copyright in the Digital Single Market Directive 2019/790 (DSMD) was one of the most controversial legislative projects in the history of European copyright. It was a fight between those who wanted to strengthen copyright enforcement on internet platforms and close the 'value gap' – and those who feared undue restrictions on freedom of expression and information. The result was a lengthy and complex provision: direct platform liability with an obligation to conclude licence contracts on the one hand – and safeguards for user freedoms on the other hand.

As a directive, it has to be transposed into the copyright law of the Member States. The Directive uses many unspecific concepts and therefore leaves discretion for Member States to specify the provisions. This applies in particular to the strongly contested relation between the obligation to prevent copyright infringements and the obligation to protect the users' freedoms: Which should prevail in case of conflict?

Some Member States have opted for a minimalist implementation, transposing Art. 17 DSMD (almost) word for word into their national copyright laws – and thus delegate the fine-tuning of the conflict between copyright protection and users' freedoms to the courts.

Germany has chosen the hard way and passed the 'Gesetz über die urheberrechtliche Verantwortlichkeit von Diensteanbietern für das Teilen von Online-Inhalten', short: UrhDaG, the Act on Copyright Content Sharing Service Providers, a very detailed implementation specifying nearly every aspect of the platform liability in great details, for example

- a comprehensive definition of an OCSSP with a safe harbour clause for excluded service providers (§ 2 et seq.);
- a detailed provision specifying the obligation to acquire contractual rights of use (§ 4);
- several provisions on direct remuneration of authors, performers and photographers;
- very detailed provisions balancing between the obligation to pre-emptively block copyright infringing material with the users' rights to freedom of expression and information (§§ 9–12), which more or less anticipated (and probably influenced) the CJEU's decision Poland/Parliament and Council (ECLI:EU:C:2022:297), including a section on uses presumably authorised by law;
- a redress system consisting of complaints procedures and an alternative dispute resolution mechanism (§§ 13–17);
- detailed obligations for measures against abuse (§ 18);
- information rights for rightholders and for the purpose of scientific research (§ 19).

Due to the very heterogeneous implementation of Art. 17 DSMD in the Member States, further rulings of the CJEU and Member State courts are to be expected. The detailed German implementation could serve as a reference and source of inspiration for the further specification of Art. 17 DSMD.

The commentary on each article begins with the current version of the article both in the German original and an English translation followed by a clear and uniformly structured analysis of the provision including the extensive (academic) discussion that accompanied the implementation procedure. The interplay of the UrhDaG with the German Copyright Act is addressed as well as the respective requirements of the CDSMD. The impact of the CJEU's first decision on Art. 17 DSMD (Poland/Parliament and Council) is already discussed in the relevant provisions.

## Preface

The commentary is based on our analysis of the UrhDaG in the German Copyright article-by-article Commentary Dreier/Schulze, 7th edition, which has been updated for this English edition. We like to thank our teams for their invaluable support, especially Helena Mahn, Maja Christmann und Lea Kwiatkowski (Team Raue) and Prof. Dr. Anna K. Bernzen, Michele Brutscher and Gregor-Rafael Görgen (Team Specht).

Benjamin Raue and Louisa Specht-Riemenschneider
Trier and Bonn, March 2024

# Authors

**Benjamin Raue** is a Professor of Private Law, Digital and IP Law at Trier University and Managing Director of the Digital Law Institute Trier (IRDT) with a special focus on platform regulation. He regularly publishes in copyright law and is co-editor and author of an in-depth article-by-article commentary Hofmann/Raue on the Digital Services Act as well as of the renowned German Copyright article-by-article Commentary Dreier/Schulze.

**Louisa Specht-Riemenschneider** is a Professor of Private Law, Data Economy Law, Data Protection Law, Law of Digitalisation and AI-Law. She regularly publishes in copyright law and is co-editor of several in-depth commentaries, one of which is the renowned German Copyright article-by-article Commentary Dreier/Schulze.

# Table of contents

# List of abbreviations

## I. Legislation

### European Union

| | |
|---|---|
| AVMSD | Audiovisual Media Services Directive |
| Brussels Ibis Regulation 1215/2012 | Regulation (EU) No. 1215/2012 of the European Parliament and the Council of 12 December 2012 on jurisdiction and the recognition and enforcement of judgments in civil and commercial matteres |
| CFR | Charter of Fundamental Rights of the European Union (2007/C 303/01) |
| DSMD | Directive (EU) 2019/790 of the European Parliament and of the Council of 17 April 2019 on copyright and related rights in the Digital Single Market and amending Directives 96/9/EC and 2001/29/EC |
| DSM-RL [EU] 2019/790 *or* DSM-RL | German abbreviation for Directive (EU) 2019/790 of the European Parliament and of the Council of 17 April 2019 on copyright and related rights in the Digital Single Market and amending Directives 96/9/EC and 2001/29/EC |
| E-Commerce Directive 2000/31/EC | Directive 2000/31/EC of the European Parliament and of the Council of 8 June 2000 on certain legal aspects of information society services, in particular electronic commerce, in the Internal Market (Directive on electronic commerce) |
| Enforcement Directive | Directive 2004/48/EC of the European Parliament and of the Council of 29 April 2004 on the enforcement of intellectual property rights |
| GDPR | Regulation (EU) 2016/679 of the European Parliament and of the Council of 27 April 2016 on the protection of natural persons with regard to the processing of personal data and on the free movement of such data, and repealing Directive 95/46/EC (General Data Protection Regulation) |
| InfoSoc Directive | Directive 2001/29/EC of the European Parliament and of the Council of 22 May 2001 on the harmonisation of certain aspects of copyright and related rights in the information society |
| Notification Directive 2015/1535 | Directive (EU) 2015/1535 of the European Parliament and of the Council of 9 September 2015 laying down a procedure for the provision of information in the field of technical regulations and of rules on Information Society services (codification) |
| Online-SatCab-RL [EU] 2019/789 | Directive (EU) 2019/789 of the European Parliament and of the Council of 17 April 2019 laying down rules on the exercise of copyright and related rights applicable to certain online transmissions of broadcasting organisations and retransmissions of television and radio programmes, and amending Council Directive 93/83/EEC |
| Rome I Regulation | Regulation (EC) No 593/2008 of the European Parliament and of the Council of 17 June 2008 on the law applicable to contractual obligations (Rome I) |
| Rome II Regulation | Regulation (EC) No 864/2007 of the European Parliament and of the Council of 11 July 2007 on the law applicable to non-contractual obligations (Rome II) |

# List of abbreviations

## Germany

| | | |
|---|---|---|
| BGB | Bürgerliches Gesetzbuch | Civil Code |
| GG | Grundgesetz | German Constitution |
| NetzDG | Netzwerkdurchsetzungsgesetz | Network Enforcement Act |
| TMG | Telemediengesetz | Telemedia Act |
| UKlaG | Unterlassungsklagengesetz | Act on Injunctive Relief |
| UrhDaG | Urheberrechts-Diensteanbieter-Gesetz | Act on Copyright Content Sharing Service Providers |
| UrhG | Urheberrechtsgesetz | Act on Copyright and Related Rights ('Copyright Act') |
| VGG | Verwertungsgesellschaftengesetz | Collecting Societies Act |
| VwGO | Verwaltungsgerichtsordnung | Code of Administrative Court Procedure |
| VwVfG | Verwaltungsverfahrensgesetz | Administrative Procedure Act |
| ZPO | Zivilprozessordnung | Code of Civil Procedure |

## II. Cited works

| | |
|---|---|
| BeckOGK/Author | Beck-online Großkommentar |
| BeckOK UrhR/Author | Beck Online-Kommentar Urheberrecht |
| Dreier/Schulze/Author | Dreier/Schulze (eds), Urheberrechtsgesetz: UrhG, 7th edn, 2022, C.H.Beck |
| Festschrift für M. Walter | v. Lewinski/Wittmann (eds.), Urheberrecht! – Festschrift für Michel Walter, 2018, Medien und Recht |
| Grüneberg/Author | Grüneberg (ed), Bürgerliches Gesetzbuch: BGB, 81st edn, 2022, C.H.Beck |
| Immenga/Mestmäcker/Author | Immenga/Mestmäcker (eds), Wettbewerbsrecht, Vol.3, 6th edn 2020, C.H.Beck |
| Köhler/Bornkamm/Feddersen/Author | Köhler/Bornkamm/Feddersen (eds), Gesetz gegen den unlauteren Wettbewerb: UWG, 39th edn, 2021, C.H.Beck |
| Liesching | Liesching, Netzwerkdurchsetzungsgesetz, 1st online edn, 2018, Nomos |
| Loewenheim/Meessen/Riesenkampff/Kersting/Meyer-Lindemann/Author | Loewenheim/Meessen/Riesenkampff/Kersting/Meyer-Lindemann (eds), Kartellrecht, 4th edn, 2020, C.H.Beck |
| MüKoBGB/Author | Säcker et al. (eds), Münchener Kommentar zum Bürgerlichen Gesetzbuch, C.H.Beck<br>Vol. 1: §§ 1–240 BGB, 9th edn 2021<br>Vol. 2: §§ 241–310 BGB, 9th edn 2022<br>Vol. 7: §§ 705–853 BGB, 8th edn 2020 |
| Raue Schadensberechnung | Raue, Die dreifache Schadensberechnung, 1st edn, 2017, Nomos |
| Schack UrhR/UrhebervertragsR | Schack, Urheber- und Urhebervertragsrecht, 10th edn, 2021, Mohr Siebeck |
| Schricker/Loewenheim/Author | Schricker/Loewenheim (eds), Urheberrecht, 6th edn, 2020, C.H.Beck |
| Simitis/Hornung/Spiecker gen. Döhrmann/Author | Simitis/Hornung/Spiecker gen. Döhrmann (eds), Datenschutzrecht, 1st edn, 2019, Nomos |
| Spindler/Schmitz/Author | Spindler/Schmitz (eds), Telemediengesetz, 2nd edn, 2018, C.H.Beck |

| | |
|---|---|
| Stieper Rechtfertigung ...... | Stieper, Rechtfertigung, Rechtsnatur und Disponibilität der Schranken des Urheberrechts, 1st edn, 2009, Mohr Siebeck |
| Walker UKlaG ................. | Walker, Unterlassungsklagengesetz, 1st edn, 2016, Nomos |

## III. General abbreviations and abbreviated literature

| | |
|---|---|
| ABl. | Amtsblatt (Official Journal) |
| AfP | Archiv für Presserecht (journal) |
| AG | attorney general |
| Alt. | alternative |
| Art. | Article |
| B2B | business-to-business |
| BB | Betriebs-Berater (journal) |
| BGH | Bundesgerichtshof (Federal Court of Justice) |
| BMJV | Bundesministerium der Justiz und für Verbraucherschutz (German Federal Ministry of Justice and Consumer Protection) |
| BT-Drs. | Bundestagsdrucksache (official document of the Federal Parliament) |
| BVerfG | Bundesverfassungsgericht (Federal Constitutional Court) |
| cf. | confer |
| CJEU | Court of Justice of the European Union |
| CR | Computer und Recht (journal) |
| DiskE | Diskussionsentwurf (Discussion Proposal) |
| DiskE II | 2. Diskussionsentwurf (2nd Discussion Proposal) |
| DPMA | Deutsches Patent- und Markenamt (German Patent and Trade Mark Office) |
| e.g. | exempli gratia (for example) |
| ECHR | European Court of Human Rights |
| edn | edition |
| eds | editors |
| EEA | European Economic Area |
| EIPR | European Intellectual Property Review (journal) |
| et al. | et alii (and others) |
| et seq. | et sequens (and the next one) |
| et seqq. | et sequentes (and those that follow) |
| EU | European Union |
| EuZW | Europäische Zeitschrift für Wirtschaftsrecht (journal) |
| fn. | footnote |
| GRUR | Gewerblicher Rechtsschutz und Urheberrecht (journal) |
| GRUR Int. | GRUR International: Journal of European and International IP law |
| GRUR-Prax | Gewerblicher Rechtsschutz und Urheberrecht, Praxis im Immaterialgüter- und Wettbewerbsrecht (journal) |
| Harv. J. L. & Tech | Harvard Journal of Law & Technology |
| IIC | International Review of Intellectual Property and Competition Law (journal) |
| jipitec | Journal of Intellectual Property, Information Technology and Electronic Commerce Law |
| JIPLP | Journal of Intellectual Property Law & Practice |
| JZ | JuristenZeitung (journal) |
| K&R | Kommunikation & Recht (journal) |
| LG | Landgericht (Regional Court) |
| MMR | MultiMedia und Recht (journal) |
| mn. | margin number |
| MPI | Max Planck-Institut (German research institute) |
| MR-Int | Medien und Recht International (journal) |
| NJ | Neue Justiz (journal) |
| NJW | Neue Juristische Wochenschrift (journal) |
| No. | number |
| Nos | numbers |

## List of abbreviations

| | |
|---|---|
| OCSSP | online content sharing service provider |
| OJ | Official Journal |
| OLG | Oberlandesgericht (Higher Regional Court) |
| RefE | Referentenentwurf (proposal of the BMJV) |
| RegE | Regierungsentwurf (government draft) |
| RW | RW Rechtswissenschaft (journal) |
| sent. | sentence |
| sub. | subsection |
| subpara. | subparagraph |
| subs | subsections |
| UFITA | Archiv für Medienrecht und Medienwissenschaft (journal) |
| Vol. | Volume |
| Vor | Vorbemerkung (introduction) |
| WCT | WIPO Copyright Treaty |
| WPPT | WIPO Performances and Phonograms Treaty |
| WRP | Zeitschrift Wettbewerb in Recht und Praxis (journal) |
| ZGE | Zeitschrift für Geistiges Eigentum (journal) |
| ZRP | Zeitschrift für Rechtspolitik (journal) |
| ZUM | Zeitschrift für Urheber- und Medienrecht (journal) |

# A. INTRODUCTION

**Bibliography: Art. 17 DSMD**: Becker, 'Von der Freiheit, rechtswidrig handeln zu können', ZUM 2019, 636; Dreier, 'Die Schlacht ist geschlagen – ein Überblick', GRUR 2019, 771; Frosio, 'Reforming the C-DSM Reform: A User-Based Copyright Theory for Commonplace Creativity', IIC 2020, 709; Geiger/Jütte, 'Platform Liability Under Art. 17 of the Copyright in the Digital Single Market Directive, Automated Filtering and Fundamental Rights: An Impossible Match', GRUR Int. 2021, 517; Gerpott, 'Artikel 17 der neuen EU-Urheberrechtsrichtlinie: Fluch oder Segen?', MMR 2019, 420; Gielen/Tiessen, 'Die neue Plattformhaftung nach der Richtlinie über das Urheberrecht im digitalen Binnenmarkt', EuZW 2019, 639; Grisse, 'After the storm – examining the final version of Article 17 of the new Directive (EU) 2019/790', JIPLP 2019, 887; Hentsch, 'Die Umsetzung der Urheberrechts-Richtlinie aus Sicht der Games-Branche', MMR 2019, 351; Hofmann, 'Die Plattformverantwortlichkeit nach dem neuen europäischen Urheberrecht – "Much Ado About Nothing"?', ZUM 2019, 617; Hofmann, 'Fünfzehn Thesen zur Plattformhaftung nach Art. 17 DSM-RL', GRUR 2019, 1219; Holznagel, 'Verfassungsrechtliche Fragen der Umsetzung von Art. 17 DSM-RL', ZUM 2020, 1; Houareau, 'Die EU-Urheberrechtsrichtlinie aus Sicht der Musikindustrie', MMR 2019, 635; Husovec/Quintais, 'How to License Article 17? Exploring the Implementation Options for the New EU Rules on Content-Sharing Platforms under the Copyright in the Digital Single Market Directive', GRUR Int. 2021, 325; Jäger, 'Die unionsrechtskonforme Umsetzung der Sperrobliegenheiten nach Art.17 DSM-RL', ZUM 2021, 903; Kaesling, 'Die EU-Urheberrechtsnovelle – der Untergang des Internets?', JZ 2019, 586; Kaesling/Knapp, '"Massenkreativität" in sozialen Netzwerken', MMR 2020, 816; Kaesling/Knapp, 'Umsetzung der urheberrechtlichen Verantwortlichkeit von Upload-Plattformen', MMR 2021, 11; Leistner, 'European Copyright Licensing and Infringement Liability Under Art. 17 DSM-Directive', ZGE 2020, 123; Leistner, 'Filtertechnologien und das Urheberrecht – Acht Thesen zur Umsetzung des Art. 17 DSM-RL mit einem Vorschlag für ein komplementär menschlich-algorithmisches Durchsetzungssystem für OCSP-Plattformen', ZUM 2020, 505; Leistner, 'Der Referentenentwurf zur Umsetzung der DSM-RL und die Theorie vom Sui generis-Charakter des Art. 17 DSM-RL', ZUM 2020, 897; Metzger/Senftleben, 'Comment of the European Copyright Society – Selected Aspects of Implementing Article 17 of the Directive on Copyright in the Digital Single Market into National Law', jipitec 2020, 115; Nordemann, 'Upload Filters and the EU Copyright Reform', IIC 2019, 275; Nordemann/Waiblinger, 'Art. 17 DSM-RL – Spannungsverhältnis zum bisherigen Recht?', GRUR 2020, 569; Pappi, 'Neue Möglichkeiten der Rechtewahrnehmungen bei Plattformnutzungen', ZUM 2020, 11; Peifer, 'Sharing-Plattformbetreiberhaftung im Urheberrecht (Art. 17 DSM-RL)', GRUR-Prax 2019, 403; Peters/Schmidt, 'Das Ringen um Upload-Filter geht in die 2. Runde', GRUR Int. 2019, 1006; Pravemann, 'Art. 17 der Richtlinie zum Urheberrecht im digitalen Binnenmarkt', GRUR 2019, 783; Raue/Steinebach, 'Uploadfilter – Funktionsweisen, Einsatzmöglichkeiten und Parametrisierung', ZUM 2020, 355; Raue, 'Die Zähmung der Uploadfilter – Konsequenzen aus dem EuGH-Urteil Polen/Parlament und Rat zu Art. 17 DSM-RL', ZUM 2022, 624; Rauer/Bibi, 'Die neue Verantwortlichkeit von Upload-Plattformen', WRP 2020, 1533; Senftleben, 'Filterverpflichtungen nach der Reform des europäischen Urheberrechts – Das Ende der freien Netzkultur?', ZUM 2019, 368; Senftleben, 'The Original Sin – Content 'Moderation' (Censorship) in the EU', GRUR Int. 2020, 339; Sesing, 'Digitaler Binnenmarkt zwischen Urheber- und Telemedienrecht', MMR 2019, 788; Schaper/Verweyen, 'Die Europäische Urheberrechtsrichtlinie 2016/0280 (COD)', K&R 2019, 433; Schonhofen/Kimmich, 'Wird das Internet kaputt gefiltert? – Die täterschaftliche Haftung von Plattformbetreibern nach Art. 17 der Richtlinie über das Urheberrecht im digitalen Binnenmarkt', WRP 2019, 1415; Schwartmann/Hentsch, 'Stufenkonzept gegen Overblocking durch Upload-Filter – Ein erster Vorschlag zur Umsetzung von Art. 17 DSM-RL', MMR 2020, 207; Senftleben, 'Art. 17 der DSM-RL und neue Impulse für die Verbesserung der urheberrechtlichen Dateninfrastruktur in Europa', GRUR 2022, 221; Specht-Riemenschneider, 'Plattformbetreiberhaftung auf dem Prüfstand – Mit gemeinsamen Leitlinien in die Zukunft?', MMR 2020, 137; Specht-Riemenschneider, Grundlegung einer verbrauchergerechten Regulierung interaktionsmittelnder Plattformfunktionalitäten, 2020, available at <https://www.svr-verbraucherfragen.de/wp-content/uploads/SVRV_Stellungnahme_Regulierung_Plattformfunktionalit%C3%A4ten.pdf> (last accessed 8.12.23); Specht-Riemenschneider, Leitlinien zur nationalen Umsetzung des Art. 17 DSM-RL aus Verbrauchersicht, 2020, available at <https://www.vzbv.de/sites/default/files/downloads/2020/11/05/2020-06-12-specht-final-art_17.pdf> (last accessed 8.12.23); Spindler, 'Die neue Urheberrechts-Richtlinie der EU, insbesondere "Upload-Filter" – Bittersweet?', CR 2019, 277; Spindler, 'Die neue Urheberrechts-Richtlinie der EU' (Teil 1), WRP 2019, 811; Spindler, 'Die neue Urheberrechts-Richtlinie der EU' (Teil 2), WRP 2019, 951; Spindler, 'The Liability system of Art. 17 DSMD and national implementation', jipitec 2019, 344; Spindler, Gutachten zur Urheberrechtsrichtlinie (DSM-RL), 2019; Spindler, 'Art. 17 DSM-RL und dessen Vereinbarkeit mit primärem Europarecht', GRUR 2020, 253; Spindler, 'Upload-Filter: Umsetzungsoptionen zu Art. 17 DSM-RL', CR 2020, 50; Steinbrecher, 'Die EU-Urheberrechtsrichtlinie aus Sicht der Digitalwirtschaft', MMR 2019, 639; Steindl, 'Verstoßen Upload-Filter gegen die Meinungsäußerungsfreiheit?', MR-Int 2021, 166; Stieper, 'Die Richtlinie über das Urheberrecht im digitalen Binnenmarkt', ZUM 2019, 211; Stieper, 'Ein angemessener Interesseausgleich im Verhältnis von Kreativen zu Rechteinhabern und Verwertungsgesellschaften?', ZUM 2019, 393; Stieper, 'Die Umsetzung von Art. 17 VII DSM-RL in deutsches Recht (Teil 1) – Brauchen wir eine Schranke für Karikaturen, Parodien und Pastiches?', GRUR 2020, 699; Stieper, 'Die Umsetzung von Art. 17 VII DSM-RL in deutsches Recht (Teil 2) – Entwurf einer Schranke für Karikaturen, Parodien und Pastiches', GRUR 2020, 792; Schröder, 'Niemand hat die Absicht, eine Mauer zu errichten – verschärfte Kontrollen durch Filterpflichten', K&R 2021, 313; Volkmann, 'Art. 17 Urh-RL und die Upload-Filter: verschärfte Störerhaftung oder das Ende der Freiheit im Internet?', CR 2019, 376; Wandtke, 'Grundsätze der Richtlinie über das Urheberrecht im digitalen Binnenmarkt', NJW 2019, 1841; Wandtke/Hauck, 'Art. 17 DSM-Richtlinie – Ein neues Haftungssystem im Urheberrecht', ZUM 2019, 627; Wandtke/Hauck, 'Ein neues Haftungssystem im Urheberrecht – Zur Umsetzung von Art. 17 DSM-RL in einem "Urheberrechts-Diensteanbieter-Gesetz"', ZUM 2020, 671; Weiden, 'Aktuelle Berichte – August 2020', GRUR 2020, 829; Weidert/Uhlenhut/von Lintig, 'Kampf gegen Upload-Filter – Teil 1: Aktuelle Rechtslage der Betreiberhaftung', GRUR-Prax 2019, 269; Weidert/Uhlenhut/von Lintig, 'Kampf gegen Upload-Filter – Teil 2: Die neue Urheberrechtsrichtlinie', GRUR-Prax 2019, 295; Würtenberger/Freischem, 'Stellungnahme des GRUR-Fachausschusses für Urheber- und Verlagsrecht zur Umsetzung der EU-RL im Urheberrecht (DSM-RL [EU] 2019/790 und Online-SatCab-RL [EU] 2019/789)', GRUR 2019, 1140.

**Discussion Proposal of the Federal Ministry of Justice (Diskussionsentwurf – DiskE):** Becker, 'Automatisierte Rechtsdurchsetzung im Umsetzungsentwurf zu Art. 17 DSM-RL', ZUM 2020, 681; Döhl, 'Das neue Bearbeitungsregime, kunstspezifisch betrachtet', ZUM 2020, 740; Hansen, 'Der urhebervertragsrechtliche Regelungskomplex im "Diskussionsentwurf" zur Umsetzung der DSM-RL aus Sicht der Film- und Fernsehbranche – Eine kritische Würdigung', ZUM 2020, 692; Hofmann, 'Plattformregulierung im Lichte des Unionsrechts', ZUM 2020, 665; Wandtke/Hauck, 'Ein neues Haftungssystem im Urheberrecht – Zur Umsetzung von Art. 17 DSM-RL in einem "Urheberrechts-Diensteanbieter-Gesetz"', ZUM 2020, 671; Würtenberger/Freischem, 'Stellungnahme des GRUR-Fachausschusses für Urheber- und Verlagsrecht zum Diskussionsentwurf eines Zweiten Gesetzes zur Anpassung des Urheberrechts an die Erfordernisse des digitalen Binnenmarktes vom 24.6.2020', GRUR 2020, 1063.

**Proposal of the Federal Ministry of Justice (Referentenentwurf – RefE):** Conrad/Nolte, 'Schrankenbestimmungen im Anwendungsbereich des UrhDaG', ZUM 2021, 111; Leistner, 'Der Referentenentwurf zur Umsetzung der DSM-RL und die Theorie vom Sui-generis-Charakter des Art. 17 DSM-RL', ZUM 2020, 897; Max-Planck-Institut (MPI, prepared by Hilty/Kaiser/Moscon/Richter/Stumpf/Sutterer), Stellungnahme zum Referentenentwurf vom 2. September 2020, available at <https://pure.mpg.de/rest/items/item_3263936_1/component/file_3263937/content> (last accessed 12.3.2024, cited as MPI Stellungnahme zum RefE); Würtenberger/Freischem, 'Stellungnahme des GRUR-Fachausschusses für Urheber- und Verlagsrecht zum RefE des DSM-Umsetzungsgesetzes', GRUR 2021, 37.

**Government draft (Regierungsentwurf – RegE):** Bischoff/Brost, 'Internetpiraterie bei Live-Sportübertragungen', MMR 2021, 303; Hohnholz, 'Was sind uns Kreative wert?', ZUM 2021, 519; Klass, 'Der Kampf ums Urheberrecht', ZRP 2021, 74; Metzger/Pravemann, 'Der Entwurf des UrhDaG als Umsetzung von Art. 17 DSM-RL – Ein gesetzgebungstechnischer Drahtseilakt', ZUM 2021, 288; Stieper, 'Vergüten statt Verbieten – Vergütungspflichten im UrhDaG nach dem Regierungsentwurf zur Umsetzung der DSM-RL', ZUM 2021, 387.

**UrhDaG:** Frey/Rudolph, 'Das Urheberrechts-Diensteanbieter-Gesetz – ein Überblick', MMR 2021, 671; Hofmann, 'Das neue Urheberrechts-Diensteanbietergesetz', NJW 2021, 1905; Janal, 'Friendly Fire? Das Urheberrechts-Diensteanbieter-Gesetz und sein Verhältnis zum künftigen Digital Services Act', GRUR 2022, 211; Lennartz/Möllers, 'Vogelfreie Werkteile', GRUR 2021, 1109; Metzger/Pravemann, 'Die finale Version des UrhDaG – Auf die Plätze, filtern, los?', ZUM 2021, 755; Möller-Klapperich, 'Die Haftung von Online-Plattformen nach dem UrhDaG', NJ 2021, 350; Möller-Klapperich, 'Urheberrecht in der Plattformökonomie – Haftungsverteilung und Prozeduralisierung im neuen UrhDaG', AfP 2021, 384; Raue, 'Die Zähmung der Uploadfilter – Konsequenzen aus dem EuGH-Urteil Polen/Parlament und Rat zu Art. 17 DSM-RL', ZUM 2022, 624; Rauer/Bibi, 'Das neue Urheberrechts-Diensteanbieter-Gesetz', BB 2021, 1475; Spindler, 'Die Umsetzung von Art. 17 DSM-Richtlinie in deutsches Recht – Das UrhDaG' (Teil 1), WRP 2021, 1111; Spindler, 'Die Umsetzung von Art. 17 DSM-Richtlinie in deutsches Recht – Das UrhDaG' (Teil 2), WRP 2021, 1245; Wandtke/Hauck, 'Verantwortlichkeit und Haftung – Das Urheberrechts-Diensteanbieter-Gesetz im Kontext des allgemeinen Urheberrechts', ZUM 2021, 763; v. Welser, 'Plattformhaftung nach dem Urheberrechts-Diensteanbieter-Gesetz (UrhDaG)', GRUR-Prax 2021, 463.

**General contributions on platform liability:** Frosio, 'From horizontal to vertical: an intermediary liability earthquake in Europe', JIPLP 2017, 565; Hofmann, 'Kontrolle oder nachlaufender Rechtsschutz – wohin bewegt sich das Urheberrecht?', GRUR 2018, 21; Hofmann/Specht-Riemenschneider, 'Verantwortung von Online-Plattformen', ZGE 2021, 48; Hofmann/Sprenger, 'Privatisierung der Rechtsdurchsetzung', UFITA 2021, 149; Holznagel, 'Put-back-Ansprüche gegen soziale Netzwerke: Quo Vadis?', CR 2019, 518; Leistner/Metzger, 'The EU Copyright Package: A Way Out of the Dilemma in Two Stages', IIC 2017, 381; Müller-Terpitz, 'Filter als Gefahr für die Meinungspluralität? – Verfassungsrechtliche Erwägungen zum Einsatz von Filtertechnologien', ZUM 2020, 365; Suwelack, 'Leistungsschutzrecht und Upload-Filter aus ökonomischer Perspektive', MMR 2018, 582; Wagner, 'Haftung von Plattformen für Rechtsverletzungen' (Teil 1), GRUR 2020, 329; Wagner, 'Haftung von Plattformen für Rechtsverletzungen' (Teil 2), GRUR 2020, 447; Weiden, 'Aktuelle Berichte – April 2019', GRUR 2019, 370.

**Content**



## I. Legislative history

The UrhDaG implements Art. 17 DSMD (→ mn. 8) into German law. The UrhDaG – 1
like the entire implementation of the DSMD – was the subject of an **extensive consultation process.**[1] On 24.6.2020, the German Federal Ministry of Justice (BMJV) published the first version of the UrhDaG in the **Second Discussion Proposal (2. Diskussionsent-**

[1] See Klass ZRP 2021, 4 et seq.

**wurf: 'DiskE II')**[2]. This was followed by a **proposal of the BMJV (Referentenentwurf: 'RefE')** on 13.10.2020. On 3.2.2021, the Federal Cabinet adopted the **government draft (Regierungsentwurf: 'RegE')**[3], which was amended in several parts at the suggestion of the **Committee on Legal Affairs**.[4] The **UrhDaG** is part of the *Gesetz zur Anpassung des Urheberrechts an die Erfordernisse des digitalen Binnenmarktes* (Act on the Adaptation of Copyright Law to the Requirements of the Digital Single Market) of 31.5.2021, which implemented the whole DSMD into German law. It entered into force as of **1.8.2021** (→ mn. 17).

## II. Rationale

### 1. Legislative objectives

2 The initial reason for the new legal regulation was the insight that a new provider category of upload platforms had emerged between host and content providers.[5] Although service providers do not make their own content available, their involvement is not limited to purely technical, automatic and passive measures.[6] Service provider platforms have become an essential source of access to online content. They provide broad access to cultural and creative works and enable significant social interaction.[7] It is fair to categorise them as **interaction platforms**.[8] The availability of high-quality creative content on the internet has made it difficult for copyright holders to exploit their content via other online services or to participate in the substantial advertising revenues of the platforms. Previously, service providers were only liable to a limited extent for the content of their users. Consequently, the rightholders could only prevent the availability of the content on the platforms or monetise it with considerable effort. This circumstance, termed the **value gap**[9], has led both the European Union (EU) and German legislatures to improve the **negotiating power** of rightholders by imposing direct copyright liability on platforms in order to give rightholders a fair share in the economic exploitation of their content and to facilitate the enforcement of their rights.[10] Service providers are obliged to conclude licensing agreements with rightholders willing to licence content that is typically uploaded on their platforms (Art. 17 (4)(a) DSMD; § 4 UrhDaG). One of the key objectives of the regulation was to foster the development of a **fair licensing market**.[11] Furthermore, the licensing obligation is intended to eliminate any **distortions of competition** due to the use of copyright-protected content online.[12] To the extent that rightholders are not willing to licence, platforms must ensure to the best of their ability that copyright-protected content is not made available on their platforms, while adhering to

---

[2] Available under https://www.bmj.de/SharedDocs/Downloads/DE/Gesetzgebung/DiskE/DiskE_II_Anpassung_Urheberrecht_digitaler_Binnenmarkt.html (last accessed 12.03.2024).

[3] BT-Drs. 19/27426.

[4] BT-Drs. 19/29894.

[5] BT-Drs. 19/27426, 44; Spindler WRP 2019, 951 (956).

[6] Becker ZUM 2020, 681 (683).

[7] Recital 61 sent. 2, 3 DSMD; BT-Drs. 19/27426, 44.

[8] Specht-Riemenschneider, Grundlegung einer verbrauchergerechten Regulierung interaktionsmittelnder Plattformfunktionalitäten, 2020, 21 et seqq.

[9] Leistner/Metzger IIC 2017, 381; Stieper ZUM 2017, 132; with criticism, for example, Frosio JIPLP 2016, 565 (567 et seqq.); cf. also Hofmann GRUR 2018, 21 (27 et seqq.).

[10] Recital 61 sent. 6 DSMD; BT-Drs. 19/27426, 62.

[11] Recital 61 sent. 7 DSMD; CJEU C-401/19, ECLI:EU:C:2022:297 mn. 29 – Poland/Parliament and Council.

[12] BT-Drs. 19/27426, 131.

high industry standards. Large amounts of content made publicly available can hardly be manually controlled with proportionate means. Therefore, there is a widespread consensus that service providers must primarily comply with their blocking obligation with the help of filtering software (**upload filters**). Given the current state of the art, filtering software can mainly recognise the similarity of content but not its context of use and, thus, not whether user activities are covered by copyright exceptions. Therefore, there is a risk of a considerable and widespread infringement of users' rights (→ § 7 mn. 19). Since large platforms have considerable significance for cultural evolution and social discussion processes, the legislature was faced with the challenge of reconciling effective protection of intellectual property rights with the preservation of **users' rights**. The German legislature created procedural safeguards: Modified content enjoys *ex ante* safeguards under certain conditions and must be made accessible until the conclusion of a complaint procedure (§ 7 (2), §§ 9–11). Concerning content not covered by the exemption in § 9 (1), users' rights are protected by swift complaints procedures (*ex post* safeguards, §§ 14–17). However, the *ex ante* safeguards will have to be expanded on grounds of the CJEU decision Poland/Council and Parliament.[13] In addition, the German legislature has introduced **statutory remuneration rights** for authors and owners of related rights so that they can participate in the additional revenue generated (§§ 4 (3), 5 (2) and 12 (1)). In combination with the licensing obligation for the OCSSPs, they promote the concept of *Bezahlen statt Blockieren* (remuneration instead of unavailability): The UrhDaG aims to promote the use of copyright-protected content with the economic participation of the rightholders instead of automated blocking obligations.[14] Despite all the criticism, one should not forget the considerable regulatory effort shouldered by both the EU and the German legislatures. Although the considerable resistance of the multitude of stakeholders was foreseeable, they did not avoid the conflict by delegating it to later court decisions. They rather fulfilled their role in the (civil law) **democratic process** by balancing the interests through very detailed specifications and introducing safeguards for users' rights.[15] The negotiation process and the finetuning of the balance of interests will be continued in court proceedings. The beginning was made by the CJEU in its fundamental decision on the conformity of Art. 17 DSMD with the fundamental rights of the Charta.[16] However, the EU and the German legislatures have provided clear ground rules and procedural safeguards that give guidance for stakeholder negotiations and court rulings in order to allow balanced solutions. Depending on the perspective, the specific liability mechanism introduced by the UrhDaG is a **paradigm shift**[17] or '**much ado about nothing**'[18]. The truth probably lies – as it so often does – in between.

## 2. The systematic concept

The German legislature has implemented Art. 17 DSMD in a separate statute, and not 3
scattered across the UrhG.[19] According to § 1 (1), OCSSPs perform an **independent act of communication to the public** when they provide the public with access to copyrighted works uploaded by their users. OCSSPs as addressees of the UrhDaG are defined in detail

[13] CJEU C-401/19, ECLI:EU:C:2022:297 – Poland/Parliament and Council. See Raue ZUM 2022, 624.
[14] See Stieper ZUM 2021, 387 et seq.
[15] See also Specht-Riemenschneider WRP 2021/8 Editorial; Peifer GRUR-Prax 2019, 403 (405).
[16] CJEU C-401/19, ECLI:EU:C:2022:297 – Poland/Parliament and Council.
[17] Dreier GRUR 2019, 771 (775); Gerpott MMR 2019, 420 (421); Wandtke/Hauck ZUM 2020, 671.
[18] Hofmann ZUM 2019, 617 (629); see also Leistner ZGE 2020, 123 (186); Wagner GRUR 2020, 447 (450); Spindler WRP 2021, 1111 mn. 5.
[19] Cf. on other proposals: Leistner ZUM 2020, 897 (898); Specht-Riemenschneider, Leitlinien zur nationalen Umsetzung des Art. 17 DSM-RL aus Verbrauchersicht, 2020, 113 et seqq.

in §§ 2, 3: § 2 contains the actual statutory definition and § 3 enhances legal certainty by specifying some information society services that are not covered by the specific liability mechanism of the UrhDaG. §§ 5, 6 regulate the scope and application of exceptions and authorisations that allow OCSSPs and users to make copyright-protected content available to the public. § 1 (2) contains an **exemption from liability**. If the OCSSP complies with the liability mechanism set out in more detail in §§ 4, 7 and 8, its liability under copyright law for the content uploaded by users is waived. According to § 4, OCSSPs must obtain licences and accept reasonable licencing offers. According to § 7, they are obliged to block content without prior or imminent copyright infringement if the rightholders have provided them with the information necessary for automated blocking. If the OCSSP does not comply with the liability mechanisms of the UrhDaG, it is liable for copyright infringement pursuant to § 1 (1) in conjunction with §§ 97 et seqq. UrhG. However, rightholders may not claim an injunction for specific actions of the OCSSP.[20] §§ 7 (2), 9–12 attempt to balance the blocking interests of the rightholders with the broadcast interests of the users by providing clear **procedural guidelines** for the **automated blocking of content**. In order to protect the functioning of the finetuned system of checks and balances, § 18 provides sanctions for abuse of procedural rights as well as claims for damages and injunctive relief. §§ 13–17 provide guidelines for **complaint procedures** that OCSSPs must implement. § 13 (4) clarifies that affected users may access state courts at any time. The **remedies** of a violation of § 1 (1) do not emanate from the UrhDaG but from §§ 97 et seqq. of the UrhG. Enforcement is facilitated by § 20, which requires OCSSPs to provide for a **domestic agent for service** of documents. §§ 4 (3), 5 (2) and 12 (1) provide for statutory **rights to remuneration** for authors which can only be claimed via a collecting society.

### 3. Strengthened negotiating position of rightholders

4 The UrhDaG provides rightholders with a stronger negotiating position because OCSSPs now perform own acts of communication to the public under § 1 (1) when their users make copyright-protected content accessible via the platform. Although OCSSPs are exonerated from liability if they comply with the obligations under § 1 (2), these obligations also include the duty to obtain licences under § 4. Accordingly, OCSSPs are required to accept reasonable offers of licences within the meaning of § 4 (2) to avoid liability (→ § 4 mn. 4). If they refuse to obtain a licence, they face considerable liability risks. Accordingly, they are subject to a *de facto* obligation to contract in order to avoid the considerable liability consequences.[21] The negotiating position of the rightholders is further strengthened by the fact that the licensing obligation is designed one-sidedly to the detriment of the OCSSPs. In contrast, rightholders are not required to conclude corresponding licence agreements with OCSSPs; however, an exception applies to collecting societies under § 34 VGG (Collecting Societies Act) (→ § 4 mn. 3). Finally, especially § 7 **reduces the enforcement costs** for rightholders and transfers them to the OCSSPs.[22]

### 4. Protection of users' rights

5 In addition to a high level of protection for copyrights (recital 2 DSMD), the DSMD stipulates in recital 6 DSMD that a fair balance of interests must be struck with users. Although Art. 17 DSMD and the UrhDaG are primarily perceived as a restriction on

[20] See CJEU C-401/19, ECLI:EU:C:2022:297 mn. 75 – Poland/Parliament and Council.

[21] Cf. MPI Stellungnahme zum RefE, 4.

[22] Specht-Riemenschneider, Leitlinien zur nationalen Umsetzung des Art. 17 DSM-RL aus Verbrauchersicht, 2020, 35 et seq.; Kaesling/Knapp MMR 2020, 816 (817).

user rights, they contain considerable **procedural safeguards** for user rights that are specified in copyright law for the first time.[23] Pursuant to § 7 (2) sent. 1, OCSSPs must design the blocking process in such a way that they do not block the content of users that can invoke copyright exceptions, authorisations from rightholders or the public domain. § 7 (2) sent. 2, in conjunction with §§ 9–11, ensures that user rights are already respected *ex ante* when content is automatically blocked by software filters. In addition, § 5 (1) clarifies that users can rely on all **exceptions to the Copyright Act**, in particular, on the newly introduced exception for caricatures, parodies and pastiches (§ 51a UrhG). Art. 17 (7), (9) DSMD requires OCCSPs to limit their best efforts to protect copyrights to measures that do not cause the unavailability of content for which use is covered by a copyright exception or any other authorisation (→ § 7 mn. 21). Furthermore, § 6 (1) extends **authorisations** of the platforms by law to users provided they do not act in a commercial capacity or do not generate significant income. Users have an **individual subjective right** to make content available that does not infringe the copyrights of third parties (→ § 5 mn. 4, → § 9 mn. 6). Since OCSSPs within the meaning of § 2 usually have a contractual relationship with their users, users have a contractual right to not have their contributions blocked as long as they do not infringe copyright and comply with the other lawful terms of the contract.[24]

## 5. Distribution of burdens of action (*Handlungslasten*)

The UrhDaG distributes the burden to commence action between rightholders, 6
OCSSPs and users.[25] **Rightholders** must actively approach OCSSPs and offer them licences unless they are known to the OCSSPs or are collecting societies established in Germany (§ 4 (1) sent. 2). If rightholders are not willing to grant licences to an OCSSP, they may demand that their content be blocked; then they have to provide the OCSSP with the necessary information (§§ 7 (1), 8 (3); → § 7 mn. 17 et seq.). They may only demand a simple blocking pursuant to § 8 (1) if they have given the OCSSP a sufficiently substantiated notice of the unauthorised communication to the public (→ § 8 mn. 9). **OCSSPs** must acquire authorisation that meets the conditions set out in § 4 (2). As long as they are not holders of the necessary authorisations, they must apply their best efforts within the limits of proportionality to block the availability of copyright-protected content if a rightholder so requests and provides the necessary information for this purpose (§ 7 (1)). In addition, they must put an end to specifically identified infringements as soon as they have received a sufficiently substantiated notice (§ 8 (1)). To protect users' rights, OCSSPs must design their automated blocking procedures in accordance with §§ 9–11. In particular, they are required under § 9 (1) to communicate to the public presumably legitimate uses until the conclusion of a complaint procedure. Furthermore, according to § 11 (1) No. 1, they must inform users of a blocking request by a rightholder so that they can flag the content as lawful. The UrhDaG places the burden of action on users to flag permitted uses accordingly or to initiate a complaint procedure if content does not meet the requirements of § 9 (2) Nos 1, 2.[26] The latter is especially problematic when OCSSPs make it particularly simple for copyright trolls to unjustifiably appropriate a legal position that users must arduously challenge.[27]

[23] Specht-Riemenschneider, Leitlinien zur nationalen Umsetzung des Art. 17 DSM-RL aus Verbrauchersicht, 2020, 11.

[24] Cf. BGH 29.7.2021 – III ZR 179/20, NJW 2021, 3179 mn. 28 – Hassrede (hate speech).

[25] Cf. Kaesling/Knapp MMR 2020, 816 (817 et seqq.).

[26] Specht-Riemenschneider, Leitlinien zur nationalen Umsetzung des Art. 17 DSM-RL aus Verbrauchersicht, 2020, 48 et seq. and passim.

[27] Becker ZUM 2019, 636 (640).

### 6. Relationship between UrhG and UrhDaG

7 The relationship between § 1 (1) UrhDaG and the concept of communication to the public in the UrhG is not entirely trivial. Due to the different subject matters of the legislation, it is difficult to give a simple, clear-cut answer. Rather, distinctions must be made according to the individual regulatory aims.[28] **§ 1 (1)** now stipulates that OCSSPs that meet its requirements perform an **independent act of communication**. The wording 'performs an act of communication to the public' (*gibt Werke öffentlich wieder*) in comparison with the general wording of exploitation rights of the UrhG 'The ... right is ...' (*Das ...recht ist...*) shows that § 1 (1) does not confer an exploitation right.[29] It is rather a sector-specific legal definition of the act of communication that could also have been included in § 15 (2) No. 3 UrhG. This result is supported by the fact that § 97 (1) UrhG has remained unchanged and does not include rights under the UrhDaG. If the requirements of § 1 (1) are met and the OCSSP cannot exculpate itself under § 1 (2) in conjunction with §§ 4, 7–11, it infringes the **right of communication to the public under § 15 (2) UrhG**, possibly in the manifestations of §§ 19a or 20 UrhG. Therefore, for other requirements, exceptions and remedies not regulated in the UrhDaG, reference must be made to the UrhG (in more detail → § 1 mn. 5, 8–10). Actions by **service providers** that **are not OCSSPs within the meaning of § 2** are governed by the general liability mechanism of § 15 (2) UrhG (in more detail → § 1 mn. 6). The same applies to uploads and other acts of users (in more detail → § 1 mn. 7).

## III. EU law

### 1. Art. 17 DSMD

8 The **Commission's proposal** for platform liability in copyright law[30] caused considerable controversy over the relationship between copyright protection and user freedoms and was 'marked by intensive lobbying campaigns on the part of the economic operators concerned and demonstrations of opposition from part of civil society, academic circles and advocates for freedom of expression'.[31] In the adopted version of **Art. 17 DSMD**[32], provisions to protect user freedoms were included. They are intended to ensure that contractually or statutorily permitted uses are not prevented by automatic filtering procedures. Art. 17 DSMD is structured as follows: **Sub. 1** states that OCSSPs perform an independent act of communication to the public and must therefore obtain authorisation from the rightholder when their users upload copyrighted works to their platform. **Sub. 2** extends to users of the service an OCSSP's authorisation for communication to the public unless the users are acting on a commercial basis or their activity generates significant revenues. **Sub. 3** specifies that OCSSPs cannot invoke the liability privilege of Art. 14 E-Commerce Directive 2000/31/EC, which will be replaced by Art. 6 DSA. **Sub. 4** establishes duty of care requirements that OCSSPs must comply with if a rightholder has not granted them authorisation. Accordingly, they may be exempted from liability if they have made

[28] Also Nordemann/Waiblinger GRUR 2020, 569 (573).

[29] Stieper ZUM 2021, 387 (393); Wandtke/Hauck ZUM 2020, 671 (673); Specht-Riemenschneider GRUR 2021, 1066; see, however: Peifer GRUR-Prax 2019, 403.

[30] Art. 13 DSMD proposal, COM(2016) 593 final.

[31] AG Saugmandsgaard Øe C-401/19, ECLI:EU:C:2021:613 mn. 23 – Poland/Parliament and Council.

[32] For an overview of the compromise proposals and their development, see Specht-Riemenschneider, Leitlinien zur nationalen Umsetzung des Art. 17 DSM-RL aus Verbrauchersicht, 2020, 21 et seq., 24 et seqq.

best efforts to obtain authorisation (lit. a), have made best efforts in accordance with high industry standards of professional diligence to ensure that the subject matter is not available on their platform on the basis of information from the rightholder (lit. b) and acted expeditiously to remove an uploaded subject matter and prevent its future upload upon receipt of a specific and sufficiently substantiated notice (lit. c). **Sub. 5** indicates the aspects that must be considered in specifying the obligations under sub. 4 and that the principle of proportionality must be taken into account. **Sub. 6** contains exemptions for start-ups. **Sub. 7** contains safeguards to protect users' rights and mandates in subpara. 1 that cooperation between OCSSPs and rightholders must not have the effect of blocking content lawfully uploaded by users. Subpara. 2 requires Member States to provide for a quotation, caricature, parody and pastiche exception for uses on platforms. According to **sub. 8 subpara. 1**, the application of the article must not lead to a general monitoring of uploaded content. Subpara. 2 contains provisions for rightholders' claims for information against OCSSPs. **Sub. 9** lays down extensive requirements for complaint and redress procedures and stipulates again in subpara. 3 that the Directive must not in any way interfere with the legitimate use of content and, in subpara. 4, that OCSSPs must inform their users accordingly. **Sub. 10** requires the Commission to engage in a stakeholder dialogue and to issue application guidelines (→ mn. 10). Art. 17 DSMD is specified in **recitals 61–69 DSMD** and complemented by the **legal definition of** OCSSPs in **Art. 2 No. 6 DSMD**.

### 2. Level of harmonisation

Art. 17 DSMD is, in principle, a **fully harmonising provision** with little discretion **9**
for Member States.[33] However, its wording contains a number of general **legal terms** (e.g., the principle of proportionality in sub. 5) that the Member States can specify when transposing the provision, as long as they do not compromise the objective of the provision and its practical effectiveness and comply with the requirements of the fundamental rights of the Union.[34] The German legislature has made extensive use of this presumed discretion, for example, in the exemptions for small OCSSPs in §§ 2 (3), 7 (5) (→ § 2 mn. 27) and the specification of the licensing obligation in § 4 (→ § 4 mn. 19) as well as in the procedural safeguarding of user rights in §§ 7 (2) sent. 2, 9–11 (→ § 7 mn. 24; → § 9 mn. 1). The **copyright platform regulation** in the EU remains rather **fragmented** (→ mn. 16) because other Member States have opted for different implementation models[35], some of which are incompatible with the German solution. So far, Art. 17 DSMD has clearly failed to achieve one goal: to create a harmonised digital single market. It is possible that the CJEU will rectify this constructive error by imposing stricter requirements and restricting the room that the Member States have for discretion.

### 3. Commission guidelines

The Commission published its Guidance on Art. 17 of Directive (EU) 2019/790 on **10**
Copyright in the Digital Single Market on 4.6.2021.[36] It prepared the guidelines in cooperation with the Member States and in consideration of the stakeholder dialogue.

---

[33] Metzger/Pravemann ZUM 2021, 755 (761); Spindler CR 2020, 50 mn. 2; Peters/Schmidt GRUR Int. 2019, 1006 (1011).

[34] Cf. CJEU C-516/17, ECLI:EU:C:2019:625 mn. 28 et seq. – Spiegel Online/Volker Beck; Würtenberger/Freischem GRUR 2019, 1140 (1153).

[35] Cf. the overview in Metzger/Pravemann ZUM 2021, 755 (761 et seq.).

[36] COM(2021) 288 final.

The intention was to support a correct and uniform implementation of Art. 17 DSMD in the Union. However, the guidelines were published three days before the end of the transposition deadline and this did not particularly support its purpose. The guidance is a **formal communication of the Commission** based on the mandate of the Union legislature in Art. 17 (10) DSMD. It carries great factual weight but is nevertheless **not a legally binding document**.[37] Therefore, it is neither binding on the Member States nor the CJEU.[38]

### 4. Compliance with fundamental rights

11 Poland's **action for annulment** of Art. 17 (4)(b) and (c) DSMD (alternatively, of the entire article) was **unsuccessful**.[39] As the liability regime in sub. 4, limited by the protection of users' rights in subs 7, 9, can be interpreted in conformity with the fundamental rights of the Charta, the specific liability mechanism of Art. 17 DSMD is compatible with the right to freedom of expression and information (Art. 11 CFR).[40] For more details → § 7 mn. 3.

### 5. Relationship to the InfoSoc Directive

12 The relationship between Art. 17 DSMD and the InfoSoc Directive has been controversially discussed[41], and it has a strong impact on the relationship between the UrhDaG and the UrhG (→ mn. 7). Here, a distinction must be made between the different objects of regulation. The **complaint and redress mechanism** in Art. 17 (9) DSMD is an independent provision for which there is no equivalent in the InfoSoc Directive. Art. 17 (2) DSMD contains a **statutory extension of licences** granted to OCSSPs to non-commercially acting users, which exempts the liability of the latter under Art. 3 InfoSoc Directive but, at the same time, confirms their liability in all other cases.[42] Art. 17 (1), (4–6) DSMD, on the other hand, exclusively addresses the act of communication to the public and the duty of care of the OCSSPs. This is a **sector-specific special provision** that supersedes Art. 3 InfoSoc Directive in its scope of regulation.[43] However, only the **act of communication** of the OCSSPs within the meaning of Art. 3 (1, 2) InfoSoc Directive is subject to the regulation, so that Art. 17 (1) DSMD functionally assumes the role of a new Art. 3 (3) InfoSoc Directive.[44] Apart from that, the remaining requirements of Art. 3 and the other provisions of the InfoSoc Directive must be met. This is supported by the wording, the context and the recitals and, in particular, by the aim of Art. 17 DSMD to create legal certainty.[45] It would be detrimental to legal certainty if apart from the actual regulatory scope, it was not possible to use the established acquis of Union copyright law. Therefore, the DSMD and, thus, Art. 17 'shall leave intact and shall in no way affect existing rules laid down [...] in particular Directives [...] 2001/29/EC [...]' (Art. 1 (2) DSMD). In particular, the

[37] COM(2021) 288 final EN, 1; Peters/Schmidt GRUR Int. 2019, 1006 (1010).

[38] CJEU C-189/02 P et al., ECLI:EU:C:2005:408 mn. 209 et seq. – Dansk Rørindustri/Commission; C-310/99, ECLI:EU:C:2002:143 mn. 52 – Italy/Commission.

[39] CJEU C-401/19, ECLI:EU:C:2022:297 – Poland/Parliament and Council.

[40] AG Saugmandsgaard Øe C-401/19, ECLI:EU:C:2021:613 mn. 157 et seq., 204 et seq. – Poland/Parliament and Council. Likewise Specht-Riemenschneider, Leitlinien zur nationalen Umsetzung des Art. 17 DSM-RL aus Verbrauchersicht, 2020, 11, 39 et seqq.

[41] See Husovec/Quintais GRUR Int. 2021, 325.

[42] Peifer GRUR-Prax 2019, 403 (404).

[43] Leistner ZUM 2020, 897 (902).

[44] Leistner ZUM 2020, 897 (904).

[45] In detail: Leistner ZUM 2020, 897 (901 et seq.); Hofmann ZUM 2020, 665 (669 et seq.); Becker ZUM 2020, 681 (685).

acquis limits the Member States' discretion in the creation of provisions on exceptions, for which they must resort to the exhaustive catalogue of the InfoSoc Directive and the DSMD. Since Art. 17 (1) DSMD does not regulate acts of copyright use by **platforms** that are **not OCSSPs** within the meaning of Art. 2 No. 6 DSMD or of **users**, their liability under Art. 3 InfoSoc Directive remains unaffected.[46] Against this background, the opposing opinion[47] that Art. 17 DSMD is a fundamentally independent provision to which, for example, Art. 5 InfoSoc Directive is not applicable,[48] is not convincing.

## IV. International scope

### 1. Applicable law in transborder cases

§ 1 (1) as well as the statutory rights for remuneration (§§ 4 (3), 5 (2) and 12 (1)) 13
regulate the scope of copyright protection, with the result that the applicable law is determined according to the *lex loci protectionis* principle (Art. 8 (1) in conjunction with Art. 15(a) Rome II Regulation).[49] The same applies to liability rules (Art. 15(b) Rome II Regulation), so that the requirements for the **exemption from liability** in § 1 (2) in conjunction with §§ 4, 7–11 are also based on the *lex loci protectionis* principle.[50] Following the *lex loci protectionis* principle, the applicable law is determined by a formal qualification based on the plaintiff's claim. Accordingly, the law of the jurisdiction (or jurisdictions) is applicable for which territory copyright **protection is claimed.**[51] It is then a question of the applicable substantive law whether the asserted act falls within the territorial scope of application of the substantive copyright.[52] The **country of origin principle** of the E-Commerce Directive is **not applicable to the** copyright liability of service providers (Art. 3 (3) E-Commerce Directive in conjunction with Annex, indent 1).[53] The restriction on contractual agreements (§ 22) by which the parties wish to alter provisions of the UrhDaG falls within the scope of the **law applicable to contractual obligations** as a prerequisite for validity of the agreement (Art. 10 (1) Rome I Regulation). The provision is applicable if the contract or term is governed by German law under the Rome I Regulation.[54] Furthermore, § 22 is to be regarded as an overriding mandatory provision within the meaning of Art. 9 Rome I Regulation. Its function is not limited to the balancing of individual interests but also serves the public interest that content remains available on platforms that is exempted from copyright protection by exceptions.[55]

### 2. Territorial scope of application of the UrhDaG

The territorial scope of application of the right of communication to the public 14
under § 15 (2) UrhG in conjunction with § 1 (1) UrhDaG is established whenever either the **act of communication** to the public has **taken place in Germany** or the

[46] Recital 64 sent. 3 DSMD; Becker ZUM 2020, 681 (685).
[47] BT-Drs. 19/27426, 130; Husovec/Quintais GRUR Int. 2021, 325.
[48] On this in detail: Leistner ZUM 2020, 897 (902 et seq.).
[49] Spindler WRP 2021, 1245 mn. 31; Dreier/Schulze/Raue UrhG Vor § 120 mn. 48.
[50] BT-Drs. 19/27426, 48; see also Metzger/Senftleben jipitec 2020, 115 mn. 64.
[51] BGH 21.9.2017 – I ZR 11/16, GRUR 2018, 178 mn. 13 – Vorschaubilder III; Dreier/Schulze/Raue UrhG Vor § 120 mn. 65.
[52] Dreier/Schulze/Raue UrhG Vor § 120 mn. 49, 99 et seq.
[53] See also Dreier/Schulze/Raue UrhG Vor § 120 mn. 52.
[54] Cf. the overview Dreier/Schulze/Raue UrhG Vor § 120 mn. 71 et seq.
[55] For general information on the requirements Dreier/Schulze/Raue UrhG Vor § 120 mn. 80.

**contents are accessible in Germany.**[56] In the latter case, the act has to disclose the intention of the OCSSP to target users in Germany.[57]

### 3. International jurisdiction

15 OCSSPs with their seat in the EU may be sued at their **general place of jurisdiction** (place of the statutory seat, central administration or principal place of business, Art. 63 (1) Brussels Ibis Regulation 1215/2012) or at the place of **special jurisdiction** pursuant to Art. 7 No. 2 Brussels Ibis Regulation 1215/2012.[58] A place where the relevant damage occurred exists according to the CJEU in Germany if an infringement of § 15 (2) UrhG in conjunction with § 1 (1) UrhDaG is alleged and the website of the OCSSP can (also) be accessed in Germany.[59] If OCSSPs are domiciled in Iceland, Norway or Switzerland, international jurisdiction is governed by the same principles of the **Lugano Convention**; if OCSSPs are domiciled outside these states and outside the EU, the international jurisdiction of German courts is governed by the German Civil Procedure Code (**ZPO**).[60]

### 4. Evaluation

16 In the application of these principles, the UrhDaG applies to OCSSPs regardless of their domicile in Germany insofar as they provide or offer their services in Germany.[61] OCSSPs are cumulatively liable under the copyright laws of all jurisdictions in which their platforms can foreseeably be accessed.[62] The copyright law applicable to upload platforms is thus composed as a **mosaic** of different copyright laws. Due to diverse implementations, the platform regulations differ among EU Member States (→ mn. 9). If platforms do not want to comply with the strictest regulation across the Union – or if this proves to be impossible – they will have to use geo-blocking measures to fragment their services within the Union.[63] Art. 17 DSMD imposed stricter liability rules for OCSSPs but failed to harmonise the copyright platform regulations across the EU. The intended creation of a common digital single market remains a desideratum. It is foreseeable that the CJEU – again – will be forced to act as a 'substitute legislature'.[64]

## V. Application in time

17 The UrhDaG entered into force on **1.8.2021** (Art. 5 sent. 2 Act on the Adaptation of Copyright Law to the Requirements of the Digital Single Market (*Gesetz zur Anpassung des Urheberrechts an die Erfordernisse des digitalen Binnenmarktes*)). The liability of OCSSPs for acts that took place before the entry into force of the UrhDaG is exclusively based on the UrhG.

---

[56] Dreier/Schulze/Raue UrhG Vor § 120 mn. 115 et seq.

[57] Cf. CJEU C-173/11, ECLI:EU:C:2012:642 mn. 39 – Football Dataco/Sportradar; OLG München GRUR-RR 2011, 1 (2) – Videodateien; LG Hamburg ZUM 2016, 887 (890).

[58] See Dreier/Schulze/Raue UrhG Vor § 120 mn. 22 et seqq. for more details.

[59] See CJEU C-441/13, ECLI:EU:C:2015:28 mn. 34 – Hejduk; BGH 21.4.2016 – I ZR 43/14, GRUR 2016, 1048 mn. 18 – An Evening with Marlene Dietrich.

[60] Dreier/Schulze/Raue UrhG Vor § 120 mn. 41, 42.

[61] BT-Drs. 19/27426, 48.

[62] Spindler GRUR 2020, 253 (260); with criticism: Metzger/Pravemann ZUM 2021, 755 (761).

[63] Metzger/Pravemann ZUM 2021, 755 (761); cf. also the criticism in Lennartz/Möllers GRUR 2021, 1109 (1113).

[64] See Jotzo ZGE 2017, 447.

# B. COMMENTARY

## Part 1
## General provisions

### § 1
### Communication to the public; liability of the service provider

**(1) A service provider (§ 2) performs an act of communication to the public when it gives the public access to copyright-protected works uploaded by its users.**

**(2) [1]If the service provider fulfils its obligations under § 4 and §§ 7 to 11 in accordance with high industry standards of professional diligence, taking into account the principle of proportionality, it shall not be responsible for the act of communication to the public. [2]In particular, the following aspects shall be taken into account**
**1. the type, the audience and the size of the service,**
**2. the type of works uploaded by the users of the service,**
**3. the availability of suitable means to fulfil the obligations; and**
**4. the costs for the service provider for the means under number 3.**

**(3) The service provider may not invoke § 10 sentence 1 of the Telemedia Act.**

**(4) A service provider whose main purpose is to engage in or to facilitate copyright infringement may not rely on subsection 2.**

## Teil 1
## Allgemeine Vorschriften

### § 1
### Öffentliche Wiedergabe; Verantwortlichkeit des Diensteanbieters

**(1) Ein Diensteanbieter (§ 2) gibt Werke öffentlich wieder, wenn er der Öffentlichkeit Zugang zu urheberrechtlich geschützten Werken verschafft, die von Nutzern des Dienstes hochgeladen worden sind.**

**(2) [1]Erfüllt der Diensteanbieter seine Pflichten nach § 4 und den §§ 7 bis 11 nach Maßgabe hoher branchenüblicher Standards unter Beachtung des Grundsatzes der Verhältnismäßigkeit, so ist er für die öffentliche Wiedergabe urheberrechtlich nicht verantwortlich. [2]Hierbei sind insbesondere zu berücksichtigen**
**1. die Art, das Publikum und der Umfang des Dienstes,**
**2. die Art der von den Nutzern des Dienstes hochgeladenen Werke,**
**3. die Verfügbarkeit geeigneter Mittel zur Erfüllung der Pflichten sowie**
**4. die Kosten, die dem Diensteanbieter für Mittel nach Nummer 3 entstehen.**

**(3) Auf § 10 Satz 1 des Telemediengesetzeskann sich der Diensteanbieter nicht berufen.**

**(4) Ein Diensteanbieter, dessen Hauptzweck es ist, sich an Urheberrechtsverletzungen zu beteiligen oder sie zu erleichtern, kann sich auf Absatz 2 nicht berufen.**

**Bibliography:** See the bibliography in the Introduction.

**Content**

# I. General remarks

## 1. Objective and structure

### a) Objective

1 Under the **liability regime of** the **UrhG** and the **InfoSoc Directive**, a service provider is only liable for acts of communication to the public by its users if it does not comply with the necessary duty of care[1] or plays an 'indispensable' role 'in full knowledge of the consequences of its action' in the process of the act of communication to the public.[2] The legislature has taken the element of the indispensable role of the platform providers, expanded its definition and created a new type of platform service provider with a special liability for copyright infringements.[3] The **new liability mechanism** is

[1] BGH 15.8.2013 – I ZR 80/12, GRUR 2013, 1030 mn. 29 et seqq. – File-Hosting-Dienst (file hosting service).

[2] CJEU C-682/18 and C-683/18, ECLI:EU:C:2021:503 mn. 68, 77 et seq. – YouTube and Cyando; C-610/15, ECLI:EU:C:2017:456 mn. 26 et seq. – Stichting Brein (Pirate Bay); BGH 10.1.2019 – I ZR 267/15, GRUR 2019, 813 mn. 39 – Cordoba II.

[3] Metzger/Pravemann ZUM 2021, 288 (290).

structured in such a way that service providers within the meaning of § 2 (OCSSPs) perform their own act of communication to the public when their users upload copyright-protected content. This **primary liability** is justified by the fact that OCSSPs take an **active role** (structuring the content/advertising) and **economically profit** from the availability of these works on their platforms.[4] OCSSPs may compete with other online content services (§ 2 (1) No. 4) because they provide the public with access to a large amount of copyright-protected content (§ 2 (1) No. 1). The introduction of increased duty of care requirements for OCSSPs is justified because they economically benefit from the attractiveness of the content uploaded by their users (→ § 2 mn. 3).[5] However, since it is not their own content, OCSSPs can exempt themselves from liability if they comply with the liability mechanisms defined in §§ 1 (2), 4, 7–11 in accordance with high industry standards. Providing a content sharing platform to its users as such does not interfere with the economic or personal interests of the rightholders. The liability is justified by the increased risk of copyright infringement (*Haftung für gefahrerhöhendes Verhalten*). § 1 (2) in conjunction with §§ 4, 7–11 defines the relevant duty of care for OCSSPs. The remaining risk for copyright infringement that exists despite a reasonable duty of care is the necessary price to pay for the freedom of speech, information and art on internet platforms.[6]

#### b) Accessoriness to user action

Pursuant to § 1 (1), by providing the platform and the technical process to make the content (automatically) accessible to the public, the OCSSPs perform their own act of communication to the public. However, liability requires that copyright-protected content is uploaded by the users of the service. Without the (subsequent) action of its users, there is no liability for OCSSPs. Therefore, a **preparatory or supporting act** is promoted to an act that is relevant under copyright law. In interpreting the further conditions for liability, it must therefore be taken into account that OCSSPs provide a platform that third parties use for their own (potentially) copyright infringing acts. In principle, the liability of the OCSSPs may not go beyond the liability of the user as the primary source of copyright infringement.[7] Although § 1 (1) technically promotes the previous secondary liability of service providers to a direct liability of OCSSPs, it remains as a **liability for accessory actions.** This has two consequences: First, the service provider can exempt itself from the liability if it complies with high industry standards (§ 1 (2)). Second, if its users act lawfully, the platform may not be subjected to stricter liability (§§ 5, 6, → § 6 mn. 10).[8] A stricter liability could create incentives to no longer make the platform available for lawful communication or to restrict lawful uses (→ § 5 mn. 7).[9] The regulation of the platform would then indirectly have a detrimental effect on the freedoms of users. 2

### 2. EU law

Sub. 1 implements **Art. 17 (1) subpara. 1 DSMD.**[10] Sub. 2 implements the requirement of **Art. 17 (4), (5) DSMD,**[11] according to which Art. 17 (4) DSMD requires that 3

---

[4] Hofmann ZUM 2020, 665 (666); Schack UrhR/UrhebervertragsR mn. 858.

[5] Cf. also BGH 15.8.2013 – I ZR 80/12, GRUR 2013, 1030 mn. 44 et seq. – File-Hosting-Dienst (file hosting service).

[6] Cf. Peifer GRUR-Prax 2019, 403 (404).

[7] Cf. Hofmann ZUM 2020, 665 (666).

[8] Cf. also BT-Drs. 19/27426, 42: 'be liable for the communication to the public of unlawful uploads […]'; cf. also Wandtke NJW 2019, 1841 (1845 et seq.).

[9] Conrad/Nolte ZUM 2021, 111 (115); see, however: Metzger/Pravemann ZUM 2021, 288 (297).

[10] Explained in recital 64 sent. 1 DSMD.

[11] Recital 64 sent. 2 and 66 subpara. 1 sent. 4, subpara. 2 DSMD.

'best efforts' (French: *meilleure efforts*) must always be made to comply with the liability mechanism, meaning best possible efforts (inaccurately translated in the German version as 'all efforts' (German: *alle Anstrengungen*); the specification that this should be done in accordance with high industry standards is only applicable to qualified blocking in lit. b of the Directive;[12] however, it is not clear why this should not also apply to the other two obligations so that this is a reasonable specification by the German legislature. Sub. 3 implements **Art. 17 (3) subpara. 1 DSMD**[13]; sub. 4 is based on **recital 62 subpara. 2 sent. 2 DSMD.**[14]

### 3. Relationship to UrhG/InfoSoc Directive/International Treaties

#### a) Differentiated approach

4 The relationship of Art. 17 DSMD/UrhDaG to the concept of communication to the public of the InfoSoc Directive/the UrhG was one of the most controversial topics during the legislative process.[15] Due to the complexity of the regulatory matter, general answers should be avoided. Rather, a distinction should be made according to the respective regulatory complexes.[16] However, it is clear that the liability of OCSSPs is not determined by **Art. 8 WCT** and **Art. 14 WPPT.**[17]

#### b) Communication to the public

5 **aa) Communication to the public by the OCSSP.** The act of communication to the public (*gibt Werke öffentlich wieder*) is linked to the respective definition in **§ 15 (2) UrhG/Art. 3 InfoSoc Directive**. The German legislature decided against an independent liability concept, choosing instead a sector-specific 'clarification'[18] of the liability concept in § 15 (2) UrhG/Art. 3 InfoSoc Directive and thus integrated the liability of OCSSPs into the existing model of communication to the public. However, it follows from the YouTube/Cyando decision of the CJEU[19] that it is an **extension of the existing liability concept.**[20] If the conditions of § 1 (1)/Art. 17 (1) DSMD are met, the legislature has now bindingly defined that OCSSPs perform their own act of communication.[21] In that case, it is no longer necessary to examine the 'several complementary criteria' for the act of communication to the public, 'which are not autonomous and are interdependent'.[22] In all other respects, however, the **additional elements** of communication to the public under § 15 (2) UrhG/Art. 3 InfoSoc Directive must be met, for which one can refer to the case law of the CJEU and BGH (→ mn. 11 et seq.).[23] The UrhDaG does not contain an independent exploitation right because it only defines the act of communication to the public. The exploitation right is derived

---

[12] Hofmann NJW 2021, 1905 mn. 7, 28; Hofmann ZUM 2020, 665 (666); Spindler WRP 2021, 1111 mn. 7.

[13] Explained in recital 65 sent. 1 DSMD.

[14] BT-Drs. 19/27426, 131.

[15] Cf. for example Nordemann/Waiblinger GRUR 2020, 569; in detail: Husovec/Quintais GRUR Int. 2021, 325–348.

[16] Also Nordemann/Waiblinger GRUR 2020, 569 (573).

[17] Husovec/Quintais GRUR Int. 2021, 325 (332 et seq.).

[18] Recital 64 sent. 1 DSMD; BT-Drs. 19/27426, 130; Stieper ZUM 2021, 387 (393); Nordemann/Waiblinger GRUR 2020, 569 (573 et seq.); see, however: Husovec/Quintais GRUR Int. 2021, 325: completely independent liability mechanism.

[19] CJEU C-682/18 and C-683/18, ECLI:EU:C:2021:503 mn. 60–102 – YouTube and Cyando.

[20] Previously Husovec/Quintais GRUR Int. 2021, 325 (328); Grisse JIPLP 2019, 887 (890 et seq.).

[21] Peifer GRUR-Prax 2019, 403.

[22] For more on the latter, see: CJEU C-682/18 and C-683/18, ECLI:EU:C:2021:503 mn. 66 et seq. – YouTube and Cyando.

[23] Cf. also Stieper ZUM 2021, 387 (393); Wandtke/Hauck ZUM 2020, 671 (673).

from §§ 15 (2), 19a, 20 UrhG in conjunction with § 1 (1) UrhDaG. Remedies for an infringement are provided by §§ 97 et seq. UrhG.[24] However, with regard to the act of communication, the provisions of the UrhDaG/Art. 17 DSMD are exhaustive and are thus ***leges speciales*** within their scope of application.[25] With regard to copyright-protected content uploaded by users, OCSSPs within the meaning of § 2 are only liable under the conditions of the UrhDaG.[26] Thus, if they comply with the liability standards set in § 1 (2) in conjunction with §§ 4, 7–11, they cannot be held liable under § 15 (2) UrhG.[27] Insofar as the UrhDaG does not contain any specific provisions, one has to rely on the provisions of the UrhG/InfoSoc Directive for the liability of the OCSSP.[28] **Outside the scope of application of the UrhDaG**, OCSSPs are liable according to the general rules set in the UrhG/InfoSoc Directive, in particular for their own content.[29]

**bb) Acts by service providers not covered by the UrhDaG.** Service providers that do 6
not meet the criteria of § 2 are liable according to the general rules of the UrhG/InfoSoc Directive (Art. 1 (2) DSMD).[30] Art. 17 DSMD is not intended to affect the concept of communication to the public in other acts of Union legislation.[31] Nevertheless, **indirect conclusions** can be drawn on OCSSP liability from the UrhDaG/Art. 17 DSMD because the Union legislature has undertaken a comprehensive **balancing of the interests concerned** and has also specified the **principle of proportionality.**[32] A comprehensive balancing of interests that takes into account the principle of proportionality is also required for the liability concept of Art. 3 InfoSoc Directive[33]; thus, the basic principles of intermediary liability laid down in Art. 17 DSMD are suitable for generalisation.[34] In principle, the UrhDaG and Art. 17 DSMD introduce a stricter form of liability for service providers that economically profit from the copyright-protected content uploaded by their users. *A fortiori*, the **liability exceptions** of the UrhDaG should be applied to other intermediaries.[35] As the UrhDaG/Art. 17 DSMD aims to introduce a stricter liability mechanism for OCSSPs, it is not convincing that service providers that do not meet the criteria of § 2 should be liable in a stricter way than OCSSPs. In addition, conclusions can be drawn about the **distribution of the burden of action** (*Handlungslasten*), for example, the specific information the rightholders must provide for the intermediary to block content (→ § 7 mn. 7).

**cc) Acts of the users.** Contrary to the explanatory memorandum (*Regierungsbegrün-* 7
*dung*)[36] of the UrhDaG, users of OCSSPs **remain liable** for the upload of copyright-protected content under the general rules of the UrhG because users are not addressees

[24] BT-Drs. 19/27426, 44, 131.

[25] BT-Drs. 19/27426, 130; COM(2021) 288 final EN, 2; Schack UrhR/UrhebervertragsR mn. 859; Leistner ZUM 2020, 897 (901 et seq.); Metzger/Pravemann ZUM 2021, 288 (290); Hofmann ZUM 2020, 665 (666).

[26] Cf. Wandtke/Hauck ZUM 2019, 627 (635).

[27] Specht-Riemenschneider GRUR 2021, 1066.

[28] BT-Drs. 19/27426, 44, 131; Leistner ZUM 2020, 897 (901).

[29] Hofmann NJW 2021, 1905 mn. 5; Grisse JIPLP 2019, 887 (892).

[30] Recital 64 sent. 3 DSMD; COM(2021) 288 final EN, 2; Nordemann/Waiblinger GRUR 2020, 569 (571); Leistner ZUM 2020, 505 (506 et seq.).

[31] Recital 64 sent. 3 DSMD (French: *n'affecte pas*); Grisse JIPLP 2019, 887 (891).

[32] Cf. AG Saugmandsgaard Øe C-401/19, ECLI:EU:C:2021:613 mn. 44 – Poland/Parliament and Council.

[33] Cf. CJEU C-682/18 and C-683/18, ECLI:EU:C:2021:503 mn. 64 – YouTube and Cyando; CJEU C-275/06, ECLI:EU:C:2008:54 mn. 68 – Promusicae/Telefonica.

[34] Specht-Riemenschneider GRUR 2021, 1066 et seq.

[35] Spindler GRUR 2020, 253 (261); see, however: Nordemann/Waiblinger GRUR 2020, 569 (571).

[36] BT-Drs. 19/27426, 130.

of the UrhDaG/Art. 17 DSMD with regard to their own acts of exploitation[37]. An exception is § 6 (1), which implements Art. 17 (2) DSMD. § 5 (1) is only a clarification that users may invoke the copyright exceptions of the UrhG for their acts of communication to the public (→ § 5 mn. 1). In addition, according to § 12 (3), the user's liability is suspended during the complaint procedure (→ § 12 mn. 2, 20), although it is not entirely clear to what extent this is in conformity with the provisions of the InfoSoc Directive. The other user-related provisions of the UrhDaG only address the relationship between users and OCSSPs and not the liability of users vis-à-vis rightholders.

**c) Exceptions**

8 § 1 (2) (and Art. 17 DSMD) exempts the act of communication to the public from liability if the OCSSP fulfils certain duties of care. Beyond that, the UrhDaG does **not** contain **any copyright exceptions** for OCSSPs. However, Art. 17 (7) and (9) subpara. 3 DSMD clarify that neither the cooperation between OCSSPs and rightholders nor the liability of OCSSPs shall affect **legitimate uses** in any way, in particular those that fall within the scope of the copyright exceptions set out in EU law. Under the InfoSoc Directive, it was commonly accepted that other intermediaries, such as newspapers, book publishers, and television and radio stations were covered by the copyright exceptions on which their authors or producers can rely to lawfully include copyright-protected content in their works. This can be generalised that redistribution of lawful content is lawful. It follows from Art. 17 (9) subpara. 3 DSMD that this should not change. Therefore, OCSSPs may also invoke the copyright exceptions of the UrhG/InfoSoc Directive according to §§ 5 (1), 6 (2) that make the use of copyright-protected content by its users lawful (→ § 6 mn. 10).[38] However, this is only a **clarification** because the OCSSPs can invoke the copyright exceptions of the UrhG in any case.[39]

**d) Authorisations**

9 According to § 4, OCSSPs that perform an act of communication to the public require the authorisation of the rightholder (also Art. 17 (1) DSMD). Here, the question arises as to how the introduction of § 1 (1) affects the **existing authorisation** that rightholders had granted to OCSSPs for the communication of their content to the public within the meaning of § 15 (2) UrhG before the UrhDaG came into force. If § 1 (1) UrhDaG is seen as a subset of communication to the public under § 15 (2) UrhG (→ mn. 5), then the authorisation for the act of communication by the OCSSPs under the UrhDaG is no different from that under the UrhG.[40] A previously **unknown type of use** (*unbekannte Nutzungsart*) within the meaning of § 31a UrhG requires that the new type of use differs from previously known uses to such an extent that the new form of exploitation of the work can only be permitted on the basis of a new decision by the author with knowledge of these new possibilities of use.[41] The previous licence agreements were based on the legal assessment that service providers were subject to a take-down as well as a stay-down obligation of copyright-infringing content after sufficient notice.[42] Consequently, the permanent use and economic exploitation of works on

---

[37] Stieper ZUM 2021, 387 (389 et seq.); Leistner ZUM 2020, 897 (901, 905); Becker ZUM 2020, 681 (685); Grisse JIPLP 2019, 887 (891).

[38] Hofmann NJW 2021, 1905 mn. 10; Husovec/Quintais GRUR Int. 2021, 325 (330); Wandtke/Hauck ZUM 2020, 671 (676); Grisse JIPLP 2019, 887 (891); see, however: BT-Drs. 19/27426, 130.

[39] Stieper ZUM 2021, 387 (389 et seq.).

[40] Likewise Stieper ZUM 2021, 387 (393).

[41] BGH 4.7.1996 – I ZR 101/94, GRUR 1997, 215 (217) – Klimbim; Dreier/Schulze/Schulze UrhG § 31a mn. 35.

[42] Cf. Holzmüller ZUM 2017, 301 (302).

platforms under the previous copyright liability mechanism was also only possible on the basis of a licence agreement with the rightholders. The UrhDaG improves the legal position and the negotiating power of the rightholders as they can now demand qualified blocking from the OCSSP before an unauthorised use of the protected content occurs (§ 7 (1)). However, the authorised use does not fundamentally differ from the previously permitted use.

**e) Remedies**

The remedies (in particular, **removal, injunction, damages**) for an unauthorised communication to the public pursuant to § 1 (1) are derived from **§§ 97 et seq. UrhG.**[43] As liability for indirect causation contributions is stricter than in all other cases of intellectual property infringement, it has been proposed that the **standard of fault** for liability for damages be raised and that infringers' profits be excluded in the calculation of damages.[44] Both restrictions are permitted by EU law: the standard of fault in Art. 13 (1) Enforcement Directive ('knowingly, or with reasonable grounds to know') is more generous than the *de facto* strict liability of German intellectual property law.[45] Concerning the infringers' profits, Art. 13 (1) sent. 2 lit. (a) Enforcement Directive states that they only have to be 'taken into account' but not disgorged as under the case law of the BGH.[46] In particular, it should be taken into account that it is very difficult for OCSSPs to determine in advance which specific measures will be required of them under the 'high industry standards of professional diligence' (→ mn. 27 et seq.; → § 7 mn. 14 et seq.). Even according to the conventional standard of fault in German law, it is questionable whether noncompliance with uncertain objective standards of care can be considered as individually negligent behaviour before they are specified by courts.[47] **10**

## II. Communication to the public (sub. 1)

### 1. OCSSP's independent act of communication to the public

An OCSSP as defined in § 2 performs an act of communication to the public when it provides the public with access to copyright-protected content uploaded by its users. This is an **independent act of communication to the public**[48], which, in addition to making available to the public (§ 19a UrhG), also covers broadcasting (§ 20 UrhG) and all other forms of communication to the public within the meaning of § 15 (2)/Art. 3 InfoSoc Directive.[49] The **act of providing access** to the public on the platform is to be regarded as the act of communication to the public.[50] Knowledge of the actual copyright infringement by its user is not required. The OCSSP is, therefore, liable under copyright law for infringements committed by its users via the service (→ mn. 1). In principle, it is liable for **all** copyright-protected **content that is accessible via the platform.**[51] For its **11**

[43] BT-Drs. 19/27426, 44; for §§ 7 and 8 see, however: Metzger/Pravemann ZUM 2021, 288 (292).

[44] Cf. Schricker/Loewenheim/Leistner UrhG § 97 mn. 56m, 96; Ohly ZUM 2017, 793 (801); Specht-Riemenschneider, Leitlinien zur nationalen Umsetzung des Art. 17 DSM-RL aus Verbrauchersicht, 2020, 64 et seq. with further references.

[45] Raue Schadensberechnung, 102 et seq.; Dreier GRUR Int. 2004, 706 (707). Cf. on the liability standard Dreier/Schulze/Specht-Riemenschneider UrhG § 97 mn. 78.

[46] Raue Schadensberechnung, 107 et seq., 129 et seqq. with further references.

[47] Cf. Hofmann GRUR 2019, 1219 (1222).

[48] BT-Drs. 19/27426, 44.

[49] Nordemann/Waiblinger GRUR 2020, 569 (573 et seq.).

[50] Wandtke/Hauck ZUM 2020, 671 (673).

[51] BT-Drs. 19/27426, 42.

own content, the OCSSP is liable pursuant to § 15 (2) UrhG. For content uploaded by its users, § 1 (1) UrhDaG extends the previously existing liability regime.

### 2. Act of communication to the public

12 § 1 (1) specifies in a binding manner the conditions under which an OCSSP performs an **act of communication** of a work within the meaning of the two-step concept of communication to the public of the CJEU.[52] As a result, the examination previously required under § 15 (2) UrhG as to whether the OCSSP has an 'indispensable' role 'in full knowledge of the consequences of its action' in the process of the act of communication to the public is no longer necessary.[53] The other requirements of the concept of communication to the public are to be construed as in the context of § 15 (2) UrhG/ Art. 3 InfoSoc Directive.[54]

### 3. Access

13 An OCSSP gives access to the public if it provides members of the public with the **opportunity to perceive** copyright-protected content.[55] In this case, it is irrelevant whether members of the public actually use the opportunity of access or not.[56]

### 4. To copyright-protected works and subject matter

14 The OCSSP is responsible for access to all **copyright-protected content**, with the liability for copyright-protected **works** resulting from § 1 (1) and the protection of **related rights** from § 21 (1). Of course, OCSSPs are not liable for content in the public domain, regardless of whether the content does or does not meet the thresholds of copyright protection under the UrhG or whether the term of protection has expired.[57] Content that sufficiently differs from pre-existing works and subject matter and, therefore, can be classified as free use of the pre-existing works (§ 23 (1) sent. 2 UrhG) is also not included in the liability mechanism.[58] If a rightholder makes unjustified claims thereunder, he or she is liable according to the principles of unjustified property right warning.[59] Repeated unjustified blocking requests shall result in exclusion from the procedure under §§ 7 and 8 pursuant to § 18 (1) (→ § 18 mn. 7 et seq.).

### 5. Public

15 The concept of 'public' has a quantitative and a qualitative dimension. In quantitative terms, access must be given to an **indeterminate number of potential recipients**

[52] E.g. CJEU C-682/18 and C-683/18, ECLI:EU:C:2021:503 mn. 66 – YouTube and Cyando; C-392/19, ECLI:EU:C:2021:181 mn. 29 – VG Bild-Kunst; C-610/15, ECLI:EU:C:2017:456 mn. 24 – Stichting Brein (Pirate Bay); BGH 10.1.2019 – I ZR 267/15, GRUR 2019, 813 mn. 39 – Cordoba II; Peifer GRUR-Prax 2019, 403.

[53] CJEU C-682/18 and C-683/18, ECLI:EU:C:2021:503 mn. 68, 77 et seq. – YouTube and Cyando; C-610/15, ECLI:EU:C:2017:456 mn. 26 et seq. – Stichting Brein (Pirate Bay); BGH 10.1.2019 – I ZR 267/15, GRUR 2019, 813 mn. 39 – Cordoba II.

[54] Wandtke/Hauck ZUM 2020, 671 (673).

[55] See BGH 21.9.2017 – I ZR 11/16, GRUR 2018, 178 mn. 19 – Vorschaubilder III.

[56] CJEU C-161/17, ECLI:EU:C:2018:634 mn. 20 – Land Nordrhein-Westfalen/Renckhoff; BGH 10.1.2019 – I ZR 267/15, GRUR 2019, 813 mn. 39 – Cordoba II.

[57] COM(2021) 288 final EN, 19; Husovec/Quintais GRUR Int. 2021, 325 (330); Wandtke/Hauck ZUM 2020, 671 (676).

[58] BT-Drs. 19/27426, 135.

[59] See Dreier/Schulze/Specht-Riemenschneider UrhG § 97a mn. 10.

consisting of a **fairly large number of people.**[60] In qualitative terms, a 'new public' must be addressed.[61] In this respect, it is sufficient that the content is stored on the OCSSP's own server or in any other way in the **OCSSP's access sphere**[62], no matter if it is accessible elsewhere on the internet with the consent of the rightholder.[63] According to § 2 (1) No. 1, an OCSSP meets this requirement by definition because it must 'store' the protected content and, thus, make it available from within its sphere of access (→ § 2 mn. 12).

### 6. Uploaded by its users

The special liability mechanism of the UrhDaG is only applicable if the copyright- 16
protected content is uploaded by the **users of** the OCSSP 'who act autonomously and who are responsible for their own actions'.[64] The users must determine whether the uploaded content is made available to other internet users or users of the service. The **OCSSP** is liable for its own content under § 15 (2) UrhG.[65] In any case, this includes content uploaded by the OCSSP's own employees or by third parties at the instruction of the OCSSP's employees. Whether user content may be treated as the platform's own content because of the concept of appropriation (*Zueigenmachen*)[66] is questionable. This is a concept yet unknown to EU law, and therefore, it is unclear to what extent German courts may use this concept alongside the very specific provisions of § 1 (1) in conjunction with § 2 (1) Nos 2, 3.[67]

### 7. Burden of proof

According to general principles, the **rightholder** must prove that the requirements 17
of § 1 (1) are met (i.e., that the content is protected by copyright and the conditions of liability are met by the service provider) and that he or she is entitled to exercise the right. On the burden of proof for the **liability exemption** in § 1 (2) → mn. 37.

## III. Liability exemption (sub. 2)

### 1. Compliance with the duties of care according to §§ 4, 7–11 (sent. 1)

#### a) Exemption of liability

OCSSPs within the meaning of § 2 generally provide services that are in the **public** 18
**interest**, as they are a 'means of providing wider access to cultural and creative works and offer great opportunities for cultural and creative industries to develop new business models'; at the same time, they 'generate challenges' for copyright-protected

---

[60] See CJEU C-392/19, ECLI:EU:C:2021:181 mn. 31 – VG Bild-Kunst; C-682/18 and C-683/18, ECLI:EU:C:2021:503 mn. 69 – YouTube and Cyando; BGH 10.1.2019 – I ZR 267/15, GRUR 2019, 813 mn. 42 – Cordoba II.

[61] See CJEU C-392/19, ECLI:EU:C:2021:181 mn. 32 – VG Bild-Kunst; BGH 10.1.2019 – I ZR 267/15, GRUR 2019, 813 mn. 43 – Cordoba II.

[62] BGH 21.9.2017 – I ZR 11/16, GRUR 2018, 178 mn. 19 – Vorschaubilder III; Schricker/Loewenheim/v. Ungern-Sternberg UrhG § 19a mn. 60.

[63] CJEU C-161/17, ECLI:EU:C:2018:634 mn. 46 et seq. – Land Nordrhein-Westfalen/Renckhoff.

[64] See CJEU C-682/18 and C-683/18, ECLI:EU:C:2021:503 mn. 71 – YouTube and Cyando.

[65] Nordemann/Waiblinger GRUR 2020, 569 (571).

[66] BGH 12.11.2009 – I ZR 166/07, 2010, 616 mn. 32 – Marions-Kochbuch; Dreier/Schulze/Specht-Riemenschneider UrhG § 97 mn. 41 et seqq.

[67] Affirming: Nordemann/Waiblinger GRUR 2020, 569 (571).

content.[68] By offering services, they only set an indirect, accessory condition for copyright infringements for which third parties are directly responsible.[69] Therefore, an OCSSP can **avoid liability** if it can demonstrate that it has **complied with** certain **duties of care**[70], which the UrhDaG defines in more detail in § 1 (2) and in §§ 4, 7–11. The liability exemption is not applicable to OCSSPs that support copyright piracy and that have the main purpose of enabling copyright infringement (§ 1 (4); → mn. 39). If an OCSSP **fulfils the duty of care obligations of the UrhDaG**, it cannot be held liable for copyright infringement on its platform, and it is neither subject to injunctive relief nor to damages.[71] Because the services provided by OCSSP are in the public interest, the duty of care is **not** an **obligation of result** that copyright-protected content is not available on their platform without authorisation.[72] They are **only** subject to an **obligation of means** as they must make best efforts to achieve that goal when organising their services.[73]

**b) Fulfilment of obligations under §§ 4, 7–11**

19 An OCSSP is not liable if it fulfils its **cumulative obligations** under §§ 4, 7–11. Accordingly, it is obliged:

- under § 4, to make best efforts to **obtain** an **authorisation** from the rightholders;
- under § 7, **to ensure the unavailability** of specific content by making best efforts to block or to remove content for which it has not obtained an authorisation to use (→ mn. 20), whereby when using automated means, presumably legitimate content must be made available according to § 9 (1) until the complaint procedure has been concluded; and
- under § 8, **to end the availability** of such content after a duly substantiated notice.

An OCSSP must fulfil these obligations in accordance **with high industry standards of professional diligence**, the determination of which must take into account the principle of proportionality.

**c) Further exemptions from liability**

20 In addition to complying with the duty of care requirements of the UrhDaG, an OCSSP is also **not liable for** making copyright-protected content available to the public in the **following cases:**

- when the OCSSP has concluded a **licence agreement** with the **rightholder** or has obtained other authorisation[74] for the content to be made accessible via its service. It is irrelevant whether the content is that of a user or of a third party; the authorisations of third parties also extend to the acts of communication by the platform's users if they are not acting on a commercial basis (→ § 6 mn. 3, 5). In the case of contracts concluded before the entry into force of the UrhDaG, whether the public communication pursuant to § 1 (1) is a **previously unknown type of use** (→ mn. 9) is to be considered;
- when the **user** has obtained authorisation from the **rightholder** to communicate to the public the content via an OCSSP (§ 6 (2), → § 6 mn. 1);

[68] Recital 61 sent. 3 DSMD; BT-Drs. 19/27426, 44.

[69] COM(2021) 288 final EN, 2.

[70] BT-Drs. 19/27426, 44.

[71] BT-Drs. 19/27426, 130 et seq.

[72] Cf. recital 66 subpara. 2 sent. 4 DSMD; CJEU C-401/19, ECLI:EU:C:2022:297 mn. 78 – Poland/Parliament and Council.

[73] Cf. recital 66 subpara. 2 sent. 2 DSMD; Hofmann ZUM 2020, 665 (666); Hofmann ZUM 2019, 617 (625).

[74] See Dreier/Schulze/Schulze UrhG § 31 mn. 6.

- when the **user** can rely on a **statutory permission** for his or her communication to the public[75] (contested, → § 5 mn. 3); and
- **during the** conduct of a **complaint procedure** (§ 12 (2) sent. 1, → § 12 mn. 18 et seq.) or until the expiry of the time limit for a decision on the complaint.

**d) High industry standards**

Platform operators must generally take those appropriate technical measures 'that can be expected from a reasonably diligent operator in its situation in order to counter credibly and effectively copyright infringements on that platform'.[76] In contrast, OCSSPs within the meaning of § 2 must comply with **high industry standards** (German: *hohe branchenübliche Standards*; French: *normes élevées du secteur en matière*). As this is a newly introduced standard, there is uncertainty about the level of care to be applied; in the end, this will have to be determined by the CJEU.[77] The new standard of care is an **autonomous notion of EU law** and must consequently be autonomously determined.[78] Therefore, established standards of German law cannot simply be applied for its specification, such as the generally recognised 'rules of technology' (*Regeln der Technik*), the 'state of the art' (*Stand der Technik*) or the 'state of science and technology' (*Stand von Wissenschaft und Technik*). In addition, **differentiated answers** for the **respective obligations** of §§ 4, 7–11 will have to be found because the standards applied to contract negotiations are different from those applied to the blocking of content. The following explanation is more appropriate for the latter. 21

**aa) Industry standards.** The standards of the respective industry are relevant.[79] The **industry** to which an OCSSP belongs is to be assessed according to the perception of the market participants (*Verkehrsanschauung*). In this context, the other providers to which the respective service provider otherwise refers can be considered, for example, regarding technology, design and advertising. 22

**bb) High standards.** OCSSPs must meet high standards.[80] This does not mean an above-average fulfilment of the obligations in a statistical sense[81] because this would only be possible for an individual and not for all OCSSPs. In any case, they will have to observe the **usual diligence** expected of an economic operator in their situation in order to credibly and effectively counter copyright infringements on their platform.[82] Because OCSSPs are required to meet 'high' standards, they must aim for the **high end of the usual measures.**[83] Therefore, an OCSSP cannot argue *per se* that other industry members do not use certain existing technologies, especially if they are not OCSSPs within the meaning of § 2. In the case of new services, if no customary practices have yet developed or if the provider is unique, it must use the available technologies. From the various options available, it must choose the most effective means, even if these are more expensive than the next best solutions. However, a limit is drawn by the **principle of proportionality**. The costs of the measures as well as the size and financial strength of the service must be considered and set in relation to the increase in effectiveness (sub. 2 Nos 1, 4). 23

---

[75] Hofmann ZUM 2020, 665 (666).

[76] CJEU C-682/18 and C-683/18, ECLI:EU:C:2021:503 mn. 84 – YouTube and Cyando.

[77] Spindler CR 2019, 277 (286); Kaesling/Knapp MMR 2021, 11 (12).

[78] Cf. COM(2021) 288 final EN, 8; Spindler CR 2020, 50 (54).

[79] Peters/Schmidt GRUR Int. 2019, 1006 (1009).

[80] See also Spindler CR 2019, 277 (286 et seq.).

[81] See also Spindler CR 2020, 50 (54).

[82] Cf. the general obligations for platform operators under Art. 3 InfoSoc Directive, CJEU C-682/18 and C-683/18, ECLI:EU:C:2021:503 mn. 84 – YouTube and Cyando.

[83] Cf. Peters/Schmidt GRUR Int. 2019, 1006 (1009).

#### e) Best efforts

24 The first benchmarks for high industry standards can be found in recital 66 subpara. 2 DSMD. Accordingly, an OCSSP must make **best efforts** (French: *meilleurs efforts*)[84] and **take all steps** that a diligent operator would take to ensure that no unauthorised works are available on its service. Under the InfoSoc Directive, a service provider is already obliged to do everything 'technically and economically reasonable' to prevent copyright infringements on its platform.[85] Thus, the service provider must employ **proven industry practices**[86] (German: *bewährte [proven] Verfahren in der Branche*; French: *meilleures [best] pratiques du secteur*; English: *best industry practices*), and it follows from the English and French versions of the Directive that OCSSPs must aim for a high standard. Therefore, OCSSPs must use the applicable technology that is best available in industry practice.[87] In deciding on the appropriate measures, its effectiveness has to be taken into account.[88] This has a twofold effect. First, an OCSSP must take effective measures to the extent they are reasonable; second and conversely, it does not have to take measures that are ineffective. Furthermore, an OCSSP does not have to go beyond the mandatory and do more than what is necessary.[89] Thus, if an effective measure was taken, a demand cannot be made of an OCSSP to do even more, especially if this would not have had an effect on the specific infringement. Similarly, an OCSSP does not have to use unproven technologies but must observe **future relevant** developments (German: *einschlägige Entwicklungen*; French: *évolutions pertinents*).[90] According to general standards, the **impossible** cannot be required of any OCSSP. Thus, if there is no reliably functioning filtering technology for certain types of content, the provider cannot be required to use it (→ mn. 32).

#### f) Principle of proportionality

25 The principle of proportionality must be taken into account in specifying best efforts. According to general principles, a measure must be appropriate and necessary to ensure that copyright-protected content is not unlawfully made available through the service. In addition, the effectiveness of the measure must be proportionate to the effort it entails and, thus, be proportionate in a strict sense.[91] In the words of the CJEU, 'where there is a choice between several appropriate measures, recourse must be had to the least onerous, and the disadvantages caused must not be disproportionate to the aims pursued'.[92] This is a general principle of both German and EU law.[93] Accordingly, OCSSPs may not be required to take **measures** that are **'excessively costly'** or **'unnecessarily complicated or**

[84] In German: *alle Anstrengungen*, which literally and inaccurately translates to 'all efforts', → § 1 mn. 3.

[85] BGH 15.8.2013 – I ZR 80/12, GRUR 2013, 1030 mn. 47 – File-Hosting-Service (file hosting service); 12.7.2012 – I ZR 18/11, GRUR 2013, 370 mn. 31 – Alone in the Dark.

[86] Recital 66 subpara. 2 sent. 2 DSMD; AG Saugmandsgaard Øe C-401/19, ECLI:EU:C:2021:613 mn. 66 – Poland/Parliament and Council.

[87] Cf. Spindler CR 2019, 277 (286), who tends to be more generous.

[88] Recital 66 subpara. 2 sent. 2, 5 DSMD; this is a general principle of EU law, cf. e.g. CJEU C-324/09, ECLI:EU:C:2011:474 mn. 136 – L'Oréal/eBay et al.; further, CJEU C-682/18 and C-683/18, ECLI:EU:C:2021:503 mn. 84 – YouTube and Cyando.

[89] Recital 66 subpara. 2 sent. 5 DSMD.

[90] Recital 66 subpara. 2 sent. 2 DSMD.

[91] CJEU C-401/19, ECLI:EU:C:2022:297 mn. 65 – Poland/Parliament and Council; CJEU C-336/19, ECLI:EU:C:2020:1031 mn. 64 – Centraal Israëlitisch Consistorie van België; AG Saugmandsgaard Øe C-401/19, ECLI:EU:C:2021:613 mn. 118 – Poland/Parliament and Council.

[92] CJEU C-401/19, ECLI:EU:C:2022:297 mn. 65 – Poland/Parliament and Council.

[93] For more on the latter, see: CJEU C-275/06, ECLI:EU:C:2008:54 mn. 68 – Promusicae/Telefonica.

**costly'**.[94] They may not be required to take measures that '**economically jeopardise**' their legitimate business model or '**disproportionately complicate** their activities'.[95] On the other hand, by passing the UrhDaG/Art. 17 DSMD, the legislatures decided that OCSSPs as defined in § 2 must meet **high industry standards** that go beyond the requirements that host providers must meet. Therefore, OCSSPs can be expected to make a high but reasonable effort, including the associated costs, to reduce the risks for copyright-protected content to an acceptable level. Consequently, they can be expected to do more than service providers that do not meet the requirements of § 2. § 1 (2) sent. 2 contains a **non-exhaustive list** ('in particular') **of criteria** that may be considered in the necessary balancing of interests.

**g) Multipolar interests**

In the regulation of internet platforms, there is a triangle or quadrangle of rights and interests among rightholders, OCSSPs, users and the general public. These interests need to be **appropriately and fairly balanced.**[96] To strike a fair balance of interests, it always has to be considered which interests are affected by the measures to be taken.[97] On the one hand, there is the **interest of the rightholder** to adequately participate in the economic exploitation of the copyright-protected content and receive effective legal protection (Art. 17 (2) CFR; Art. 14 (1) GG). On the other hand, the freedom of the OCSSP to conduct a business must be respected (Art. 16 CFR; Art. 12 GG).[98] In addition, Art. 17 (7–9) DSMD and its implementation in §§ 7 (2), 9–11 specify that the **interest of users** and the **public** in being able to make lawful content publicly accessible must be taken into account when determining specific obligations of the OCSSPs.[99] In particular, the fundamental rights to freedom of expression, art and information as well as the protection of personal data must be taken into account (Art. 8, 11 CFR; Art. 2, 5 GG). In addition, the **particular importance of the internet** as 'one of the principal means by which individuals exercise their right to freedom of expression and information' must be considered.[100] Not only the content of the communication participates in the protection of freedom of expression and information but also the means of dissemination.[101] Internet platforms enable individuals, in particular, to share and receive information independently of traditional gatekeepers, thereby 'providing an unprecedented platform for the exercise of freedom of expression'.[102] 26

[94] Generally for online services, see: CJEU C-324/09, ECLI:EU:C:2011:474 mn. 139 – L'Oréal/eBay and others; C-360/10, ECLI:EU:C:2012:85 mn. 46 – SABAM/Netlog.

[95] BGH 12.7.2012 – I ZR 18/11, GRUR 2013, 370 mn. 22 – Alone in the Dark, with further references.

[96] CJEU C-401/19, ECLI:EU:C:2022:297 mn. 20 et seq. – Poland/Parliament and Council. Further, CJEU C-682/18 and C-683/18, ECLI:EU:C:2021:503 mn. 64 – YouTube and Cyando; C-70/10, ECLI:EU:C:2011:771 mn. 44 et seqq. – Scarlet/SABAM; C-360/10, ECLI:EU:C:2012:85 mn. 43 – SABAM/Netlog; C-324/09, ECLI:EU:C:2011:474 mn. 143 – L'Oréal/eBay et al.

[97] See also Hofmann ZUM 2019, 617 (625 et seq.); Raue/Steinebach ZUM 2020, 355 (356 et seqq.).

[98] CJEU C-401/19, ECLI:EU:C:2022:297 mn. 75 – Poland/Parliament and Council; COM(2021) 288 final EN, 8.

[99] CJEU C-401/19, ECLI:EU:C:2022:297 mn. 80 et seq. – Poland/Parliament and Council; Wandtke/Hauck ZUM 2020, 671 (672); Kaesling/Knapp MMR 2021, 816 et seq.

[100] CJEU C-401/19, ECLI:EU:C:2022:297 mn. 45–47 – Poland/Parliament and Council; CJEU C-682/18 and C-683/18, ECLI:EU:C:2021:503 mn. 65 et seq. – YouTube and Cyando.

[101] CJEU C-401/19, ECLI:EU:C:2022:297 mn. 46 – Poland/Parliament and Council; ECHR CE:ECHR:2015:1201JUD004822610 mn. 52 – Cengiz and Others v. Turkey.

[102] CJEU C-401/19, ECLI:EU:C:2022:297 mn. 46 – Poland/Parliament and Council.

## 2. Criteria to be considered (sent. 2)

27 The aspects listed in § 1 (2) sent. 2 must be taken into account in specifying the obligations of OCSSPs in light of proportionality and a balancing of the interests. § 1 (2) sent. 2 contains a **non-exhaustive list** of criteria to be considered to **interpret** the legal terms and **specify the duties** under §§ 4, 7–11.[103] Therefore, reasonable measures in a specific case may differ depending on the OCSSP or the type, scope or audience of the respective service. The German legislature assumed that not all OCSSPs would use the same technical means.[104] According to the CJEU, the resources and abilities available to the OCSSP must be taken into account in determining the specific measures, and they must be balanced with 'other obligations and challenges which they will encounter in the exercise of their activity'.[105] Therefore, as a general rule, **no specific measures** can be demanded of the OCSSPs. It is for the service provider to decide how to achieve the required results with the means at its disposal and how to balance the conflicting interests. The principle of proportionality must be taken into account.[106]

### a) The type, the audience and the size of the service (No. 1)

28 The reasonable effort of the OCSSP must take into account the type of service. This has several dimensions. On the one hand, the **extent of the competition** with other online content providers and, thus, the economic potential of the OCSSPs to deprive them of customers can be considered. The more competitive its service and the higher the number of users of its service, the more the OCSSP can be expected to make greater efforts (because it is targeting the same audience as existing content providers and makes available similar content on its service). Conversely, the smaller the service and the lesser the overlap in terms of target groups and available content, the less effort is required. The same applies to ancillary services offered alongside the main purpose of § 2 (1) No. 1 or to categories of content that are uploaded to the platform only in small quantities (on this → § 2 mn. 4). In addition, the **size of the service** (German: *Umfang des Dienstes*; French: *taille du service*), and thus, its **economic resources**, must be taken into account. OCSSPs may not be required to take measures that '**economically jeopardise**' their legitimate business model or '**disproportionately complicate** their activities'.[107] The legislatures have determined that standards of conduct may be differentiated according to the economic capacity of the OCSSP. As a specification of this principle, **start-ups** and **small OCSSPs** (within the meaning of § 2 (2), (3)) are exempted in principle from the obligations of § 7 (1) (§ 7 (4), (5) → § 2 mn. 25 et seqq., → § 7 mn. 27 et seq.). The criticism has been raised that this would relativise objective standards of conduct.[108] However, the **differentiation** is **in line** with the regulatory aim of the UrhDaG and Art. 17 DSMD. The substitution potential (→ § 2 mn. 18 et seqq.), and thus, the potential to impair the value of copyright-protected content of other paying content providers, usually increases with the size and economic performance of a provider. Furthermore, the criterion strengthens competition. It lowers the market entry barriers and, thus, the possibility for smaller OCSSPs to compete with large OCSSPs even after the start-up privilege in § 2 (3) has expired.

---

[103] BT-Drs. 19/27426, 131.

[104] BT-Drs. 19/27426, 137.

[105] On this and the following, see: CJEU C-401/19, ECLI:EU:C:2022:297 mn. 75 – Poland/Parliament and Council.

[106] CJEU C-401/19, ECLI:EU:C:2022:297 mn. 36, 57, 65 et seq. – Poland/Parliament and Council.

[107] Cf. BGH 12.7. 2012 – I ZR 18/11, GRUR 2013, 370 mn. 22 – Alone in the Dark.

[108] Spindler CR 2019, 277 (287).

**b) The type of works uploaded by the users of the service (No. 2)**

**aa) Impact on available technical measures.** The type of content uploaded by users can give rise to various differentiations. For example, the type of content has an influence on the available filtering technologies, which are more or less robust depending on the type of uploaded content and can cause different effort and costs (→ mn. 32). 29

**bb) Attractiveness of the content.** The interests of the rightholders are affected above all else by the making available of **up-to-date content** that is still in the primary exploitation phase[109], such as current movies, music that is in the charts or live streams of music or sporting events (cf. on the latter also § 7 (2) sent. 3, → § 7 mn. 25). Here, the OCSSPs can be expected to make greater efforts than in the case of less current content. One can also differentiate according to the attractiveness of the content for the OCSSPs' users. It is reasonable to expect OCSSPs to more closely monitor content that is very **frequently accessed** than content in the long tail that is rarely accessed. This differentiation is also in line with § 2 (1) No. 4/recital 62 subpara. 1 sent. 2 DSMD, according to which an essential reason for the increased duty of care is that OCSSPs compete with other online content providers. Conversely, modified, substantially abridged or otherwise **altered content does** not affect the interests of rightholders to the same extent as original content that is made available.[110] The rules on the communication to the public of presumably legitimate uses in §§ 9 et seqq. of the Copyright Act (→ § 10 mn. 1) are also based on these considerations. These criteria can be parameterised (date of publication, self-assessment of criticality by [trusted] rightholders, number of downloads/visits, degree of conformity with the original) and considered, for example, in the setting of upload filters; the reaction of the filtering software can then be modified, for example, to automatically block the content or to inform the rightholder.[111] 30

**cc) The significance of the content to the users' fundamental rights.** When balancing the different interests, the importance of the uploaded (and potentially blocked) content to the users' freedoms of communication and information must be taken into account. An essential aspect in this regard is the **time criticality** of the content[112], which can be of particular importance due to the very dynamic attention curves on the internet.[113] The **interference** with users' rights is more severe when blocking content that is related to a current political discussion or any other **current issue** of public interest.[114] The same applies if a live stream of a current social, cultural or political event is to be blocked.[115] This can be succinctly described as 'censorship by the passage of time'.[116] 31

**c) The availability of suitable means to fulfil the obligations (No. 3)**

The availability of suitable and effective means (German: *geeignete und wirksame Mittel*; French: *moyens adaptés et efficaces*) has a significant influence on the duty of care. Of course, OCSSPs cannot be required to do the **impossible**. They can only use the technology that is available. Therefore, the DSMD clarifies that with regard to different types of content and specific circumstances of use, there may not exist suitable technol- 32

---

[109] Raue/Steinebach ZUM 2020, 355 (356, 363).
[110] Cf. also MPI Stellungnahme zum RefE, 18.
[111] See Raue/Steinebach ZUM 2020, 355 (357, 363).
[112] Hofmann/Specht-Riemenschneider ZGE 2021, 48 (97).
[113] Leistner ZUM 2020, 505 (512).
[114] Senftleben ZUM 2019, 369 (373); Raue/Steinebach ZUM 2020, 355 (363).
[115] Gielen/Tiessen EuZW 2019, 639 (645).
[116] Weiden GRUR 2019, 370 (371 et seq.).

ogies that enable qualified *ex ante* blocking of content under § 7.[117] The OCSSPs' increased duty of care exists only because and to the extent that suitable means (at proportionate cost, No. 4) are available.[118] According to the explanatory memorandum of the UrhDaG (*RegE*), an OCSSP can use manual, semi-automated or fully automated procedures.[119] It is technically possible to identify identical content using cryptographic hash procedures and **similar content** using robust hash procedures.[120] However, the technical possibilities and the effort required vary considerably depending on the type of media. According to the current **state of the art**,[121] it is impossible – with reasonable effort – to recognise individual still images of videos or individual sound elements that are included, for example through sampling, in a piece of music. In addition, a large number of individual images must be processed for videos, which requires considerable storage and processing capacities. Therefore, according to the current state of the art, the methods for feature recognition usually become less accurate with increasing playing time or data volume. To the extent that **automatic content filtering is not possible** with proportionate means and non-machine monitoring is disproportionate, rightholders may only demand *ex post* blocking pursuant to § 8, even according to high industry standards. However, OCSSPs are obliged to observe the **evolving state of the art** (→ mn. 24).[122]

**d) The costs for the service provider (No. 4)**

33 The proportionality test shall factor in the costs incurred by the OCSSPs as a result of the respective measures. This is a **general principle of both German and EU law**. This means that no measures may be imposed on OCSSPs that are 'excessively costly' or 'unnecessarily complicated'.[123] On the other hand, the legislature decided by adopting UrhDaG/Art. 17 DSMD that OCSSPs within the meaning of § 2 must meet high standards that are customary in the industry, which goes beyond the requirements that other host providers must meet. Therefore, OCSSPs can be required to make a **high, but reasonable effort**, including the associated costs, to reduce the risks of copyright-protected content to an acceptable level. They can also be expected to use measures that go beyond the measures that online services that do not meet the requirements of § 2 are obliged to use; however, the expected efforts must remain **reasonable**.[124] In this context, the other factors listed in Nos 1–3 must be taken into account, in particular, the size and economic capacity of the OCSSP as well as the type, audience and scope of its service. Therefore, the explanatory memorandum of the UrhDaG assumes that not all OCSSPs will use the same technical means.[125] With regard to **costs**, OCSSPs that develop and operate their own technologies will have to be differentiated from those that must licence externally developed technologies. In the latter case, the reasonableness may depend on the corresponding cost models, for example, whether smaller OCSSPs can refrain from automatically screening such content with filtering technology that is significantly modified or rarely accessed by other users and, thus, has little or no impact on the financial interests of rightholders and other content providers.[126] According to the

[117] Recital 66 subpara. 2 sent. 4 DSMD; Spindler CR 2019, 277 (287).

[118] Wagner GRUR 2020, 447 (451); Hofmann GRUR 2019, 1219 (1225).

[119] BT-Drs. 19/27426, 137.

[120] Raue/Steinebach ZUM 2020, 355 (358).

[121] Cf. the overview in Raue/Steinebach ZUM 2020, 355 (360 et seq.).

[122] Recital 66 subpara. 2 sent. 3 DSMD.

[123] Generally for online services, CJEU C-324/09, ECLI:EU:C:2011:474 mn. 139 – L'Oréal/eBay et al; C-360/10, ECLI:EU:C:2012:85 mn. 46 – SABAM/Netlog.

[124] BT-Drs. 19/27426, 137.

[125] BT-Drs. 19/27426, 137.

[126] Raue/Steinebach ZUM 2020, 355 (357, 364).

explanatory memorandum to the UrhDaG, OCSSPs must expect costs of EUR 0.05–0.1 per reviewed content for the licensing of filtering software, depending on the content.[127]

**e) Enabling legitimate uses (Art. 17 (7) DSMD)**

Art. 17 (7) DSMD requires Member States to ensure that legitimate uses that do not infringe copyright or related rights may not be blocked as a result of cooperation between OCSSPs and rightholders. Although this objective of the Directive is not explicitly listed in the non-exhaustive (→ mn. 27) list of § 1 (2) sent. 2, it must be **taken into account** in interpreting the high standards customary in the sector (→ § 7 mn. 16).[128] This obligation is rooted in the obligation to comply with the fundamental rights of the CFR as well of the German *Grundgesetz* (GG), and it is an obligation of **result.**[129] §§ 7 (2) sent. 1 and 8 (2) clarify this for **blocking**. Permitted uses must also not interfere with the **licensing efforts** of § 4 (→ § 4 mn. 41, → § 5 mn. 1). In the Commission's view, filtering by automatic content recognition technology ('upload filters') should not lead to the unavailability of permitted uses; thus, only obviously infringing uploads should be blocked. In principle, presumably legitimate content should be allowed to go online and only be blocked *ex post* based on a human assessment should the rightholders object to the upload.[130] 34

## 3. Individual cases

**a) Video platforms**

According to the general standard of Art. 3 InfoSoc Directive, a video platform, such as YouTube, takes **appropriate technological measures** to credibly and effectively counter copyright infringements on the platform[131] if the platform: 35

- clearly **informs users** in its general terms of service and every time an infringing content is uploaded that it is **forbidden to post copyright-protected content**;
- calls upon its users in its 'community guidelines' **to respect copyright**;
- warns users who upload copyright-infringing content that their **accounts** will be **suspended in the event of repeated infringements**;
- facilitates the prevention and cessation of copyright infringements with **technical provisions**, such as a **notification button**, a **special alert procedure** and a **content verification and recognition programme** that facilitates the identification and designation of such content; and
- immediately **deletes** or **blocks access to** infringing content when it becomes aware of it.

It remains to be **seen** whether OCSSPs will be required to **go** beyond the described prevention and reporting measures (this would mean that the licensing obligation of § 4 is the only far-reaching innovation of the special liability mechanism). OCSSPs are still allowed to organise the content uploaded by the users (§ 2 (1) No. 2) and to advertise it within the meaning of § 2 (1) No. 3 (otherwise they would not be OCSSPs). However, they may neither facilitate the unauthorised sharing of copyright-protected content nor pursue a business model that promotes such sharing; this is the basis on which the CJEU has not objected to YouTube's business model (on the latter also → mn. 39).[132]

---

[127] BT-Drs. 19/27426, 63.

[128] COM(2021) 288 final EN, 20.

[129] CJEU C-401/19, ECLI:EU:C:2022:297 mn. 78, 85 – Poland/Parliament and Council; COM(2021) 288 final EN, 20.

[130] COM(2021) 288 final EN, 20; Raue ZUM 2022, 624.

[131] CJEU C-682/18 and C-683/18, ECLI:EU:C:2021:503 mn. 93 et seq. – YouTube and Cyando; C-401/19, ECLI:EU:C:2022:297 mn. 27 – Poland/Parliament and Council.

[132] CJEU C-682/18 and C-683/18, ECLI:EU:C:2021:503 mn. 95 et seq. – YouTube and Cyando.

#### b) Other platforms

36 As a rule, pure sharehosters are not OCSSPs within the meaning of § 2 (→ § 2 mn. 16). The CJEU has not yet decided whether **sharehosters**, such as Uploaded, take appropriate technical measures to combat copyright infringement in a credible and effective way.[133] However, it must be assumed that it is not sufficient in terms of high industry standards for an OCSSP to merely inform its users in its general terms of use that they may not infringe copyright via the platform.

### 4. Burden of proof

37 In contrast to indirect liability for infringements of legal interests under § 823 (1) of the German Civil Code (BGB)[134] or *Störerhaftung* (breach of duty of care) under intellectual property law, the infringement of the duties of care in § 1 (2) UrhDaG is not a condition for liability but a possibility for the OCSSP to avoid liability. This has an impact on the **burden of proof**, which § 1 (1), (2) UrhDaG shifts at least in principle from the rightholder to the **OCSSP**. The OCSSP must prove – if necessary, with the help of experts – that it has complied with high industry standards of professional diligence.[135] OCSSPs should thus document their efforts.[136] However, the criteria of § 1 (2) sent. 2 may not only intensify the duties of care but also reduce them. It is, therefore, appropriate to distribute the burden of proof in this regard according to the respective effect.[137] Deviating from the general burden of proof rule, the **rightholder** must prove facts that intensify liability. Insofar as facts originate in the OCSSP's sphere of influence, rightholders benefit from the secondary burdens of disclosure (*sekundäre Darlegungslasten*) of the OCSSP.

## IV. Exclusion of the host provider privilege (sub. 3)

38 According to § 1 (3), OCSSPs are expressly **precluded from** invoking the **liability privilege of** the **host provider in § 10 (1) TMG**, which will be replaced by Art. 6 DSA. Therefore, it is irrelevant whether OCSSPs assume an active role within the meaning of § 10 (1) TMG/Art. 14 E-Commerce Directive.[138] The liability privilege of the TMG is functionally replaced by the liability exemption in § 1 (2).[139] This reflects the midway position of OCSSPs between host and content providers: they are no longer host providers because of their more active role, but they also do not offer their own content like content providers.

## V. OCSSPs with copyright-infringing main purpose (sub. 4)

39 An OCSSP cannot invoke the liability exemption in § 1 (2) if its main purpose is to participate in or facilitate copyright infringement; in short, if it pursues a **business model based on copyright infringement**.[140] All circumstances of the individual case

[133] CJEU C-682/18 and C-683/18, ECLI:EU:C:2021:503 mn. 100 – YouTube and Cyando.

[134] Cf. generally MüKoBGB/Wagner, 8th edn 2020, BGB § 823 mn. 89.

[135] Leistner ZGE 2020, 123 (136); Nordemann/Waiblinger GRUR 2020, 569 (574); Spindler CR 2019, 277 (286 et seq.).

[136] Rauer/Bibi BB 2021, 1475 (1477).

[137] Spindler CR 2019, 277 (287 et seq.).

[138] See CJEU C-682/18 and C-683/18, ECLI:EU:C:2021:503 mn. 103 et seqq. – YouTube and Cyando; Husovec/Quintais GRUR Int. 2021, 325 (329).

[139] Cf. Nordemann/Waiblinger GRUR 2020, 569 (574); Volkmann CR 2019, 376 (378).

[140] Hofmann ZUM 2020, 665 (666); Bischof/Brost MMR 2021, 303 (305).

must be considered to come to this conclusion.[141] The OCSSP is then liable under § 1 (1) for all copyright-infringing content uploaded by its users. This changes little as such a service provider performed an act of communication to the public according to Art. 3 InfoSoc Directive.[142] Consequently, the case law of the CJEU on Art. 3 InfoSoc Directive can be used to specify this provision. It is sufficient for a copyright-infringing principal purpose that a **very large amount of** the **content** offered via the OCSSP is published **without the consent of the rightholder**[143] or the **main or predominant** use consists in making protected content illegally available to the public.[144] Advertising statements of the OCSSP may be included in the assessment.[145] An OCSSP should not be enabled to 'hide' behind a few legal offers.[146] A business model is based on copyright infringements if **90 % of the content** is made accessible by users in a copyright infringing manner.[147] In such a case of an **infringement-oriented business model**, general knowledge of copyright infringements is sufficient.[148] Irrespective of a high proportion of copyright infringing content, a copyright-infringing main purpose may also be established by the fact that the **operator's business model is** based on the availability of infringing content on its platform.[149]

## § 2
## Service providers

**(1) Service providers within the meaning of this Act are providers of services within the meaning of Article 1 subsection 1 lit. b of Directive (EU) 2015/1535 of the European Parliament and of the Council of 9 September 2015 laying down a procedure for the provision of information in the field of technical regulations and of rules on Information Society services (OJ L 241, 17.9.2015, p. 1), which**

1. **main purpose is, exclusively or at least in part, to store and give the public access to a large amount of copyright-protected content uploaded by third parties,**
2. **organise the content within the meaning of number 1,**
3. **promote the content within the meaning of number 1 for profit-making purposes and**
4. **compete with online content services for the same target groups.**

## § 2
## Diensteanbieter

**(1) Diensteanbieter im Sinne dieses Gesetzes sind Anbieter von Diensten im Sinne des Artikels 1 Absatz 1 Buchstabe b der Richtlinie (EU) 2015/1535 des Europäischen Parlaments und des Rates vom 9. September 2015 über ein Informationsverfahren auf dem Gebiet der technischen Vorschriften und der Vorschriften für die Dienste der Informationsgesellschaft (ABl. L 241 vom 17.9.2015, S. 1), die**

1. **es als Hauptzweck ausschließlich oder zumindest auch verfolgen, eine große Menge an von Dritten hochgeladenen urheberrechtlich geschützten Inhalten zu speichern und öffentlich zugänglich zu machen,**
2. **die Inhalte im Sinne der Nummer 1 organisieren,**
3. **die Inhalte im Sinne der Nummer 1 zum Zweck der Gewinnerzielung bewerben und**
4. **mit Online-Inhaltediensten um dieselben Zielgruppen konkurrieren.**

---

[141] Nordemann/Waiblinger GRUR 2020, 569 (573).

[142] Cf. CJEU C-610/15, ECLI:EU:C:2017:456 mn. 36 et seqq. – Stichting Brein (Pirate Bay).

[143] CJEU C-610/15, ECLI:EU:C:2017:456 mn. 45 – Stichting Brein (Pirate Bay).

[144] CJEU C-682/18 and C-683/18, ECLI:EU:C:2021:503 mn. 100 – YouTube and Cyando.

[145] CJEU C-527/15, ECLI:EU:C:2017:300 mn. 50 et seq. – Stichting Brein/Wullems (Filmspeler).

[146] See BGH 26.11.2015 – I ZR 174/14, GRUR 2016, 268 mn. 55 – Störerhaftung des Accessproviders.

[147] Nordemann/Waiblinger GRUR 2020, 569 (573); cf. also BGH 26.11.2015 – I ZR 174/14, GRUR 2016, 268 mn. 56: a total share of 4 % of legitimate content is negligible.

[148] Schricker/Loewenheim/Leistner UrhG § 97 mn. 96 d.

[149] CJEU C-682/18 and C-683/18, ECLI:EU:C:2021:503 mn. 101 – YouTube and Cyando.

**(2) Start-up service providers are service providers with an annual turnover within the European Union of up to 10 million euro whose services have been available to the public in the European Union for less than three years.**

**(3) Small service providers are service providers with an annual turnover within the European Union of up to 1 million euro.**

**(4) [1]For the calculation of the turnover of start-up service providers and small service providers, the Commission Recommendation of 6 May 2003 concerning the definition of micro, small and medium-sized enterprises (OJ L 124, 20.5.2003, p. 36) shall apply. [2]The relevant turnover is that of the previous calendar year.**

**(2) Startup-Diensteanbieter sind Diensteanbieter mit einem jährlichen Umsatz innerhalb der Europäischen Union von bis zu 10 Millionen Euro, deren Dienste der Öffentlichkeit in der Europäischen Union seit weniger als drei Jahren zur Verfügung stehen.**

**(3) Kleine Diensteanbieter sind Diensteanbieter mit einem jährlichen Umsatz innerhalb der Europäischen Union von bis zu 1 Million Euro.**

**(4) [1]Für die Berechnung des Umsatzes von Startup-Diensteanbietern und kleinen Diensteanbietern ist die Empfehlung der Kommission vom 6. Mai 2003 betreffend die Definition der Kleinstunternehmen sowie der kleinen und mittleren Unternehmen anzuwenden (ABl. L 124 vom 20.5.2003, S. 36). [2]Maßgeblich ist jeweils der Umsatz des vorangegangenen Kalenderjahres.**

Article 1
Directive (EU) 2015/1535

**(1) For the purposes of this Directive, the following definitions apply: […].**

**b) 'service' means any Information Society service, that is to say, any service normally provided for remuneration, at a distance, by electronic means and at the individual request of a recipient of services.**

**For the purposes of this definition:**

**i) 'at a distance' means that the service is provided without the parties being simultaneously present;**

**ii) 'by electronic means' means that the service is sent initially and received at its destination by means of electronic equipment for the processing (including digital compression) and storage of data, and entirely transmitted, conveyed and received by wire, by radio, by optical means or by other electromagnetic means;**

**iii) 'at the individual request of a recipient of services' means that the service is provided through the transmission of data on individual request.**

**An indicative list of services not covered by this definition is set out in Annex I; (…)**

Artikel 1
Richtlinie (EU) 2015/1535

**(1) Für die Zwecke dieser Richtlinie bezeichnet der Ausdruck: […]**

**b) "Dienst" eine Dienstleistung der Informationsgesellschaft, d. h. jede in der Regel gegen Entgelt elektronisch im Fernabsatz und auf individuellen Abruf eines Empfängers erbrachte Dienstleistung.**

**Im Sinne dieser Definition bezeichnet der Ausdruck**

**i) "im Fernabsatz erbrachte Dienstleistung" eine Dienstleistung, die ohne gleichzeitige physische Anwesenheit der Vertragsparteien erbracht wird;**

**ii) "elektronisch erbrachte Dienstleistung" eine Dienstleistung, die mittels Geräten für die elektronische Verarbeitung (einschließlich digitaler Kompression) und Speicherung von Daten am Ausgangspunkt gesendet und am Endpunkt empfangen wird und die vollständig über Draht, über Funk, auf optischem oder anderem elektromagnetischem Wege gesendet, weitergeleitet und empfangen wird;**

**iii) "auf individuellen Abruf eines Empfängers erbrachte Dienstleistung" eine Dienstleistung die durch die Übertragung von Daten auf individuelle Anforderung erbracht wird.**

**Eine Beispielliste der nicht unter diese Definition fallenden Dienste findet sich in Anhang I; (…)**

**Bibliography:** See the bibliography in the Introduction.

**Content**



# I. General remarks

## 1. Objective

In § 2, the UrhDaG introduces the concept of 'service provider' (*Diensteanbieter*), 1
which is a **new category** of information society services between host and content providers.[1] The DSMD calls them **service providers for sharing online content**, which is commonly abbreviated as **OCSSP** (online content-sharing service providers). § 2 contains the **legal definition** of the OCSSP in **sub. 1** and, thus, the addressee of the special liability mechanism and other duties of the UrhDaG. An OCSSP provides its users with a technical service through which its users can make large amounts of copyright-protected content publicly available (sub. 1 No. 1). However, the special liability mechanism under the UrhDaG only applies to service providers that take an **active role.**[2]

[1] BT-Drs. 19/27426, 43.
[2] Cf. Metzger/Pravemann ZUM 2021, 288 (290).

Therefore, they must organise the content and advertise it with the aim of making **profits** (sub. 1 Nos 2, 3, → mn. 17). Their business model must aim at making money from copyrighted content uploaded by third parties.[3] At the same time, their service must **compete with** other online content services that are usually subject to a fee (sub. 1 No. 4, → mn. 18 et seqq.). The definition primarily applies to video platforms such as YouTube and audio platforms such as Soundcloud. Social networks were also mentioned as addressees in the legislative process,[4] although it is doubtful whether they would meet all the requirements of sub. 1.[5] Generally, a case-by-case assessment is necessary.[6] Because the UrhDaG imposes considerable obligations on OCSSPs, **§ 3** creates a **safe harbour** in the form of a **non-exhaustive list of examples**. It excludes the information society services mentioned therein from the scope of application of the UrhDaG, and in that way, it specifies the definition of § 2 (1) in a binding manner. **§ 2 (2)** and **(3)** provide the **legal definition** of **start-up** and **small OCSSPs**. Although both types of service providers fall within the scope of the UrhDaG, they are only subject to limited obligations. The explanatory memorandum of the UrhDaG assumes that in the medium term, there will be **thirteen OCSSPs** as defined in § 2, seven of which will be large OCSSPs as defined in § 2 (1), two start-up OCSSPs as defined in § 2 (2) and four small OCSSPs as defined in § 2 (3).[7]

### 2. EU law requirements

2 The definition of OCSSP in sub. 1 implements the definition in **Art. 2 No. 6 subpara. 1 DSMD**, which specifies recital 62 subpara. 1 DSMD. The definition of information society service by reference to Art. 1 (1)(b) of Directive 2015/1535 is provided by **Art. 2 No. 5 DSMD**. The criterion of competition with other online service providers in sub. 1 No. 4 is not included in the definition of Art. 2 No. 6 DSMD but can be based on **recital 62 subpara. 1 sent. 2 DSMD** (on this → mn. 19).[8] The Commission recommends that the Member States include the concretisations of the recitals in their transposition.[9] The definition of a start-up OCSSP is derived from **Art. 17 (6) subpara. 1 DSMD**, which is explained in recital 67. The category of small OCSSPs is an original creation of the German legislature with no equivalent in the DSMD. It can be justified as a provider-oriented concretisation of the principle of proportionality from **Art. 17 (5) DSMD.**[10] Its conformity with the Directive is disputed, but convincing (→ mn. 27).

## II. OCSSPs (sub. 1)

### 1. Cumulative requirements

3 Only providers that provide information society services as defined in Notification Directive 2015/1535 and **cumulatively fulfil the requirements of Nos 1–4** are subject to the specific liability mechanism of the UrhDaG.[11] If any one of the requirements is

[3] BT-Drs. 19/27426, 44.
[4] Wandtke/Hauck ZUM 2020, 671 (672).
[5] Husovec/Quintais GRUR Int. 2021, 325 (327) with further references.
[6] Cf. recital 63 DSMD; COM(2021) 288 final EN, 4.
[7] BT-Drs. 19/27426, 61.
[8] BT-Drs. 19/27426, 131; with criticism: Wandtke/Hauck ZUM 2020, 671 (672).
[9] COM(2021) 288 final EN, 4.
[10] BT-Drs. 19/27426, 131.
[11] COM(2021) 288 final EN, 4; Wandtke/Hauck ZUM 2020, 671 (672).

not met, a service provider is liable solely under the general requirements of the Copyright Act (→ § 1 mn. 6). Whether the conditions are met depends on the actual activity of the OCSSP.[12]

### 2. Uniform concept of an OCSSP

It is still unclear how differentiated the characteristics of an OCSSP must be applied if the service provider offers different services (→ mn. 14) and different content (→ mn. 10, 21).[13] According to the wording of § 2 (1), a provider of information society services is an OCSSP as a whole within the meaning of the UrhDaG if it meets the requirements of § 2.[14] Thus, a **uniform concept of an OCSSP** applies.[15] However, the scope of the individual obligations that affect the OCSSP can differ with regard to the different services and content. It will generally be disproportionate to extend the stricter obligations of the UrhDaG to services offered for **ancillary purposes** if those services do not compete with those of other online content services, cf. § 1 (2) Nos 1, 4.[16] The same applies to **categories of content** that are uploaded to its service only in minor quantities and do not compete with the content provided by other content providers (→ § 1 mn. 28). § 4 (2) No.1 expressly stipulates that the licensing obligation does not apply to content that is only marginally uploaded. The other obligations of the OCSSPs under the UrhDaG are subject to the proportionality test of § 1 (2) No.2. If the automated blocking of minor content that is not part of the main content uploaded on the platform causes considerable effort or costs, qualified blocking according to § 7 may be disproportionate. 4

### 3. Information society service

#### a) Service provider

Only service providers that provide an **information society service** as defined in the Notification Directive 2015/1535 fall within the scope of the UrhDaG. Art. 1 (1)(b) Notification Directive 2015/1535 defines an information society service as a service normally provided for remuneration, at a distance, by electronic means and at the individual request of the recipient. 5

#### b) Remuneration

The concept of 'remuneration' is **understood broadly**.[17] It is not required that payment for the service be made by those for whom it is performed. Payment can also be provided by third parties that, for example, book advertising[18] or pay for customer data. In addition, a remunerated information society service is provided 'in so far as they represent an economic activity'; thus, it includes any 'on line information or commercial communications, or those providing tools allowing for search, access and retrieval of data'.[19] Accordingly, a service is remunerated if it is provided for economic purposes and not purely altruistically.[20] 6

---

[12] Specht-Riemenschneider, Leitlinien zur nationalen Umsetzung des Art. 17 DSM-RL aus Verbrauchersicht, 2020, 57.

[13] Cf. Leistner ZGE 2020, 123 (145 et seq.); Leistner ZUM 2020, 505 (507 et seq.).

[14] Leistner ZGE 2020, 123 (146).

[15] See, however: COM(2021) 288 final EN, 5: 'consider each service separately'.

[16] COM(2021) 288 final EN, 5; Leistner ZGE 2020, 123 (146).

[17] Cf. on the identical concept: recital 18 sent. 3 E-Commerce Directive 2000/31/EC.

[18] CJEU C- 484/14, ECLI:EU:C:2016:689 mn. 41 et seq. – Mc Fadden.

[19] Recital 18 sent. 3 E-Commerce Directive 2000/31/EC; CJEU C-339/15, ECLI:EU:C:2017:335 mn. 36 – Luc Vanderborght.

[20] Simitis/Hornung/Spiecker gen. Döhrmann/Klement DSGVO Art. 4 No. 25 mn. 9.

#### c) At a distance

7 According to the Directive, a service is provided 'at a distance' if the service is provided **without the simultaneous physical presence** of the contracting parties. This excludes services for which users must visit specific places or facilities of the provider.

#### d) By electronic means

8 A service is provided 'by electronic means' if two conditions are met. First, it must be provided by **means of electronic processing** (including digital compression) and storage equipment that transmits data at the origin and receives data at the destination. Second, data must be entirely transmitted, conveyed and received by wire, radio, optical means or other electromagnetic means; in short, by **an electronic communications network**.

#### e) At the individual request of a recipient of services

9 A service is provided at the individual request of a recipient if the data transmission is provided on individual demand. Therefore, classic television or radio transmissions are not information society services because they are simultaneously provided to an unlimited number of individual recipients. In contrast, **all services offered via the internet** fall under the definition because they must be individually accessed.

### 4. To store and give the public access as main purpose (No. 1)

#### a) Large amounts of copyright-protected content

10 Stricter liability is only justified if one of the essential purposes (→ mn. 14) of the service provider is to provide the public with access to **large amounts** (German: *große Mengen*; French: *quantité importante*) of copyright-protected content. According to recital 63 DSMD, all essential aspects must be considered on a case-by-case basis, in particular, the **number of uploaded files** with copyright-protected content. That criterion interacts with the 'important role' the OCSSP must play in order to compete with the same target group according to No. 4 (→ mn. 22). Against this background, it makes sense that the audience of the OCSSP should also be considered in assessing whether the service provider stores and gives access to a large amount of content (recital 63 DSMD). Thus, the criterion not only has a **quantitative dimension** but also a **qualitative dimension**[21], which is also suggested by the French version of the Directive (French *quantité importante*). If a large amount of data is made accessible, but only a few users take notice of it, then the service does not significantly compete with other content providers and does not play the required important role in competition (→ mn. 21). The same applies if only singular works of a certain content category are uploaded (cf. → mn. 4). Conversely, in the case of a niche provider with specialised content, even an absolutely small number of works can be a 'large amount' if the corresponding niche content is offered almost in its entirety.[22]

#### b) Uploaded by third parties

11 The content must be uploaded by third parties, but it is irrelevant whether it is content of the uploaders or of uninvolved third parties. OCSSPs are liable for their own content according to § 15 (2) UrhG, → § 1 mn. 16.

#### c) To store

12 To store (German: *speichern*; French: *stocker)* means any **permanent storage** of copyright-protected content on the OCSSP's servers or in the OCSSP's sphere of

---

[21] Nordemann/Waiblinger GRUR 2020, 569 (572).
[22] Cf. Nordemann/Waiblinger GRUR 2020, 569 (572).

influence. This requirement is not met by an OCSSP that merely links to or frames content that is stored on servers controlled by third parties.[23] The OCSSP must control the content that is made accessible.[24] Storage also covers the **temporary storage** of, for example, live casts.[25] The right of reproduction under § 16 UrhG or Art. 2 InfoSoc Directive also covers transient acts of reproduction,[26] although § 2 (1) No. 1 UrhDaG and Art. 2 No. 6 DSMD use the different term 'to store', which implies a certain permanence.[27] However, making protected content even temporarily accessible can compete with other online content services (No. 4), for example, in the case of sports broadcasts or live concerts, and severely impact their business models. In addition to the aim of the UrhDaG, § 7 (2) sent. 3 also speaks in favour of considering caching as storage. The provision enables the rightholder to prevent live transmissions without the user being able to flag the content as permitted (→ § 7 mn. 25).

**d) Give the public access**

This does not only mean 'making available to the public' within the meaning of § 19a UrhG but also **any form of (nonphysical) online access for the public**. This follows from two aspects: first, from § 1 (1) that refers to the broader concept of 'giving the public access' and, second, from the identical provisions in Art. 2 No. 6 subpara. 1 and Art. 17 (1) subpara. 1 DSMD (German: *der Öffentlichkeit Zugang verschaffen*; French: *donner au public l'accès*). § 2 (1) No.1 does **not** cover (physical) **acts of distribution**, which follows from the exemption of online marketplaces in § 3 No. 5.[28] **13**

**e) Main purpose**

The service provider must 'exclusively or at least in part' pursue the main purpose (German: *Hauptzweck*; French: *objectif principal*) of making content uploaded by users accessible to the public. Only then is it justified to impose on them the licensing obligation, the provision of filtering technology, complaint management and the other obligations of the UrhDaG. Therefore, the UrhDaG mainly covers platforms that enable their users to upload videos, music, images, texts or other content. The Act assumes that an OCSSP may pursue **different main purposes**. It is irrelevant if a service provider offers its users other services besides content sharing, such as social networking or messenger services. However, content sharing must be the predominant function of the provider.[29] Services that allow their users to post profile pictures but primarily have other functions (e.g., dating platforms) are outside the scope of application of the UrhDaG.[30] It is **unclear** whether the obligations of the UrhDaG also extend to these **ancillary services** (→ mn. 4). In any case, this can only apply if the users of the service make copyrighted objects available to the public (§ 1 (1)). The licensing obligation under § 4 only extends to repertoires of content that the OCSSP communicates to the public in more than minor quantities (§ 4 (2) No.1). It would usually be disproportionate to extend the other onerous obligations of the liability **14**

[23] Becker ZUM 2020, 681 (683).

[24] Cf. on the corresponding requirements of § 19a UrhG: BGH 21.9.2017 – I ZR 11/16, GRUR 2018, 178 mn. 19 – Vorschaubilder III.

[25] Leistner ZGE 2020, 123 (145). See, however: COM(2021) 288 final EN, 4: 'more than temporary'; Becker ZUM 2020, 681 (683) [on DiskE].

[26] Dreier/Schulze/Schulze UrhG § 16 mn. 12.

[27] Nordemann/Waiblinger GRUR 2020, 569 (571).

[28] Nordemann/Waiblinger GRUR 2020, 569 (572).

[29] COM(2021) 288 final EN, 4.

[30] See, however: Peters/Schmidt GRUR Int. 2019, 1006 (1007).

mechanisms to ancillary services if these services do not compete with other online content services (cf. § 1 (2) Nos 1, 4).[31]

#### f) Other main purpose

15 Services are **not covered** by the UrhDaG if they pursue another main purpose, in particular, the services listed in § 3 Nos. 4–7 (→ § 3 mn. 6 et seqq.). Providers of **electronic communication services** fall outside the scope of application as long as their main purpose is the provision of individual communication services or the provision of internet access (→ § 3 No. 6). The main purpose of **online marketplaces** (§ 3 No. 5) is to sell the goods or services offered thereon and not to make copyright-protected content available (→ § 3 No. 7).[32] Because of the providers mentioned in § 3, online platforms fall outside the scope of the UrhDaG, which primarily serves **professional networking** as well as **dating or flirting portals**[33], **internet forums**, discussion groups and bulletin boards[34] insofar as they do not primarily serve the exchange of copyright-protected content. B2B or private **cloud services** (§ 3 Nos. 6, 7) provide storage space and serve to network closed groups. Thus, their main purpose is other than to provide the public with access to protected content. In such cases, it is irrelevant if their users occasionally use the service to share content with the public, as long as this is not one of the essential functions of the service.

### 5. To organise and promote the content (Nos 2, 3)

#### a) Active role

16 A service provider must take an active role beyond just storing the content. It can assume an active role by organising the content (No. 2) and promoting it with the intention of making a profit (No. 3). This requirement distinguishes OCSSPs from host providers. Therefore, it is not sufficient if the service provider merely provides storage space, such as simple sharehosters.[35] The provider must make tools available to users, for example, by **structuring** the content by categorising and indexing[36] or by specifically **drawing the attention** of other users to it.[37] A search function can also contribute to an active role.[38] The aim of the efforts should be to make the content uploaded by the users **more attractive** to a larger audience (recital 62 subpara. 1 sent. 3 DSMD).[39] As a rule, the service provider must be using targeted promotion within its service.[40] Providers meet this criterion if, like social networks, they provide content in **newsfeeds**, **suggest interesting content** to their users ('other users also watched'/'this could be interesting') or provide automatic playlists.[41] This may include information provided by the provider on third-party platforms, such as blogs, forums or other forms of link lists.[42] However,

---

[31] COM(2021) 288 final EN, 5: 'consider each service separately'.
[32] Recital 62 subpara. 1 sent. 5 DSMD.
[33] Spindler WRP 2019, 951 (956).
[34] Würtenberger/Freischem GRUR 2019, 1140 (1154).
[35] Becker ZUM 2020, 681 (683); see also CJEU C-682/18 and C-683/18, ECLI:EU:C:2021:503 mn. 98 – YouTube and Cyando.
[36] Cf. CJEU C-682/18 and C-683/18, ECLI:EU:C:2021:503 mn. 82 – YouTube and Cyando; C-610/15, ECLI:EU:C:2017:456 mn. 38 – Stichting Brein (Pirate Bay).
[37] Recital 62 subpara. 1 sent. 3 DSMD.
[38] See CJEU C-682/18 and C-683/18, ECLI:EU:C:2021:503 mn. 82, 98 – YouTube and Cyando; Peters/Schmidt GRUR Int. 2019, 1006; Hofmann ZUM 2019, 617 (618); Spindler WRP 2019, 951 (956); see, however: Sesing MMR 2019, 788 (789).
[39] COM(2021) 288 final EN, 5; Metzger/Pravemann ZUM 2021, 288 (290).
[40] Nordemann/Waiblinger GRUR 2020, 569 (572); also Spindler WRP 2019, 951 (956).
[41] Becker ZUM 2020, 681 (684); Metzger/Pravemann ZUM 2021, 288 (290).
[42] See CJEU C-682/18 and C-683/18, ECLI:EU:C:2021:503 mn. 98 – YouTube and Cyando.

an advertisement of the platform, such as a general advertisement for a sharehoster or another online service, does not meet this criterion.

#### b) For profit-making purposes

In the UrhDaG and in the German version of Art. 2 No. 6 subpara. 1 DSMD, the purpose of making profit refers only to advertising (*Inhalte organisiert und zum Zweck der Gewinnerzielung bewirbt*). The English and French versions (French: *qu'il organise et promeut à des fins lucratives*) of the Directive indicate that the purpose of profit-making refers to the active role of the OCSSP in organising and promoting the content.[43] However, this point of reference is also somewhat inaccurate. The active role distinguishes an OCSSP from a host provider (→ mn. 1). The profit-making purpose distinguishes it from non-profit platforms (§ 3 Nos 1–3) and justifies the specific liability mechanism. The relevant question is whether the **making available** of copyright-protected content is **generally** carried out with the direct or indirect **aim of making a profit, not** whether **individual measures** are profit-orientated (so also recital 62 subpara. 1 sent. 4 DSMD).[44] Because the objective of making a profit is sufficient, it does not matter whether the OCSSP actually makes a profit. Therefore, start-ups can be OCSSPs even if they accept high losses in the initial phase of the enterprise in order to gain or expand customers and market shares – as long as they have the goal of being profitable in the long run. The goal of making a profit can be pursued **directly** (e.g., via user fees for the platform) or **indirectly** (e.g., via advertising or the sale of user data) (recital. 62 subpara. 1 sent. 3 DSMD).[45] On the other hand, platforms that use their revenue only to cover their costs incurred do not fall within the scope of application of the UrhDaG.[46] Therefore, all **non-commercial services** are outside the scope of application of the UrhDaG, in particular, non-commercial online encyclopaedias such as Wikipedia or corresponding scientific repositories (§ 3 Nos 1, 2)[47] as well as governmental, non-profit services.[48] In contrast, no sufficient conclusions can be drawn solely from the legal form of the OCSSP or from the fact that it is an economic operator.[49] 17

### 6. Competition with online content services (No. 4)

#### a) Competition for the same audiences

The service provider must compete with other online content services for the same target group. Only the market for **online content** is relevant. Competition with offline content providers is irrelevant according to the wording of the provision. Qualifying a service provider as an OCSSP requires an examination of whether there is an actual or potential competitive relationship with other online content services. This has a **quantitative** (→ mn. 21) and a **qualitative** (→ mn. 22) **component**. 18

#### b) Compatibility with DSMD

This criterion is not included in the definition of Art. 2 No. 6 DSMD. However, it can be based on **recital 62 subpara. 1 sent. 2 DSMD**. Accordingly, the Directive 'should 19

---

[43] COM(2021) 288 final EN, 5.

[44] Würtenberger/Freischem GRUR 2019, 1140 (1154); cf. also CJEU C-610/15, ECLI:EU:C:2017:456 mn. 46 – Stichting Brein (Pirate Bay).

[45] Peters/Schmidt GRUR Int. 2019, 1006 et seq.

[46] Cf. in particular the services mentioned in § 3 (Nos 1, 2); COM(2021) 288 final EN, 5; Nordemann/Waiblinger GRUR 2020, 569 (572).

[47] Spindler CR 2019, 277 (284).

[48] Nordemann/Waiblinger GRUR 2020, 569 (572).

[49] COM(2021) 288 final EN, 5.

target only online services that play an important role on the online content market by competing with other online content services, such as online audio and video streaming services, for the same audiences'.[50] This is a **permissible clarification**[51] because in interpreting EU law, it is not only the wording of the norm that must be taken into account but also 'its context, the objectives pursued by the rules [...]', for which purpose the recitals are an important and binding source.[52] This clarification is also included in the Commission's recommendation.[53]

### c) Criticism

20 The restricting criterion in both the DSMD and the UrhDaG contradicts their respective aims. Depending on the actual interpretation, this has the potential to considerably limit the circle of providers addressed by the UrhDaG.[54] In particular, when parts of copyright-protected works (e.g., short music or video clips) are uploaded to platforms, they are not necessarily in a competitive relationship with existing audio or video platforms. Social networks also tend not to substitute the use of video or audio platforms or professional picture agencies (but possibly the use of news providers). Nevertheless, these platforms organise and promote large amounts of copyright-protected content uploaded by users for the purpose of making a profit. They should thus be covered by the regulation that aims to provide authors with fair remuneration for the use of their content on commercial online platforms. However, the criterion has some justification because substitutable OCSSPs diminish the economic potential of competing content providers and thus the value of copyright-protected content. But the restrictive criterion must not be applied so strictly that it **impairs the practical effectiveness** of the liability mechanism.[55]

### d) Important role in the online market

21 The DSMD specifies the criterion in **quantitative terms** to the effect that the OCSSP must play an **important role** in the market for online content (recital 62 subpara. 1 sent. 2 DSMD). If the OCSSP attracts only a **small audience**, it does not play an important role in the market for online content. Apart from niche constellations, it cannot enter into serious competition with other content providers. However, one should not be too strict about the 'important role'. According to § 2 (2) UrhDaG and Art. 17 (6) DSMD, start-ups with a turnover of less than 10 million euro – and even small companies with a turnover of less than 1 million euro (§ 2 (3) UrhDaG) – can be subject to the specific liability mechanism. Therefore, providers can fall within the scope of application well below the threshold of market dominance.[56] The provision has the function of a ***de minimis* provision** and excludes OCSSPs that only play a minor role on the market from the scope of application of the UrhDaG.[57] Furthermore, categories of content that are only made available in small quantities on the service can be exempted from the UrhDaG's increased duty of care (→ mn. 4).

---

[50] BT-Drs. 19/27426, 131; critically Wandtke/Hauck ZUM 2020, 671 (672).

[51] Leistner ZGE 2020, 123 (144 et seq.); Spindler WRP 2021, 1111 mn. 10.

[52] On the last two aspects, CJEU C-263/18, ECLI:EU:C:2019:1111 mn. 38 et seq. – NUV et al./Tom Kabinet.

[53] COM(2021) 288 final EN, 4.

[54] Leistner ZGE 2020, 123 (145).

[55] Cf. CJEU C-516/17, ECLI:EU:C:2019:625 mn. 36 – Spiegel Online/Volker Beck; Specht-Riemenschneider, Leitlinien zur nationalen Umsetzung des Art. 17 DSM-RL aus Verbrauchersicht, 2020, 59.

[56] Cf. Würtenberger/Freischem GRUR 2019, 1140 (1154).

[57] Cf. also Wandtke/Hauck ZUM 2020, 671 (672).

### e) Actual or potential competitive relationship

By its type, the service must be capable of substituting, at least potentially and partially, the use of other online content services[58] because users perceive it as an equivalent means to access content online.[59] As a start, competition law concepts can be relied on for the qualitative capability for substitution. As the competition criterion has its foundations in recital 62 DSMD, only EU law concepts should be considered. According to the **demand-side oriented market concept** (*Bedarfsmarktkonzept*) **of antitrust law**, an actual or potential competitive relationship exists if services are regarded 'as interchangeable or substitutable by the consumer, by reason of the products' characteristics, their prices and their intended use'.[60] However, a narrow market definition tends to be used in antitrust law to enforce the prohibition of the abuse of a dominant position because market dominance will rarely exist in broadly defined markets.[61] One should rather rely on the broader, future-related market definition of merger control. In this context, future technical developments and expected changes in the economic or legal framework are considered.[62] A definition of competition also exists in EU **unfair competition** law to identify a 'competitor', for example, of the advertiser in the sense of Art. 2 (c) Directive 2006/114/EC. This definition requires the existence of a certain 'degree of substitution' between products, for which they need to be 'capable of meeting identical needs'; courts take into account 'not only the present state of the market but also the possibilities for development […] and the further potential […] which may be revealed by intensification of trade'.[63] The UrhDaG aims to ensure that rightholders receive appropriate remuneration for the use of their works and subject matter (recital 61 sent. 9 DSMD → Introduction mn. 2). This calls for a wide interpretation of the necessary competitive relationship. Such a relationship exists under the **UrhDaG** if the OCSSP's service can be **substituted for the offer of other online content providers** to an **economically relevant extent**, taking into account a probable further development of the market and, thus, potential competition. Both the quantity and quality of the content uploaded by the users as well as the number of users and their target group affiliation must be considered. In borderline cases, this might prove to be a demanding undertaking.[64] 22

### f) Competition for the same third-party content

§ 3 (3) (implementing Art. 2 No. 6 subpara. 2 DSMD) further specifies the concept of competition. According to this section, online platforms for open-source software do not fall within the scope of application of the UrhDaG. However, open-source software can compete with proprietary software. Platforms offering access to open-source software can compete with online services that distribute software or offer it as a service. The competition is based on the fact that the software available on the platform is usually offered with the consent of the rightholders. As a consequence, only competition for the offer of the same third-party content is relevant. The UrhDaG does not intend to impede competition between platforms by imposing strict due diligence requirements when platforms compete with lawful content, especially when users offer the content in 23

---

[58] Cf. Leistner ZGE 2020, 123 (145); Becker ZUM 2020, 681 (684).

[59] Cf. AG Saugmandsgaard Øe C-401/19, ECLI:EU:C:2021:613 mn. 15 – Poland/Parliament and Council.

[60] Commission Notice on the definition of relevant market for the purposes of Community competition law, OJ. 1997 C 372/5 mn. 7; CJEU 85/76, ECLI:EU:C:1979:36 mn. 28 – Hoffmann-La Roche; CFI T-427/08, ECLI:EU:T:2010:517 mn. 67 – CEAHR.

[61] Loewenheim/Meessen/Riesenkampff/Kersting/Meyer-Lindemann/Bergmann/Fiedler AEUV Art. 102 mn. 36.

[62] Immenga/Mestmäcker/Körber FKVO Art. 2 mn. 20 et seq.

[63] CJEU C-381/05, ECLI:EU:C:2007:230 mn. 30, 36 – De Landtsheer/CIV.

[64] Therefore, with criticism: Wandtke/Hauck ZUM 2020, 671 (672).

the form of open licences. Thus, all service providers are excluded from the scope of application of the UrhDaG if they mainly offer copyright-protected content with the **consent of the author**, for example, under a **free licence** (such as Creative Commons licences) such as for providers of licence-free images or music.

### 7. Estimated number of OCSSPs

24 The legislative memorandum of the UrhDaG assumes that in the medium term, there will be **13 OCSSPs** as defined in § 2, seven of them large OCSSPs as defined in § 1, two start-up OCSSPs as defined in § 2 (2) and four small OCSSPs as defined in § 2 (3).[65]

## III. Start-up OCSSPs (sub. 2)

25 The UrhDaG privileges start-up OCSSPs and exempts them from the obligation to block content in a qualified manner under § 7 (4). A start-up is defined by a **turnover-related criterion** and a **time-related criterion**. First, the company must not have generated more than **10 million euro in turnover** in the previous calendar year. Sub. 4 specifies the calculation of turnover in more detail (→ mn. 29 et seq.). Second, the service cannot be available to the public in the EU for **longer than three years**. After that period, the OCSSP is subject to full liability under the UrhDaG to the extent they meet the other requirements of sub. 1.[66] In order to prevent abuse, the wording of the law already requires the service as such to be taken into account. From a material point of view, it must be a new service. The privilege cannot be renewed by renaming an existing service or providing an identical service under a newly established company (recital 67 sent. 4 et seq. DSMD). It is irrelevant whether the service provider acts with the intention of circumventing the regulations or not.[67]

## IV. Small OCSSPs (sub. 3)

### 1. Objective

26 For small OCSSPs, it is rebuttably presumed under § 7 (5) that qualified blocking under § 7 (1) is a disproportionate burden, and therefore, they do not have to use filtering technology.[68] By this, the German legislature has specified the **principle of proportionality**[69] with regard to OCSSPs.[70] The liability mechanism of the UrhDaG should not prevent independent providers from operating small platforms, especially in niche areas. In terms of provider diversity, it would not be desirable if after the expiry of the start-up privilege, small service providers could only exist under the umbrella of large platform providers that are able to afford an UrhDaG-compliant infrastructure.

### 2. Conformity with EU law

27 By introducing 'small OCSSPs', the German legislature has created a **separate category of OCSSPs** that has **no counterpart in Art. 17 DSMD**. It is debatable

[65] BT-Drs. 19/27426, 61.
[66] Dreier GRUR 2019, 771 (775).
[67] See, however: Spindler CR 2019, 277 (288).
[68] BT-Drs. 19/27426, 131.
[69] § 1 (2) UrhDaG, implementing Art. 17 (5) DSMD, → § 1 mn. 29.
[70] BT-Drs. 19/27426, 131, 138.

whether the provision is a permissible specification of EU law[71] or is contrary to EU law.[72] However, a directive may provide the Member States with room for specification, particularly if it uses indeterminate legal terms. In this case, Member States may introduce statutory specifications of the EU law requirements in their national law insofar as they stay within the limits set by EU law and do not jeopardise the practical effectiveness of the regulations (→ Introduction mn. 9).[73] Art. 17 (5)(a) DSMD expressly provides that in light of the principle of proportionality, the size (German: *Umfang*; French: *taille*) of the service is to be taken into account. The start-up provision in Art. 17 (6) DSMD is thus a concretisation of the proportionality principle but it is not a conclusive one.[74] The UrhDaG's specification is also in line with recital 62 subpara. 1 sent. 2 DSMD, according to which the increased duties of care of Art. 17 DSMD should only apply to online services that play an 'important role' on the market for online content. This will typically not be the case for OCSSPs with an annual turnover of less than 1 million euro. In addition, the copyright exception for small OCSSPs is designed as a rebuttable presumption. If in an unusual case, the stated assumptions do not apply, even a small OCCSP must fulfil the obligations of § 7 (1) UrhDaG. Therefore, the limits of the start-up exemption in Art. 17 (6) DSMD are not undermined.

### 3. Small OCSSPs

Small OCSSPs are OCSSPs that have an annual turnover within the EU in the previous calendar year of **less than 1 million euro**. Sub. 4 specifies the calculation of turnover in more detail (→ mn. 29 et seq.). 28

## V. Calculation of turnover (sub. 4)

### 1. Rules for calculating turnover (sent. 1)

Commission Recommendation 2003/361/EC of 6 May 2003 concerning the definition of micro, small and medium-sized enterprises[75] is to be used to calculate the turnover of a start-up (sub. 2) and a small OCSSP (sub. 3). VAT and other indirect taxes or duties are not included in the calculation of turnover (Annex Art. 4 (1) sent. 2). It is unclear whether the rule of Annex Art. 4 (2) that states that a company only loses its status if it exceeds the threshold of 10 million euro in two consecutive business years must also be taken into account. Furthermore, the data is compiled solely on the basis of the accounts of the enterprise (Annex Art. 6 (1)). 29

### 2. Turnover of the previous calendar year (sent. 2)

Sentence 2 clarifies that only the turnover of the **previous calendar year** is relevant – not the turnover of the current calendar year or the turnover of a possibly deviating business year. For reasons of legal certainty, a start-up and a small OCSSP continue to qualify for the relief in § 7 (4) and (5) for the remainder of the first very successful 30

---

[71] Gielen/Tiessen EuZW 2019, 639 (643); Hofmann ZUM 2020, 665 (667); Hofmann ZUM 2019, 617 (625); Schack UrhR/UrhebervertragsR mn. 860.

[72] Cf. Spindler CR 2020, 50 (53); Spindler WRP 2021, 1111 mn. 11, 30.

[73] Cf. CJEU C-516/17, ECLI:EU:C:2019:625 mn. 28 et seqq. – Spiegel Online/Volker Beck; Würtenberger/Freischem GRUR 2019, 1140 (1153).

[74] See, however: Spindler CR 2020, 50 (51, 53).

[75] OJ 2003 L 124, 36.

calendar year (and, if applicable, a subsequent calendar year, → mn. 29). The calculation of the average visitors of start-ups under § 7 (4) must also be based on the previous calendar year.

**§ 3**
**Services not covered**

**This Act shall not apply in particular to**
1. **not-for-profit online encyclopaedias,**
2. **not-for-profit educational and scientific repositories,**
3. **development and sharing platforms for open-source software,**
4. **providers of electronic communications services as defined in Article 2 number 4 of Directive (EU) 2018/1972 of the European Parliament and of the Council of 11 December 2018 on the European Electronic Communications Code (OJ L 321, 17.12.2018, p. 36; L 334, 27.12.2019, p. 164),**
5. **online marketplaces,**
6. **cloud services provided between businesses, and**
7. **cloud services that allow users to upload content for their own use.**

**§ 3**
**Nicht erfasste Dienste**

**Dieses Gesetz gilt insbesondere nicht für**
1. **nicht gewinnorientierte Online-Enzyklopädien,**
2. **nicht gewinnorientierte bildungsbezogene oder wissenschaftliche Repositorien,**
3. **Entwicklungs- und Weitergabe-Plattformen für quelloffene Software,**
4. **Anbieter elektronischer Kommunikationsdienste im Sinne des Artikels 2 Nummer 4 der Richtlinie (EU) 2018/1972 des Europäischen Parlaments und des Rates vom 11. Dezember 2018 über den europäischen Kodex für die elektronische Kommunikation (ABl. L 321 vom 17.12.2018, S. 36; L 334 vom 27.12.2019, S. 164),**
5. **Online-Marktplätze,**
6 **Cloud-Dienste, die zwischen Unternehmen erbracht werden, und**
7. **Cloud-Dienste, die ihren Nutzern das Hochladen von Inhalten für den Eigengebrauch ermöglichen.**

**Bibliography:** See the bibliography in the Introduction.

**Content**



# I. General remarks

## 1. Objective

1 Because the UrhDaG imposes considerable obligations on OCSSPs, § 3 specifies the definition of § 2 (1) in a binding manner. It uses a list of **non-exhaustive examples** and excludes the information society services mentioned therein from the scope of application of the UrhDaG. On the platforms mentioned in **Nos 1–3**, copyright-protected objects may be made accessible to the public under certain circumstances. However,

these platforms do **not** operate **for profit.**[1] The platforms mentioned in **Nos 4, 6–7** do **not** provide the public with **access** to works. The business model of **online market-places** (No. 5) is not based on providing access to copyrighted objects. The statutory examples create **legal certainty for** the included services.

### 2. EU law requirements

The list of exempted services is based on Art. 2 No. 6 subpara. 2 DSMD, which is **2**
explained in recital 62 subpara. 1 sent. 4, 5 and subpara. 2 sent. 1 DSMD.

## II. Details

### 1. Non-exhaustive list

The services listed in the provision as outside the regulatory scope of the UrhDaG are **3**
exemplary and not exhaustive ('in particular').[2] Services that are not listed in § 3 but do not fulfil the requirements of § 2 still fall outside the scope of the Act.

### 2. Non-profit platforms (Nos 1, 2)

OCSSPs that make copyright-protected content available to the public but do not **4**
pursue either a direct or an indirect profit-making purpose (→ § 2 mn. 17) are excluded from the scope of application of the UrhDaG pursuant to § 2 (1) No. 3. § 3 clarifies this for non-profit **online encyclopaedias**, such as Wikipedia (No. 1), or **educational and scientific repositories** and archives (No. 2). It is irrelevant if these services generate revenue through the operation of the platform as long as they only use it to cover their own costs; the same applies to the solicitation of donations from the public.[3]

### 3. Development and sharing platforms for open-source software (No. 3)

According to the literal sense of the word, only the source code of open-source software **5**
must be made freely available in human-readable form. However, this is usually accompanied by the right to **use** and **modify the software free of charge** and **without restriction.**[4] Open-source software can compete with proprietary software; therefore, open-source platforms can compete with online services that distribute software or offer it for use as a service. However, the competition is based on the fact that the software available on the open-source platform is usually offered with the consent of the rightholders. In this respect, No. 3 specifies the constituent element of § 2 (1) No. 4. *Argumentum e contrario* to Nos 1 and 2,[5] a profit-oriented operation of such platforms is possible without stepping into the scope of the UrhDaG. This should also apply to **other platforms that usually** offer copyright-protected content under a **free licence with the consent of the author** (e.g., Creative Commons licences), such as platforms for freely usable images or sounds.

### 4. Provider of electronic communications services (No. 4)

Art. 2 No. 4 Directive 2018/1972/EU defines an 'electronic communications service' **6**
as a service normally provided for remuneration via electronic communications net-

[1] Cf. Hofmann ZUM 2019, 617 (618).
[2] BT-Drs. 19/27426, 132; COM(2021) 288 final EN, 3 et seq.
[3] COM(2021) 288 final EN, 6.
[4] Dreier/Schulze/Dreier UrhG § 69a mn. 11.
[5] This is compliant with Art. 2 No. 6 subpara. 2 DSMD.

works and includes **'internet access services'** within the meaning of Art. 2 (2) No. 2 of Regulation (EU) 2015/2120, **'interpersonal communication services'** and **services consisting** wholly or mainly in the **conveyance of signals** (in particular for broadcasting or machine-to-machine communications). Explicitly excluded from the definition are services that provide or exercise editorial control over content via electronic communications networks and services. Providers of electronic communications services are excluded from the scope of the UrhDaG because their **main purpose** is to **provide communication services** and, by definition, not to make copyright-protected content available to the public. However, that classification may change if a communication service is no longer primarily used for individual or small group communication but provides advertising-financed communication, including copyright-protected content, to large groups.[6] But even in this case, the provided content will usually not be authorised by the provider so that the provision of § 2 (1) No. 2 will not be met.

### 5. Online marketplaces (No. 5)

7 The **main purpose of online marketplaces** is **online retail** (recital 62 subpara. 1 sent. 5 DSMD).[7] Online marketplaces are primarily operated to sell goods or services and not to provide access to copyright-protected content. Therefore, they do not in any case meet the requirements of § 2 (1) Nos 1, 4. The exemption covers both providers offering their own merchandise and intermediary platforms such as eBay.[8]

### 6. Cloud services for business and personal use (Nos 6, 7)

8 Providers of business-to-business cloud services and cloud services that allow users to upload content for their own use do not make available large amounts of copyright-protected content to the public (§ 2 (1) No. 1). They are not an OCSSP nor do they perform an act of communication to the public under § 1 (1).[9] Their **main purpose** is to **make storage space available** for the **personal use of** private or commercial users. Therefore, they do not meet the requirements of § 2 (1) Nos 3, 4. It is irrelevant whether individual users occasionally use the platforms to make copyright-protected content available to the public. In these cases, the cloud service is liable under the general liability mechanism only if the rightholder has made it aware of the availability of the content to the public and it has not put an end to it.[10] However, if the service is used to share copyright-protected content with larger groups with the operator's consent on a large scale, the requirement 'for personal use' is not met. In this case, such a cloud services provider can be an OCSSP within the meaning of § 2.[11]

---

[6] See also Spindler WRP 2019, 951 (956); Würtenberger/Freischem GRUR 2019, 1140 (1155).
[7] Hofmann ZUM 2019, 617 (618).
[8] Peters/Schmidt GRUR Int. 2019, 1006 (1007).
[9] Hofmann ZUM 2019, 617 (618); Spindler CR 2019, 277 (284).
[10] BT-Drs. 19/27426, 132.
[11] Cf. Würtenberger/Freischem GRUR 2019, 1140 (1154 et seq.).

# Part 2
# Authorised uses

## § 4
## Obligation to obtain contractual rights of use; direct remuneration right of the author

(1) [1]A service provider shall be obliged to make best efforts to obtain the contractual rights of use to communicate copyright-protected works to the public. [2]The service provider fulfils this obligation provided it obtains rights of use that are

1. offered to the service provider,
2. are available through representative rightholders known to the service provider, or
3. can be acquired through collecting societies or dependent collecting entities established in Germany.

(2) Rights of use under subsection 1 sentence 2 must

1. apply to content that by its nature, the service provider manifestly communicates to the public in more than negligible quantities,
2. comprise a substantial repertoire in regard to works and rightholders,
3. cover the territorial scope of this Act and
4. allow the use on reasonable terms and conditions.

(3) [1]If the author has granted to a third party the right of communication to the public of a work, the service provider shall nevertheless pay the author an appropriate remuneration for the communication of the work to the public for the contractual authorised uses. [2]Sentence 1 shall not apply if the third party is a collecting society or the author engages the third party as a digital distributor.

(4) [1]The author may not waive the direct remuneration right under subsection 3 and may only assign it in advance to a collecting society. [2]It can only be asserted by a collecting society.

# Teil 2
# Erlaubte Nutzungen

## § 4
## Pflicht zum Erwerb vertraglicher Nutzungsrechte; Direktvergütungsanspruch des Urhebers

(1) [1]Ein Diensteanbieter ist verpflichtet, bestmögliche Anstrengungen zu unternehmen, um die vertraglichen Nutzungsrechte für die öffentliche Wiedergabe urheberrechtlich geschützter Werke zu erwerben. [2]Der Diensteanbieter erfüllt diese Pflicht, sofern er Nutzungsrechte erwirbt, die

1. ihm angeboten werden,
2. über repräsentative Rechtsinhaber verfügbar sind, die der Diensteanbieter kennt, oder
3. über im Inland ansässige Verwertungsgesellschaften oder abhängige Verwertungseinrichtungen erworben werden können.

(2) Nutzungsrechte nach Absatz 1 Satz 2 müssen

1. für Inhalte gelten, die der Diensteanbieter ihrer Art nach offensichtlich in mehr als geringfügigen Mengen öffentlich wiedergibt,
2. in Bezug auf Werke und Rechtsinhaber ein erhebliches Repertoire umfassen,
3. den räumlichen Geltungsbereich dieses Gesetzes abdecken und
4. die Nutzung zu angemessenen Bedingungen ermöglichen.

(3) [1]Hat der Urheber das Recht der öffentlichen Wiedergabe eines Werkes einem Dritten eingeräumt, so hat der Diensteanbieter für vertragliche Nutzungen gleichwohl dem Urheber eine angemessene Vergütung für die öffentliche Wiedergabe des Werkes zu zahlen. [2]Satz 1 ist nicht anzuwenden, wenn der Dritte eine Verwertungsgesellschaft ist oder der Urheber den Dritten als Digitalvertrieb einschaltet.

(4) [1]Der Urheber kann auf den Direktvergütungsanspruch nach Absatz 3 nicht verzichten und diesen im Voraus nur an eine Verwertungsgesellschaft abtreten. [2]Er kann nur durch eine Verwertungsgesellschaft geltend gemacht werden.

**Bibliography:** See also the bibliography in the Introduction.

**Content**

# I. General remarks

## 1. Objective

§ 4 specifies in subs 1 and 2 the OCSSP's **duty of care** and thus the efforts it must make to acquire rights of use for **content** uploaded on its platform. This defines the requirements that an OCSSP must meet in order to benefit from the liability exemption pursuant to § 1 (2) No. 1.[1] In the interpretation, the principle of proportionality and the criteria of § 1 (2) No. 2 must be taken into account (→ § 1 mn. 27 et seqq.).[2] It is the declared aim of both the Union and the German legislature to **strengthen the negotiating position of rightholders vis-à-vis the platforms** and to **promote** the development of a **licensing market** between rightholders and OCSSPs (recital 61 sent. 7, 8 DSMD; → Introduction mn. 2).[3] The licensing obligation is thus the core of the new liability regime.[4] The exact form of the licensing obligation will have a considerable influence on what kind of rightholder will benefit from the new liability regime.[5] For reasons of proportionality, OCSSPs cannot be expected to approach every individual rightholder. Consequently, primarily large rightholders and rightholders represented by collecting societies will benefit (see sub. 1 sent. 2 Nos 2, 3). The obligation of OCSSPs to acquire offered rights of use is **not a legal obligation that can be enforced** by the rightholders. Its infringement will establish liability under §§ 97 et seqq. UrhG, which should incentivise an OCSSP to acquire the necessary licences. § 1 (2) and § 4 share the **burden of action** between OCSSPs and rightholders. OCSSPs must obtain rights of use for communication to the public pursuant to § 1 (1) in accordance with high industry standards (sub. 1 sent. 1). However, unknown rightholders must approach an OCSSP in a first step and offer them the licences (sub. 1 sent. 2). To reduce transaction costs, OCSSPs must for reasons of **proportionality** only contract with rightholders who have a substantial repertoire of relevant rights (sub. 2). OCSSPs are not required to obtain rights that do not meet the qualification of sub. 2. In order for authors, photographers and performers to participate in the expected additional licensing revenue, **subs 3 and 4** grant authors an indispensable **direct remuneration right** against the OCSSP that can only be claimed via a collecting society. 1

## 2. Requirements under EU law

Subs 1 and 2 implement **Art. 17 (1) subpara. 2 and (4)(a) DSMD,**[6] which is specified by recital 64 sent. 2, 3 DSMD. The limitations of the licensing obligations are specifications of the principle of proportionality laid down in **Art. 17 (5) DSMD.**[7] The German legislature corrected the mistranslation of the German language version of Art. 17 (4)(a) DSMD, which speaks of *alle Anstrengungen* (all efforts) and thus deviates from the other language versions (English: *best efforts*; French: *meilleurs efforts*).[8] Subs 3 and 4 can be based on **Art. 18 (1) DSMD** (→ mn. 44),[9] specified by recital 73 DSMD. 2

---

[1] BT-Drs. 19/27426, 132.

[2] BT-Drs. 19/27426, 44 et seq., 132.

[3] BT-Drs. 19/27426, 62; COM(2021) 288 final EN, 6.

[4] Cf. Stieper ZUM 2021, 387 (392).

[5] Leistner ZGE 2020, 123 (136).

[6] BT-Drs. 19/27426, 44.

[7] For doubts about conformity with EU law, see: Spindler WRP 2021, 1111 mn. 16 et seq.; but cf. COM (2021) 288 final EN, 5, 10.

[8] BT-Drs. 19/27426, 132.

[9] BT-Drs. 19/27426, 45.

### 3. Restriction of freedom of contract

#### a) Private autonomy of the rightholders

3 The UrhDaG is **not** intended to **restrict the contractual freedom** of the **rightholders** (recital 61 sent. 10 DSMD).[10] Sub. 1 sent. 1 establishes a unilateral acquisition obligation for the OCSSP without a corresponding obligation of the rightholders to make an offer (recital 61 sent. 10 DSMD).[11] Rightholders still have the possibility to pursue exclusive exploitation strategies. They may do everything necessary to ensure that their content is not freely available on the internet. If they refuse to grant licences, however, the OCSSPs' licensing obligation also lapses.[12]

#### b) Private autonomy of the OCSSPs

4 Before the UrhDaG came into force, providers such as YouTube were already licensing content that was accessible on their platform.[13] In order to strengthen the negotiating position of rightholders, § 4 aims to **restrict** the **private autonomy of OCSSPs.**[14] If an OCSSP wants to avoid liability under § 1 (1) in conjunction with §§ 97 et seqq. UrhG, it must accept reasonable offers from the rightholders if they fulfil the requirements of sub. 2. However, § 4 does not impose an enforceable legal obligation on the OCSSP to conclude a licensing agreement (→ mn. 5). Due to the considerable liability risks, the provision nevertheless creates a ***de facto* obligation to contract.**[15] In order to maintain proportionality, sub. 2 in return imposes a high threshold that the licensing offers must meet.[16] Nevertheless, § 1 (2) and § 4 cause a **considerable encroachment on the OCSSPs' freedom to contract.**[17] The encroachment would be particularly intense if they were required to allow and pay for content on their platforms that did not fit their business concept. Therefore, the conditions for the licensing obligation must again be interpreted in light of entrepreneurial freedom (Art. 16 CFR; Art. 12 GG; → mn. 24 et seqq.). This applies, in particular, to smaller OCSSPs that do not have the market power of large OCSSPs.

#### c) No enforceable obligation

5 The German legislature has not designed the licensing duty as an enforceable obligation to contract, but as a **duty of care.**[18] OCSSPs complying with that duty are exempted from liability under § 1 (1). The consequence of non-compliance is liability for injunctions and damages.[19] A rightholder cannot force an OCSSP to conclude a licence agreement.

### 4. Relation to the blocking obligation and exceptions

#### a) Relation to blocking obligations in §§ 7, 8

6 Even if the OCSSP refuses to conclude a licence agreement on reasonable terms, the rightholder must still **provide** the **information** required for blocking under §§ 7, 8. This

[10] Metzger/Pravemann ZUM 2021, 288 (291).
[11] BT-Drs. 19/27426, 45, 65.
[12] COM(2021) 288 final EN, 10; Metzger/Pravemann ZUM 2021, 288 (291).
[13] BT-Drs. 19/27426, 62.
[14] BT-Drs. 19/27426, 133; with criticism: Hofmann ZUM 2020, 665 (667).
[15] MPI Stellungnahme zum RefE, 4.
[16] BT-Drs. 19/27426, 133.
[17] MPI Stellungnahme zum RefE, 4.
[18] BT-Drs. 19/27426, 132; Metzger/Pravemann ZUM 2021, 288 (291).
[19] Cf. Metzger/Pravemann ZUM 2021, 288 (291).

is also not an enforceable obligation. However, unless the rightholder provides the necessary information, the liability of the OCSSP is suspended insofar as it is unable to block the content without the information that was withheld (recital 66 subpara. 5 DSMD; → § 7 mn. 18).

#### b) Relation to copyright exceptions

There is widespread agreement that the **copyright exceptions of** the UrhG in favour of users also exempt the OCSSP's acts of communication to the public under § 1 (1) (→ § 1 mn. 8; → § 5 mn. 3; → § 6 mn. 10). Therefore, such acts of communication to the public are **not covered by** the author's **exclusive right**. The OCSSP is not required to acquire licences or other authorisations from rightholders for uploaded content covered by a copyright exception.[20] Due to criticism of the government draft, the legislature also refrained from making all acts of communication to the public that are covered by copyright exceptions **subject to remuneration** for the OCSSPs (for more details → § 5 mn. 5).[21] The statement in the explanatory memorandum to the UrhDaG[22] that the OCSSP must also acquire a licence from the rightholders within the scope of copyright exceptions is not reflected in the passed legislation. 7

### 5. Burden of proof

Appropriate distribution of the burden of proof is not a trivial task.[23] In principle, the **OCSSP** must prove that it has fulfilled its obligations under § 1 (2) if users have made copyright-protected content accessible via its platform without the consent of the rightholders. This includes proving that it has made the best possible efforts to acquire the necessary authorisation of use.[24] If the rightholder has made an offer to conclude a licence agreement or if licensing negotiations have taken place, the OCSSP must prove that it has conducted the **negotiations in good faith** (→ mn. 15 et seqq.) and that it was **entitled to reject an offer by the rightholder** because it did not meet the requirements of sub. 1 sent. 2 or sub. 2. When negotiating with **collecting societies**, the OCSSP may acquire a licence by paying the amount it considers to be reasonable and paying or depositing the remainder with reservation (§ 37 VGG). The appropriate royalty fee and other licensing conditions are then subject to court proceedings. Then, the collecting society has the burden of proof on the appropriateness of the licensing conditions.[25] 8

## II. Obligation of obtaining rights of use by the OCSSP (sub. 1)

### 1. Best possible efforts (sent. 1)

#### a) General

The OCSSP has no enforceable obligation to conclude a licence agreement (→ mn. 5). However, if it wants to avoid liability under § 1 (1), it must make the best possible efforts to acquire the necessary authorisation under § 4 (1) sent. 1. Therefore, the UrhDaG does **not** impose an **obligation of result**. Whether the OCSSP has made best efforts to acquire authorisation is to be assessed on the basis of a comprehensive 9

[20] Cf. Spindler WRP 2021, 1111 mn. 14.
[21] BT-Drs. 19/29894, 92.
[22] BT-Drs. 19/27426, 132.
[23] Cf. also MPI Stellungnahme zum RefE, 5.
[24] MPI Stellungnahme zum RefE, 6.
[25] See Dreier/Schulze/Raue VGG § 39 mn. 22 et seq.

**consideration of the individual facts of the case**, taking into account the principle of proportionality.[26] The German legislature has specified the necessary **efforts** in sub. 1 sent. 2. The OCSSP must only approach actively representative rightholders known to it and collecting societies; in all other cases, the rightholders must take the first step (→ mn. 19 et seqq.). Furthermore, sub. 2 limits the licensing obligation of an OCSSP to **qualified licensing offers** that meet the requirements of content, representativeness and appropriateness that have been laid down (→ mn. 29 et seqq.).

10 **aa) Compliance with the obligation by acquiring rights of use.** The OCSSP complies with the licensing obligation if it concludes a licence agreement or acquires authorisation in any other form.[27] It is irrelevant whether the licensing offer fulfils the requirements of § 4 (1) No. 2 and (2) because an authorisation by the rightholder eliminates the OCSSP's liability in any case (→ § 1 mn. 20).[28] OCSSPs can minimise their liability if they acquire individual licences from small rightholders, for example, with the help of automated processes (→ mn. 18). They can also rely on non-exclusive licences that authors grant, for example, within the framework of Creative Commons licences, or that users grant the service provider on the basis of the platform's terms of use.[29]

11 **bb) Right to reject inappropriate offers.** *Argumentum e contrario*, OCSSPs may **reject licensing offers** that do not meet the conditions listed in sub. 2. If they reject such an offer, they are exempted from liability under § 1 (2) No. 1 if in compliance with the other obligations under §§ 7–11.[30] The respective right to reject inappropriate offers to licence is recognised, for example, for collecting societies that are obliged to grant rights of use on reasonable terms under § 34 (1) sent. 1 VGG.[31]

12 **cc) Proportionality.** The principle of proportionality must be considered when specifying the best efforts to acquire contractual rights of use.[32] Pursuant to § 1 (1) sent. 2 No. 1, the size and economic resources of the OCSSP must be taken into account (→ § 1 mn. 28). Therefore, the duties of care with regard to the licensing obligation may vary according to the **size of the platform**.[33] However, this only applies to individual efforts to acquire the licences and not to the obligation to acquire as such. Start-up OCSSPs (§ 2 (2)) and small OCSSPs (§ 2 (3)) are also subject to the licensing obligation, although this must not impose disproportionate burdens on them.[34] In exceptional cases, it may be disproportionate if they had to accept a licensing offer that is reasonable according to general standards but that cannot be refinanced with the OCSSP's legitimate business model (→ mn. 25 et seq.). This objection of disproportionality may only be used with restraint as the legislature has stipulated in sub. 2 that the licensing of relevant and not too fragmented content at reasonable conditions is reasonable for OCSSPs.

**b) Negotiations in good faith**

13 As soon as an OCSSP is contacted by a rightholder (or vice versa), a **pre-contractual relationship** (*vorvertragliches Schuldverhältnis*) with mutual duties of protection

---

[26] COM(2021) 288 final EN, 9.
[27] Metzger/Senftleben jipitec 2020, 115 mn. 22.
[28] Stieper ZUM 2021, 387 (392).
[29] COM(2021) 288 final EN, 6.
[30] COM(2021) 288 final EN, 10; Stieper ZUM 2021, 387 (392).
[31] BGH 22.4.2009 – I ZR 5/07, GRUR 2009, 1052 mn. 11 – Seeing is Believing; Dreier/Schulze/Raue VGG § 34 mn. 11.
[32] BT-Drs. 19/27426, 132.
[33] COM(2021) 288 final EN, 9 et seq.
[34] COM(2021) 288 final EN, 10.

(*Schutzpflichten*, § 241 (2) BGB) arises under § 311 (2) BGB. OCSSPs are under an obligation to conduct the necessary negotiations in good faith.[35] The same applies to collecting societies in their negotiations with OCSSPs (§ 36 VGG; Art. 16 (1), (3) directive 2014/26/EU).[36] The **reciprocal duties to negotiate under § 36 VGG** are generalisable principles that can be applied in a corresponding manner to negotiations with other rightholders. Recourse can also be made to the **FRAND principles.**[37] Therefore, OCSSPs and rightholders must conduct **fair, expeditious and constructive negotiations**[38] and, in doing so, observe recognised commercial practices.[39]

**aa) Burden of action.** In principle, the OCSSP must take **proactive action to initiate licensing negotiations** if the rightholder can be easily identified and located.[40] Sub. 1 sent. 2 specifies this requirement and limits the obligation to take proactive action to rights that can be acquired through domestic collective management organisations (No. 3). The same applies to representative rightholders; however, they must be known to the OCSSP (No. 2). Conversely, the OCSSP does **not have** to **proactively search for** rightholders that it cannot easily identify and locate.[41] If such a rightholder approaches an OCSSP, the OCSSP is obliged to conclude a licence agreement with the rightholder on reasonable terms.[42] In any case, an OCSSP only has to accept offers that meet the requirements of sub. 2. Once the rightholder has expressed its willingness to licence, which party has to open the licensing negotiations with a **contractual offer** must be determined. If the negotiating partner is a collecting society, it must make an offer to the OCSSP without undue delay pursuant to § 36 (2) sent. 2 VGG if the latter has provided all the necessary information. In all other cases, the burden of action will stay with the OCSSP because sub. 1 sent. 1 unilaterally imposes the obligation to make best efforts on the OCSSP. The OCSSP must make an offer on reasonable terms to the rightholder without undue delay as soon as the latter has provided the OCSSP with the necessary information to do so. 14

**bb) Transparency and swift communication.** The obligation to negotiate in a fair, expeditious and constructive manner includes certain transparency obligations.[43] Both sides must exchange the information necessary for the negotiations and **swiftly respond** to requests from the other side.[44] The rightholders must comprehensibly explain which works and other protected subject matter belong to their repertoire.[45] Conversely, OCSSPs must be transparent in regard to the criteria they use to identify and remunerate the content used.[46] This corresponds with the right to information under § 19 (1), according to which the OCSSP must provide the rightholder with information on the contractually permitted use of its content. Both sides must justify a refusal to accept offers made by the other side (cf. § 36 (2) sent. 2 VGG). 15

---

[35] COM(2021) 288 final EN, 10.

[36] COM(2021) 288 final EN, 11; BT-Drs. 19/27426, 133.

[37] CJEU C-170/13, ECLI:EU:C:2015:477 mn. 63–69 – Huawei/ZTE; Leistner ZUM 2020, 505 (508); Metzger/Senftleben jipitec 2020, 115 mn. 20.

[38] BGH 24.11.2020 – KZR 35/17, GRUR 2021, 585 mn. 65 – FRAND-Einwand II. See also Dreier/Schulze/Raue VGG § 36 mn. 1.

[39] CJEU C-170/13, ECLI:EU:C:2015:477 mn. 65 – Huawei/ZTE.

[40] COM(2021) 288 final EN, 9.

[41] COM(2021) 288 final EN, 9.

[42] COM(2021) 288 final EN, 9.

[43] COM(2021) 288 final EN, 10.

[44] Cf. § 36 (1) sent. 2 VGG.

[45] Metzger/Senftleben jipitec 2020, 115 mn. 20.

[46] COM(2021) 288 final EN, 10.

16 **cc) Willingness to negotiate.** Contractual negotiations must be expeditiously conducted (cf. § 36 (2) VGG).[47] The obligation of good faith negotiations includes the **possibility of electronic communication** with rightholders; an information society service provider (→ § 2 mn. 5 et seqq.) would create unreasonable obstacles to the conclusion of a contract if it exclusively referred rightholders to analogue means of communication. The **OCSSP** may not use **delaying tactics**[48] and must demonstrate a continued willingness to licence.[49] The OCSSP must deal with a contractual offer by the rightholder 'in a way that shows that he is now pursuing the goal of reaching a mutually beneficial result as soon as possible'; if the rightholder does not make an offer that is reasonable within the meaning of sub. 2 No. 4, the OCSSP may not terminate the negotiations but must work towards a reasonable result.[50] If it has failed to comply with its obligations to cooperate, it may be expected to make additional efforts to ensure that a licence agreement on reasonable terms can be concluded as soon as possible.[51] Conversely, a **rightholder**[52] does not have to **actively promote the negotiations** because it has no obligation to licence its rights (→ mn. 3). In this case, the OCSSP fulfils the obligation under § 4 (1) No. 1 if it demonstrates its willingness to negotiate. It is exempt from liability under § 1 (2) if the delays in negotiations are attributable to the rightholder.

17 **dd) Conflicting reasonable offers.** Whether an offer is reasonable depends on a variety of factors that need to be considered in relation to each other. Stricter requirements in one area may be compensated by more generous conditions elsewhere; lower remuneration may be offset by other benefits. Consequently, there is usually a **range of different licensing conditions** that can be considered **reasonable.** It is not inconceivable that both the OCSSP and the rightholder would submit divergent but individually reasonable licensing offers. In this case, the question arises of whether the **OCSSP is obliged to accept** such a reasonable **licensing offer from the rightholder** in order to fulfil its licensing obligation or whether it may insist on its own reasonable offer. The wording of the law ('obtains rights of use that are 1. offered to the service provider [... (sub. 2) and] 4. allow the use on reasonable terms and conditions') and the explanatory memorandum to the UrhDaG[53] speak in favour of the first alternative. However, the private autonomy of the OCSSP argues against such an interpretation. Particularly in light of the principle of proportionality (§ 1 (2) No. 1), it may be sufficient for best efforts that the OCSSP demonstrates its willingness to acquire rights of use on reasonable terms by making a binding, reasonable licensing offer. By this, the OCSSP may retain a **residual degree of private autonomy** within the licensing obligation. Parties that benefit from a contractual obligation are generally not entitled to conclude a contract on very specific terms.[54] In this case, however, the OCSSP is still exposed to the risk that the courts will subsequently consider its counteroffer not to be reasonable. The OCSSP can avoid this risk vis-à-vis **collecting societies** by rejecting the offer but providing security for the higher remuneration demanded by the collecting society pursuant to § 37 VGG.[55] Reasonable terms are then determined in subsequent state

[47] COM(2021) 288 final EN, 10.
[48] See CJEU C-170/13, ECLI:EU:C:2015:477 mn. 65 – Huawei/ZTE.
[49] BGH 24.11.2020 – KZR 35/17, GRUR 2021, 585 mn. 67 – FRAND-Einwand II.
[50] Cf. BGH 24.11.2020 – KZR 35/17, GRUR 2021, 585 mn. 72 – FRAND-Einwand II.
[51] Cf. BGH 24.11.2020 – KZR 35/17, GRUR 2021, 585 mn. 62 – FRAND-Einwand II.
[52] This does not apply to collecting societies due to their obligations under § 36 (2) sent. 2 VGG.
[53] BT-Drs. 19/27426, 42.
[54] MüKoBGB/Busche, 9th edn 2021, Vor § 145 mn. 23; BeckOGK/Möslein, 1.5.2019, BGB § 145 mn. 52.
[55] BGH 27.10.2011 – I ZR 125/10, GRUR 2012, 711 mn. 12 – Barmen Live; Dreier/Schulze/Raue VGG § 37 mn. 2.

arbitration or court proceedings.[56] There are good arguments for applying this procedure (except for state arbitration) **by analogy to** negotiations with **other rightholders**.

**ee) Automated rights management.** OCSSPs are not obliged to acquire rights of use from rightholders that do not have a substantial repertoire (sub. 2 No. 2, → mn. 34). If they still want to acquire rights of use from such rightholders (to avoid blocking obligations), they may standardise the acquisition of rights on reasonable conditions via an online licensing tool. Without a certain degree of **standardisation** and **automation**, rights management is usually not possible at a proportionate cost. Although this weakens the negotiating position of smaller rightholders, it is an acceptable procedure because the licensing terms of the OCSSP must be reasonable even in the case of individual licensing (§ 32 UrhG). Furthermore, small rightholders have the option to assign their rights to a collecting society and strengthen their bargaining power in that way. The rights management tools must be **easy to find** and **simple to use**. **18**

## 2. Specification of the obligation to obtain rights of use (sent. 2)

Sentence 2 specifies the efforts of the OCSSP that are considered reasonable and proportionate. This is a **concretisation of the principle of proportionality** in § 1 (2), particularly of reasonable efforts and reasonable costs. The OCSSP must only **actively** approach domestic **collecting societies** (No. 3, → mn. 23) and those **representative rightholders** that are known to the OCSSP (No. 2, → mn. 21 et seq.). This specification of the obligation to obtain rights of use in light of the principle of proportionality is in conformity with the DSMD[57] (→ mn. 22) and has the additional advantage that it creates legal certainty.[58] Sub. 2 provides a further specification of the conditions under which the acquisition of rights of use is reasonable for the OCSSP (→ mn. 29 et seqq.). **19**

### a) Obligation of non-representative rightholders to make an offer (No. 1)

To keep the efforts of OCSSPs within **reasonable** limits, they are **not** generally obliged to **proactively** search for licensing offers from individual rightholders unknown to them.[59] This would only be possible with disproportionate effort due to the – by definition – large amounts of copyright-protected content uploaded by third parties (§ 2 (1) No. 1).[60] OCSSPs must in principle respond solely to such licensing offers that rightholders make to them. However, it follows from sub. 2 No. 2 that OCSSPs are only obliged to obtain rights of use for substantial repertoires. They do not have to acquire licences for individual rights.[61] **20**

### b) Representative rightholders known to the OCSSP (No. 2)

In contrast, the OCSSP must actively approach and enter into licensing negotiations with rightholders that are representative and known to the OCSSP. In conjunction with sub. 2 No. 2, a rightholder is **representative** if it can licence a **significant repertoire of rights** relevant to the OCSSP (for more details → mn. 33). Examples are major labels or film studios[62] and major press publishers.[63] **21**

---

[56] §§ 92(1) No. 1, 128 VGG.
[57] More strictly, however, COM(2021) 288 final EN, 11.
[58] Cf. Hofmann ZUM 2020, 665 (667).
[59] BT-Drs. 19/27426, 45, 133; Stieper ZUM 2021, 387 (392); Hofmann ZUM 2020, 665 (667).
[60] BT-Drs. 19/27426, 133.
[61] BT-Drs. 19/27426, 133.
[62] BT-Drs. 19/27426, 132.
[63] Stieper ZUM 2021, 387 (394).

22 The representative rightholder must be known to the OCSSP. On a *prima facie* interpretation of the wording, a rightholder is only known if the OCSSP has **positive knowledge** of its existence and how it can be contacted, for example, due to a pre-existing business relationship.[64] In this case, the general principles of the attribution of knowledge in a company are applicable.[65] In the Commission's view, however, the OCSSP is also obliged to approach **rightholders that can be easily identified and located**, at least those who have an extensive catalogue of copyright-protected content.[66] It is thus possible that the criterion of 'knowing' must be interpreted in conformity with the Directive to the effect that the best possible efforts also include obtaining an overview of the market of the main rightholders. At the same time, the explanatory memorandum to the UrhDaG forecasts that there will only be 13 OCSSPs as defined in § 2.[67] It is a reasonable effort for the major rightholders to approach these few OCSSPs and provide them with the knowledge required for No. 2. The OCSSPs must ensure that they can be easily contacted by rightholders by providing easy-to-find and clear **contact details** or corresponding contact forms.[68]

#### c) Domestic collecting societies (No. 3)

23 The OCSSP must actively approach **domestic collecting societies** (§ 2 VGG) and **dependent collecting entities** (§ 3 VGG). In contrast to No. 2, the OCSSP does not have to know the collecting society, although this is hardly conceivable in the case of domestic collecting societies. OCSSPs must also acquire the **rights of outsiders** (§ 7a VGG) from the collecting societies if a collecting society offers corresponding extended collective licences.[69] An outsider then has the possibility to make use of the right of objection under § 51 (2) VGG.[70] In this case, the OCSSP is only obliged to negotiate a licensing agreement with the outsider if it has a substantial repertoire (sub. 2 No. 2).

### 3. Refusal options of the OCSSP

24 *Argumentum e contrario* to sub. 2, OCSSPs may reject **irrelevant, too small** or **unreasonable licensing offers** (→ mn. 11). Conversely, they generally do not fulfil their obligation under sub. 1 if they reject **reasonable licensing offers as** defined in sub. 2. In this case, they do not fulfil the requirements for exemption from liability under § 1 (2) because the obligations listed there must be cumulatively fulfilled. However, it must be possible for them to reject certain licensing offers for **economic** or **content-related reasons**.[71] The OCSSP is in principle free to define content that may not be made available on its platform in its **terms of use** in a non-discriminatory manner.[72] By doing so, it defines what content 'by its nature' (sub. 2 No. 1) may be made accessible on the platform and, at the same time, restricts the scope of its licensing obligation.

---

[64] BT-Drs. 19/27426, 132.

[65] Cf. MüKoBGB/Schubert, 9th edn 2021, BGB § 166 mn. 58 et seqq.

[66] COM(2021) 288 final EN, 9; also Metzger/Senftleben jipitec 2020, 115 mn. 20.

[67] BT-Drs. 19/27426, 61.

[68] COM(2021) 288 final EN, 9.

[69] BT-Drs. 19/27426, 132; on this in more detail: Leistner ZUM 2020, 505 (509 et seq.) and Dreier/Schulze/Raue VGG § 51 mn. 5.

[70] Dreier/Schulze/Raue VGG § 51 mn. 9

[71] Hofmann ZUM 2020, 665 (667).

[72] BT-Drs. 19/27426, 133; MPI Stellungnahme zum RefE, 4; Hofmann ZUM 2020, 665 (666); cf. also BGH 29.7.2021 – III ZR 179/20, NJW 2021, 3179 mn. 58 et seqq. – Hassrede (hate speech); with criticism: Spindler WRP 2021, 1111 mn. 16.

**a) Economic reasons**

If the reasonable licence fees for a **certain type of content or genre** (such as sports rights) cannot be refinanced by their business model, OCSSPs can **prohibit** their users from making this content accessible via their service by means of its **terms of use.**[73] In this case, they do not have to licence such content because they do **not offer it by its 'nature'** (sub. 2 No. 1, → mn. 30).[74] This might be relevant, for example, if a platform wants to make sports content accessible but cannot refinance certain (premium) content; it must be possible for an OCSSP to allow the recording of amateur games or certain sports but to exclude other content such as football in licenced leagues. The OCSSP should not then be obliged under § 4 to licence the excluded content. However, the OCSSP must enforce the ban of certain content and remains obliged to effectively block the content within the framework of §§ 7, 8. 25

**b) Reasonableness**

The licensing obligation must also be interpreted in light of the **principle of proportionality** (→ § 1 mn. 27). According to § 1 (2) sent. 2 No. 4, the costs incurred by the OCSSP in fulfilling its obligations must be taken into account, and this includes the costs of acquiring rights of use under § 4. The business model of an OCSSP that wants to make certain content accessible on its platform is only legitimate if the OCSSP can pay reasonable licence fees for the content, in which case, the economic value of the use must be considered in determining the licensing fee according to general principles (→ mn. 37). This is the basic rationale of the UrhDaG, and in principle, it cannot be restricted even by considerations of proportionality. According to previous case law on platform liability, however, OCSSPs may **not be required to take measures** that are '**excessively costly**'[75] or that '**economically jeopardise**' their legitimate business model or '**disproportionately complicate** their activity'.[76] If OCSSPs are not allowed to refuse economically unreasonable licensing offers by banning the respective content from their platform (→ mn. 25), they must nevertheless in exceptional cases be allowed to reject such licensing offers that are generally reasonable but individually too costly under the **principle of proportionality** and to protect their entrepreneurial freedom (Art. 16 CFR; Art. 12 GG).[77] This can be construed by a respective interpretation of sub. 2 No. 4 (→ mn. 36) or as an exception to sub. 1 sent. 2. OCSSPs must also be allowed to **limit accessibility to licenced content in order** to limit the licence fees to a reasonable amount (→ mn. 37).[78] 26

**c) Content-related reasons**

OCSSPs should not have to offer certain media on their platform because of its content and should not have to conclude licence agreements with corresponding rightholders. This could be due to the **nature of the content** (sub. 2 No. 1). A sports portal does not have to licence cinema movies and a music portal does not have to licence sports content. In addition, an OCSSP may exclude certain content from being made available on its platform for **thematic reasons** or because of the **way it is presented**, such as if it is erotic, racist, extremist or discriminatory content.[79] If a 27

[73] BT-Drs. 19/27426, 133; MPI Stellungnahme zum RefE, 4.

[74] For doubts see: Spindler WRP 2021, 1111 mn. 16.

[75] Generally for online services, see: CJEU C-324/09, ECLI:EU:C:2011:474 mn. 139 – L'Oréal/eBay et al; C-360/10, ECLI:EU:C:2012:85 mn. 46 – SABAM/Netlog.

[76] BGH 12.7.2012 – I ZR 18/11, GRUR 2013, 370 mn. 22 – Alone in the Dark, with further references.

[77] Hofmann ZUM 2020, 665 (667).

[78] Hofmann ZUM 2020, 665 (667).

[79] Cf. Hofmann ZUM 2020, 665 (667).

platform has a certain **religious or non-religious orientation**, it cannot be expected to make content accessible that is against its beliefs. Additional restrictions are imposed on large platforms from a different angle, namely by the **increased (indirect) fundamental rights obligation.**[80] Accordingly, content restrictions must be objectively justified and may not discriminate against certain political views.[81]

## III. Rights of use subject to acquisition obligation (sub. 2)

### 1. Acquisition of contractual rights of use

28 The object of best efforts under sub. 1 is to obtain contractual rights of use for the communication to the public of copyright-protected content under § 1 (1). **Rights of use** are the rights mentioned in § 31 (1) sent. 1 UrhG.[82] Best efforts and, thus, the licensing obligation relate only to copyright-protected content, that is, **works** (§ 4 (1)) and **related rights** (§ 21 (1)). The OCSSP does not have to licence works in the public domain, and thus, it is irrelevant whether the respective protection thresholds are not met or the term of protection has expired. According to general principles, the **burden of proof** for protectability and ownership lies with the rightholder.[83] OCSSPs are only obliged to acquire rights of use for communication to the **public** under § 1 (1). The best effort obligation under the UrhDaG does **not** extend to **acts of reproduction.**[84]

### 2. Qualified licensing offers

29 Sub. 2 contains a further specification of **the licensing obligation**. It specifies in more detail the conditions under which the acquisition of rights of use is reasonable for the OCSSP. The OCSSP does not have to accept every licensing offer that meets the requirements in → mn. 27 to fulfil its obligations under § 4. Only qualified licensing offers that meet the criteria listed in Nos 1–4 trigger the licensing obligation.[85]

### 3. Content communicated to the public on the platform (No. 1)

30 The OCSSP is only obliged to acquire the rights of use for content that by its nature is manifestly communicated to the public in more than negligible quantities on its platform. On the one hand, this has a factual dimension. If users make only a certain type of content accessible on a platform, then the OCSSP must also only licence such content. On the other hand, the requirement in No. 1 also enables the OCSSP to normatively control the extent of its licensing obligation through its terms of use (→ mn. 24 et seq.). If, for example, the OCSSP prohibits in its terms of use that certain content is made accessible on its platform, this generally releases the service provider from the obligation to licence this content. An OCSSP that specialises in certain music genres or sports does not have to licence content of other music genres or other sports.[86] However, the OCSSP must enforce its terms of use. If despite the prohibition in the terms of use corresponding content is made accessible on the platform to a significant

---

[80] Cf. BVerfG NJW 2018, 1667 mn. 33 – Stadionverbot (stadium ban); BGH 29.7.2021 – III ZR 179/20, NJW 2021, 3179 mn. 65 et seqq. – Hassrede (hate speech); Raue JZ 2018, 961 (964 et seqq.).

[81] Cf. BGH 29.7.2021 – III ZR 179/20, NJW 2021, 3179 mn. 80 et seq. – Hassrede (hate speech).

[82] Dreier/Schulze/Schulze UrhG § 31 mn. 3.

[83] Cf. the comparable situation with collecting societies in Dreier/Schulze/Raue VGG § 27 mn. 13, 17.

[84] COM(2021) 288 final EN, 6.

[85] BT-Drs. 19/27426, 133.

[86] BT-Drs. 19/27426, 133; for doubts see: Spindler WRP 2021, 1111 mn. 16.

extent, the OCSSP remains obliged to licence such content. Consideration must be given to the extent to which the OCSSP is technically able to keep such content off its platform with the proportionate means at its disposal. As far as it is necessary, the rightholder will have to provide the OCSSP with the information necessary to block the content (→ § 7 mn. 18).

#### a) According to their type

In the Commission's view, the type of works (German: *Art der Inhalte*; French: *le type d'oeuvre*) must be formally distinguished according to the **category of content** (music, audio-visual content, images, texts).[87] The type of works must also be **distinguished according to its content**, for example, according to music genres, film genres, sports and text genres.[88] This is required by the entrepreneurial freedom of OCSSPs (Art. 16 CFR; Art. 12 GG) because the choice of what kind of content can or cannot be presented on the platform is essential for the OCSSP and, consequently, should limit the scope of its licensing obligation (→ mn. 4, 27). **31**

#### b) More than negligible quantities

If content is made available on the platform only in a negligible quantity, it does not trigger the OCSSP's licensing obligation. As soon as certain content is made available on the platform in a non-negligible quantity, the OCSSP must acquire rights of use for this content. It is irrelevant whether this is the **predominant** or **less frequent type of** content.[89] **32**

### 4. Substantial repertoire (No. 2)

OCSSPs only have to negotiate the licensing of rights of use with those rightholders who have a substantial repertoire that is relevant to the OCSSP (No. 1). Unlike in the Second Discussion Proposal (DiskE II → Introduction mn.1), the repertoire does not have to be representative but only substantial. Therefore, a rightholder cannot be expected to have a similarly broad repertoire as a collecting society. This criterion aims to avoid disproportionate transaction costs for the OCSSPs.[90] Therefore, the rightholder must have a considerable repertoire in terms of the number of **works** and **rightholders** that is **economically** so **significant** that the OCSSP can reasonably be expected to enter individual negotiations. The explanatory memorandum to the UrhDaG mentions major music labels or film studios as examples of rightholders that have a relevant repertoire.[91] **33**

### 5. No licensing obligation vis-à-vis small rightholders

The OCSSP is **not obliged to accept licensing offers from rightholders** that have an insignificant repertoire. Accordingly, OCSSPs are free to accept, ignore or reject licensing offers from such rightholders.[92] This restriction is a consequence of the principle of proportionality. OCSSPs should not have to deal with a large number of individual rightholders who can only licence rights of use for non-significant content.[93] If such content only generates advertising revenues of fractions of a cent, the transaction costs would be manifestly disproportionate to the generated revenues. In the light of § 1 (2) **34**

---

[87] COM(2021) 288 final EN, 10.
[88] Cf. BT-Drs. 19/27426, 133.
[89] COM(2021) 288 final EN, 10.
[90] BT-Drs. 19/27426, 133; for doubts about conformity with EU law see Spindler WRP 2021, 1111 mn. 17.
[91] BT-Drs. 19/27426, 132.
[92] Cf. Metzger/Pravemann ZUM 2021, 288 (291).
[93] BT-Drs. 19/27426, 133.

sent. 2 No. 4/Art. 17 (5)(b) DSMD, the Commission's view[94] that OCSSPs must engage with all rightholders who approach them with a licensing offer is, therefore, not convincing. If rightholders want to benefit from the licensing obligation of § 4 (1) No. 1, they must either own a substantial repertoire or assign their rights to a rightholder with a substantial repertoire or a collecting society. If no collecting societies exist in certain sectors (e.g., in the games sector), this can be an incentive to establish a corresponding collecting society.

## 6. Territorial scope (No. 3)

35 The territorial scope of § 1 (1) is limited to Germany (→ Introduction mn. 14). This limits the licensing obligation to the acquisition of **domestic rights of use.**[95] The rightholder must make licensing offers to the OCSSP limited to their use in Germany. However, if the OCSSP makes accessible the copyright-protected content to audiences in other EU Member States, a licensing obligation for those states may arise from the corresponding transposition of Art. 17 DSMD.

## 7. Reasonable terms and conditions (No. 4)

36 The OCSSP does not have to accept every licensing offer from rightholders, in particular, not at any price, but only on reasonable terms. This requirement is necessary **in light of the principle of proportionality** (→ mn. 4). At the same time, it is a basic principle of copyright law that authors shall equitably participate in the economic exploitation of their works (§ 11 (2) UrhG). For licence agreements with collecting societies, the obligation already arises from §§ 34, 39 VGG.[96] In exceptional cases, it will not be possible to reconcile these two requirements because the usual and, therefore, reasonable licensing fees cannot be earned with the OCSSP's legitimate business model. In this case, it would be disproportionate to oblige the OCSSP to conclude a corresponding licence agreement (§ 1 (2) sent. 2 No. 4), so that **reasonable conditions** under § 32 UrhG may be **unreasonable** within the meaning of No. 4 in this exceptional case (cf. also → mn. 26). However, the OCSSP remains obliged to make best efforts to block this content according to §§ 7, 8.

### a) Reasonable licence fee

37 The OCSSP must pay reasonable licence fees (cf. also recital 61 sent. 9 DSMD). Reasonableness is an indeterminate legal concept that is difficult to define in concrete terms due to different interests and perspectives. However, the provisions in § 32 UrhG and § 39 VGG and their interpretations can be of use.[97] According to § 39 (1) sent. 1 VGG, the basis for calculating a tariff should be the **economic value** of the use of the rights. Here, in addition to the (advertising) revenue of the OCSSP, other forms of economic benefits are to be taken into account, such as the increased possibility of exploiting user data due to the attractiveness of the content.[98] In order to adequately capture the economic value of the use, the tariff can take into account, for example, the number of pageviews or other relevant figures measuring the attention of users of the

---

[94] COM(2021) 288 final EN, 9.
[95] BT-Drs. 19/27426, 133.
[96] Cf. Dreier/Schulze/Raue VGG § 39 mn. 4 et seqq.
[97] Cf. on the latter: MPI Stellungnahme zum RefE, 7.
[98] Cf. Wandtke/Hauck ZUM 2020, 671 (676); Riesenhuber in Festschrift für M. Walter, 2018, 253 (257 et seqq.); Dreier/Schulze/Raue VGG § 39 mn. 7.

content (§ 39 (1) sent. 2 VGG). Collecting societies must take into account in their tariffs the **quantitative extent to which** copyright-protected content was actually used.[99] **Lump sums** are only permissible as long as there is no alternative method that can more precisely determine, measure and monitor with reasonable effort the use of the copyright-protected content.[100] Because internet platforms have extensive usage statistics, usage-based remuneration models will usually be appropriate. This may also enable OCSSPs to limit their expenditures on licences by limiting the accessibility of content subject to licensing on a volume basis (→ mn. 26).[101] Furthermore, the **direct remuneration right** to which authors, photographic images and performing artists are entitled under sub. 3 must be taken into account.[102]

**b) Nonmonetary remuneration**

The remuneration will usually consist of a **reasonable licence fee in money**. However, this is not mandatory. Rightholders may **also** authorise the use of their content in return for **nonmonetary benefits**, for example, that the OCSSP provides them with data on their audiences, increases the reach of their content or allows them to place advertising banners in their content.[103] An OCSSP may also rely on the grant of non-exclusive licences, for example, under Creative Commons licences or by users under the platform use agreement, in exchange for the use of the platform.[104] **38**

**c) Reasonable other licensing conditions**

Not only the licensing fee but all the other terms of the licence must be reasonable.[105] **39**

**d) Scope of licensing**

The OCSSP must licence the content to the extent to which it is **made accessible** on the platform. If entire songs or complete texts are usually made accessible, the OCSSP must obtain corresponding licences; if only short excerpts are uploaded on the platform that are copyrightable the scope of the licence can be correspondingly reduced.[106] If either form is common on the platform, then the mix must be reflected in the terms of the licensing agreement. **40**

**e) No restriction of lawful uses**

Pursuant to recital 66 subpara. 1 DSMD, the cooperation between OCSSPs and rightholders must not have the effect of making it difficult or impossible for users to access content via the platform that is covered by an individual licence agreement or a statutory copyright exception. Licensing terms that require the OCSSP to **restrict** these **user rights** are **not reasonable** under No. 4. Such clauses are also invalid under § 5 (1) in conjunction with § 22 (→ § 5 mn. 1). **41**

---

[99] CJEU C-372/19, ECLI:EU:C:2020:959 mn. 50 – SABAM/Weareone.World.
[100] CJEU C-372/19, ECLI:EU:C:2020:959 mn. 52.
[101] Hofmann ZUM 2020, 665 (667).
[102] BT-Drs. 19/27426, 134.
[103] Cf. COM(2021) 288 final EN, 6.
[104] COM(2021) 288 final EN, 6.
[105] See BT-Drs. 19/27426, 133. For a corresponding interpretation of § 34 (1) sent. 2 VGG, see also BGH 22.4.2009 – I ZR 5/07, GRUR 2009, 1052 mn. 10 – Seeing is Believing; Dreier/Schulze/Raue VGG § 34 mn. 11.
[106] BT-Drs. 19/27426, 132.

## IV. Direct remuneration right (sub. 3)

### 1. Regulatory objective

42 If authors do not directly grant OCSSPs the authorisation and, thus, receive an appropriate remuneration, they have an additional direct remuneration right against the OCSSP pursuant to sub. 3. The legislature assumes that the claim does not increase the total remuneration for the rights of use because the direct remuneration right must be considered in the amount of the licence between the user and the OCSSP (→ mn. 37).[107] However, sub. 3 is intended to ensure in this constellation that **authors, photographers** and **performing artists** receive a **fair share of the additional remuneration** that derivative rightholders obtain through licence agreements with OCSSPs.[108] It is questionable whether this would otherwise be guaranteed, especially if authors have received a fixed sum in return for the licensing of their rights to the derivative rightholder.[109]

### 2. EU law requirements

43 Art. 17 DSMD does not contain a remuneration right for the author. Subs 3 and 4 are based on **Art. 18 (1) DSMD**.[110] This is in conformity with the Directive because Art. 17 DSMD does not prescribe who should benefit from the additionally generated royalties.[111] Moreover, Union copyright law is generally author friendly.

### 3. Entitled persons

44 The holders of the direct remuneration right are **authors** who have granted the corresponding rights of use (exclusively) to a third party and therefore have **no direct contractual relationship with the OCSSP**. Conversely, authors who grant an authorisation to anyone (and, thus, also to the OCSSP) free of charge, for example, through Creative Commons licences, are not entitled to a direct remuneration right.[112] § 21 (1) also allows holders of related rights to benefit from the direct remuneration right, but according to § 21 (2), this is limited to the related rights of the **photographer** and the **performer**, which are not exclusively commercial rights but also have a root in the law of personality.

### 4. Exceptions (sent. 2)

45 The direct remuneration right does not exist in cases in which collecting societies or digital distributors grant the OCSSP the rights of use. The reasoning behind this is that **collecting societies** must in any case pay each author a fair share of the revenue according to § 27 VGG.[113] **Digital distributors** are OCSSPs that licence rights in bundled form, in particular, to online platforms, and act on behalf and in the interest

---

[107] BT-Drs. 19/27426, 134.

[108] BT-Drs. 19/27426, 45, 133 et seq.; Hohnholz ZUM 2021, 519 (523); Spindler WRP 2021, 1111 mn. 19.

[109] Metzger/Pravemann ZUM 2021, 288 (290); with criticism: Hansen ZUM 2020, 692 (699).

[110] BT-Drs. 19/27426, 45, 134.

[111] Metzger/Pravemann ZUM 2021, 288 (290); Metzger/Senftleben jipitec 2020, 115 mn. 59 et seq.; Spindler WRP 2021, 1111 mn. 19; see, however: Houareau MMR 2019, 635 (636 et seq.).

[112] BT-Drs. 19/29894, 92.

[113] Cf. BT-Drs. 19/29894, 96; Spindler WRP 2021, 1111 mn. 20.

of authors in return for a commission fee.[114] They thus provide a service only to the authors, and this ensures that the authors receive an appropriate share of the revenue.

## V. Assertion of renumeration right by collecting society (sub. 4)

### 1. Non-waivable right and assignable only to collecting society (sent. 1)

Authors and holders of related rights may not waive the remuneration right of sub. 3 and may only assign it in advance to a collecting society. This regulation technique has become customary for statutory remuneration rights. It ensures that authors actually benefit from these rights.[115] This reflects the protective function of collecting societies in favour of authors.[116] **46**

### 2. Mandatory assertion by collecting society (sent. 2)

The remuneration right can only be asserted by a collecting society. On the one hand, this reduces transaction costs for the OCSSPs and, on the other hand, ensures that the remuneration rights are enforced and that the revenue benefits the authors. The legislature has instructed collecting societies not to apply existing **distribution keys** to the revenues of this direct remuneration claim without further examination.[117] They must **examine** whether the use of certain repertoires on upload platforms significantly differs from the forms of use on which the existing distribution keys are based. They are in any case obliged under § 27 (1) VGG to distribute the revenue as **fairly** as possible in regard to the actual **use and performance**.[118] For this purpose, the collecting societies right to information against OCSSPs pursuant to § 41 (1) sent. 1 VGG has been extended with regard to the direct remuneration rights of the UrhDaG. **47**

## § 5
## Statutorily permitted uses; remuneration of the author

**(1) The communication to the public of works and parts of works protected by copyright by the user of a service provider shall be permitted for the following purposes:**
**1. for quotations under § 51 of the Copyright Act,**
**2. for caricatures, parodies and pastiches under § 51a of the Copyright Act and**
**3. for statutorily permitted cases of communication to the public under Division 1 Subdivision 6 of the Copyright Act not covered by numbers 1 and 2.**

**(2) [1]The service provider shall pay the author an appropriate remuneration for the communication to the public under subsection 1**

## § 5
## Gesetzlich erlaubte Nutzungen; Vergütung des Urhebers

**(1) Zulässig ist die öffentliche Wiedergabe von urheberrechtlich geschützten Werken und Teilen von Werken durch den Nutzer eines Diensteanbieters zu folgenden Zwecken:**
**1. für Zitate nach § 51 des Urheberrechtsgesetzes,**
**2. für Karikaturen, Parodien und Pastiches nach § 51a des Urheberrechtsgesetzes und**
**3. für von den Nummern 1 und 2 nicht erfasste gesetzlich erlaubte Fälle der öffentlichen Wiedergabe nach Teil 1 Abschnitt 6 des Urheberrechtsgesetzes.**

**(2) [1]Für die öffentliche Wiedergabe nach Absatz 1 Nummer 2 hat der Diensteanbieter dem Urheber eine angemessene Ver-**

[114] BT-Drs. 19/29894, 91 et seq.
[115] BT-Drs. 19/29894, 92.
[116] More on that, see Dreier/Schulze/Raue VGG Vor VGG mn. 5.
[117] BT-Drs. 19/27426, 134.
[118] BT-Drs. 19/29894, 92; Dreier/Schulze/Raue VGG § 27 mn. 12.

**number 2. [2]The claim to remuneration is not waivable and can only be assigned in advance to a collecting society. [3]It can only be asserted by a collecting society. [4]§ 63a subsection 2 of the Copyright Act and § 27a of the Collecting Societies Act shall apply.**

**(3) The service provider shall notify the user of the statutory permissions under subsection 1 in its general terms and conditions.**

**gütung zu zahlen. [2]Der Vergütungsanspruch ist nicht verzichtbar und im Voraus nur an eine Verwertungsgesellschaft abtretbar. [3]Er kann nur durch eine Verwertungsgesellschaft geltend gemacht werden. [4]§ 63a Absatz 2 des Urheberrechtsgesetzes und § 27a des Verwertungsgesellschaftengesetzes sind anzuwenden.**

**(3) Der Diensteanbieter hat den Nutzer auf die gesetzlichen Erlaubnisse nach Absatz 1 in seinen Allgemeinen Geschäftsbedingungen hinzuweisen.**

**Bibliography:** Conrad/Nolte, 'Schrankenbestimmungen im Anwendungsbereich des UrhDaG', ZUM 2021, 111; Positionspapier der Urheberrechtswissenschaft: Zitate und Parodien müssen vergütungsfrei bleiben!, available at <https://www.zar.kit.edu/downloads/News/Positionspapier%20der%20Urheberrechtswissens.pdf> (last accessed 12.3.2024); Stieper, 'Die Umsetzung von Art. 17 VII DSM-RL in deutsches Recht (Teil 2)', GRUR 2020, 792; Stieper, 'Vergüten statt Verbieten – Vergütungspflichten im UrhDaG nach dem Regierungsentwurf zur Umsetzung der DSM-RL', ZUM 2021, 387. – See also the bibliography in the Introduction.

**Content**



# I. General remarks

## 1. Objective

1 According to § 5 (1), users who use copyright-protected content on OCSSP platforms can rely on all the copyright exceptions of the UrhG. This is an expression of the necessary **balancing of interests** between rights in **intellectual property** protected by fundamental rights and **user's interests** protected, in particular, by freedom of opinion and information.[1] The **classification of § 5 (1)** is unclear. On the one hand, the wording 'by the user' *(durch den Nutzer)* addresses copyright relevant acts by **users.**[2] On the other hand, both the copyright relevant acts by the user and their exemption by the copyright exceptions are governed by the UrhG, not by the UrhDaG (→ § 1 mn. 7).

[1] BT-Drs. 19/27426, 135.

[2] Metzger/Pravemann ZUM 2021, 288 (293).

With regard to the user, § 5 (1) primarily has a clarifying function.[3] However, it is a helpful reminder that not only Art. 5 InfoSoc Directive but also Art. 17 (7) DSMD must be taken into account when interpreting the copyright exceptions in light of EU law.[4] In conjunction with § 6 (2), § 5 (1) clarifies that the communication to the public by **OCSSPs** (§ 1 (1)) is also exempted by the copyright exceptions on which users may rely for their communication (→ § 1 mn. 8).[5] Therefore, § 5 (1) primarily has significance because of the **remuneration provision** in sub. 2, which obliges OCSSPs to pay reasonable remuneration for communication to the public that is exempted on the basis of the caricature, parody and pastiche exception (§ 51a UrhG). In addition, sub. 3 contains a **contract law provision** that obliges the OCSSP to draw the attention of its users to the statutory permissions of sub. 1 in its general terms and conditions. In a Union law compliant interpretation, this constitutes a contractual right of the users against the platform to make relevant content accessible on the platform (→ mn. 12). Furthermore, according to Art. 17 (7) subpara. 1 and recital 66 subpara. 1 DSMD, cooperation between OCSSPs and rightholders must not make it difficult or impossible for users to make content that is not or no longer protected by copyright or covered by a statutory copyright exception or a licence agreement accessible via the platform.[6] Therefore, § 5 (1) in conjunction with § 22 precludes **contractual agreements** that prohibit the OCSSP or its users for copyright reasons from making available on the platform **content that is not** protected by copyright or is covered by a legal or contractual **authorisation.**[7]

### 2. EU law requirements

Sub. 1 implements **Art. 17 (7) subpara. 2(a)** and **(b) DSMD** in Nos 1 and 2 and the 2
general requirement of **Art. 17 (7) subpara. 1** and **(9) subpara. 3 DSMD** in No. 3, which are explained in recital 66 subpara. 1 sent. 6, 7, and recital 70 subpara. 1 DSMD. The remuneration obligation of sub. 2 is not required by the DSMD but can be based on **recital 36 InfoSoc Directive.**[8] Sub. 3 implements **Art. 17 (9) subpara. 4 DSMD.**

## II. Permissible communication to the public (sub. 1)

### 1. Permitted use

The users of the OCSSPs can rely on **all copyright exceptions** of the UrhG for their 3
communication to the public on platforms (No. 3). The special emphasis on the quotation exception in No. 1 and the caricature, parody and pastiche exception in No. 2 is, strictly speaking, superfluous (and a remnant of an earlier version of the provision), but it highlights the corresponding provision in Art. 17 (7) subpara. 2 DSMD. The statutory exemption of user acts extends to the **acts of communication to the public of OCSSPs** under § 1 (1) (§ 6 (2); → § 6 mn. 10).[9] For the scope of the exemption, reference can be made to the relevant commentaries on the UrhG, particularly to § 51a UrhG.[10] The explanatory memorandum of the UrhDaG also indicates that

[3] Stieper ZUM 2021, 387 (389); Becker ZUM 2020, 681 (687).
[4] Cf. on the latter: COM(2021) 288 final EN, 19.
[5] BT-Drs. 19/27426, 45, 136; see also → § 1 mn. 8.
[6] COM(2021) 288 final EN, 19 et seq.
[7] See also AG Saugmandsgaard Øe C-401/19, ECLI:EU:C:2021:613 mn. 163 – Poland/Parliament and Council; Leistner ZGE 2020, 123 (166).
[8] Stieper GRUR 2020, 792 (795); with criticism: Conrad/Nolte ZUM 2021, 111 (115 et seq.).
[9] BT-Drs. 19/27426, 45, 136.
[10] For example Dreier/Schulze/Dreier UrhG § 51 a.

the exemptions are intended to enable '**current social practices of creative engagement with pre-existing content**', in particular, through memes.[11]

### 2. User rights

4 In general, copyright exceptions do not constitute subjective rights.[12] It remains to be seen whether the statutory permissions of the copyright exceptions in the context of the UrhDaG will become **subjective, enforceable rights of the users** against the OCSSPs. The requirements of Art. 17 (7) and (9) DSMD favour this interpretation.[13] Accordingly, the Member States must ensure that users can at least rely on the quotation, caricature, parody or pastiche exception (Art. 17 (7) DSMD). Member States must also ensure that the users can assert the use of a copyright exception in court (Art. 17 (9) subpara. 2 sent. 5 DSMD). This presupposes the existence of a statutory or contractual right of the user. **Contractual rights** of the user to make rightful content accessible on the platform (if the use is covered by copyright exceptions or licensing agreements) arise under sub. 3 from the contract between the OCSSP and the user (→ mn. 12).[14] Contractual terms limiting that use are invalid pursuant to sub. 1 in conjunction with § 22 (→ mn. 1). In particular, a clause would be invalid permitting OCSSPs to block content only on grounds of an (unfounded) rightholder complaint of copyright infringement.[15] A **statutory right of a user against the OCSSP** to communicate content on the platform arises from § **9 (1)**, at least in automated procedures (→ § 9 mn. 6).

## III. Remuneration rights (sub. 2)

### 1. Right to remuneration for caricatures, parodies and pastiches (sent. 1)

5 Sub. 2 sent. 1 grants authors and holders of related rights (in connection with § 21 (1)) a statutory right to remuneration for communication to the public if the communication is covered by a copyright exception. However, the claim to remuneration **only** arises for permitted uses according to sub. 1 No. 2 for **caricatures, parodies and pastiches**. Other uses exempted by copyright exceptions, in particular, **quotations, public speeches, incidental works** or uses within the scope of the **freedom of panorama**, remain **free of remuneration** even if they are made accessible via an OCSSP. **The government draft (RegE,** → Introduction mn. 1) had provided for remuneration for all uses exempted by copyright exceptions. After considerable criticism from civil society and legal scholars,[16] the Bundestag, at the suggestion of the Committee on Legal Affairs,[17] limited the remuneration obligation **to avoid an incentive for overblocking**. The obligation to pay remuneration was primarily introduced **for**

---

[11] BT-Drs. 19/27426, 135.

[12] Stieper Rechtfertigung, 99 et seq., 168 et seqq.; Schricker/Loewenheim/Stieper UrhG Vor § 44a mn. 56 et seqq.

[13] Hofmann/Specht-Riemenschneider ZGE 2021, 48 (82); cf. also Wagner GRUR 2020, 447 (452); Holznagel ZUM 2020, 1 (4).

[14] Cf. BGH 29.7.2021 – III ZR 179/20, NJW 2021, 3179 mn. 28 – Hassrede (hate speech); Volkmann CR 2019, 376 (382 et seq.); Raue JZ 2018, 961 (969 et seq.); cf. also Becker ZUM 2020, 681 (686).

[15] AG Saugmandsgaard Øe C-401/19, ECLI:EU:C:2021:613 mn. 163 – Poland/Parliament and Council; Leistner ZUM 2020, 505 (511).

[16] Cf., for example, 'Positionspapier der Urheberrechtswissenschaft: Zitate und Parodien müssen vergütungsfrei bleiben!'; Stieper ZUM 2021, 387 (390 et seq.); see, however: MPI Stellungnahme zum RefE, 9 et seq.

[17] BT-Drs. 19/29894, 92.

**pastiche**[18] because, here, even minor deviations from the original can fall into the scope of the copyright exception.[19] In order to be able to take account of everyday culture in the 'social web', on the one hand, and the interests of rightholders, on the other hand, particularly with regard to the three-step test, the UrhDaG has opted for a remunerated copyright exception. It remains to be seen whether this will lead to a more generous interpretation of the copyright exception and, therefore, to the inclusion of common cultural practices of the web, such as meme culture, in the scope of the exception.[20] **Caricatures** and **parodies** have so far been regarded as free use within the scope of application of the former § 24 UrhG and have been possible without remuneration. In order to avoid difficulties of demarcation, especially in the case of social media use, the Legal Committee has included both of the copyright exceptions in the remuneration obligation.[21]

### 2. Debtor of remuneration

Although it is primarily the user who performs the exempted act of use, the **OCSSP** 6 **alone** is liable for remuneration.[22] The exemption of the user is justified because it is primarily the OCSSP that economically profits from the attention generated by the use of the protected content.

### 3. Criticism

The introduced remuneration right indirectly puts a price tag on the exercise of 7 fundamental communication rights.[23] The justification for the existing remuneration-free copyright exceptions is primarily that the interests of the general public outweigh the individual interests of the rightholders in the **necessary balancing of interests**, especially if the primary exploitation of the work or subject matter is hardly affected.[24] Remuneration rights create **incentives for** OCSSPs to design their business model in a way that **minimises the uses that are subject to remuneration**.[25] Particularly in the case of platforms with substantial market shares, users have hardly any alternative options due to the network effects if they want their content to be visible. Therefore, internet platforms play an important role in the social communication process, so that they are of particular importance for freedom of expression and information.[26] Furthermore, other intermediaries, such as newspaper or book publishers as well as television and radio broadcasters, are not subject to remuneration when they distribute content exempted by copyright exceptions, even if they earn money from it. The fact that the same or similar content is now distributed via a different (online) distribution channel does not change the underlying balancing of interests.[27] Therefore, the remuneration obligation must above all be considered in the context of its genesis of the UrhDaG[28] and is not suitable for generalisations.

---

[18] BT-Drs. 19/29894, 92.

[19] Dreier/Schulze/Dreier UrhG § 51a mn. 19.

[20] Dreier/Schulze/Dreier UrhG § 51a mn. 21. With criticism: Stieper ZUM 2021, 387 (391).

[21] BT-Drs. 19/29894, 92; with criticism: Metzger/Pravemann ZUM 2021, 755 (757).

[22] BT-Drs. 19/27426, 136.

[23] Schack UrhR/UrhebervertragsR mn. 862.

[24] Dreier/Schulze/Dreier UrhG § 51 mn. 1; Stieper ZUM 2021, 387 (390) with further references.

[25] Conrad/Nolte ZUM 2021, 111 (115); also Metzger/Pravemann ZUM 2021, 288 (297).

[26] CJEU C-401/19, ECLI:EU:C:2022:297 mn. 45–47 – Poland/Parliament and Council; CJEU C-682/18 and C-683/18, ECLI:EU:C:2021:503 mn. 65, 77 – YouTube and Cyando.

[27] Stieper ZUM 2021, 387 (390 et seq.).

[28] Cf. MPI Stellungnahme zum RefE, 9.

### 4. Appropriate remuneration

8 The parties to the necessary remuneration negotiations are given the extraordinarily demanding task of determining the equitable remuneration in a practically manageable form.[29] The setting of tariffs of collecting societies is regulated in § 39 VGG. According to § 39 (1) sent. 1 VGG, the **monetary benefits** generated by the exploitation should generally be used as the **basis for calculating** tariffs.[30] However, according to § 39 (1) sent. 2 VGG, other factors may also be used to calculate the benefits generated by the use.[31] The explanatory memorandum to the UrhDaG indicates that a **market price** for the use of the protected content is to be used as a basis for remuneration (→ § 12 mn. 12).[32] For this purpose, the **price of a usual licence** is to be used in a first step and then, in a second step, **deductions are to be** made because the work has been used in a transformative form or only in parts. In the latter case, whether the part of the work has a particularly high recognition value or generates special attention is to be taken into account, as may be the case with the chorus of a song or the catchphrase of a film. In a third step, the **economic impact** must be taken into account, that is, the attention generated in the form of pageviews or other relevant figures measuring the attention as well as the monetisation in the form of advertising. This can have the effect of both increasing and decreasing remuneration. Pursuant to § 41 (1) sent. 1 VGG, the OCSSP must provide the collecting societies with **data** on individual content views.[33] The explanatory memorandum to the UrhDaG assumes that the costs to provide this data are proportionate because they are essentially 'anyway' costs since the platforms already collect and evaluate the necessary data.[34] The reference to the corresponding relief of § 60h (3) sent. 1 UrhG in the RefE[35] is no longer included in the adopted version (also → § 12 mn. 12). Due to the legislative history, a **lump-sum calculation**, for example, based on a representative user sample, is generally inadmissible.[36] An equitable remuneration can **only be** demanded **once**, even if it should arise from several bases of claims, for example, from § 12 (1) (→ § 12 mn. 17).

### 5. Non-waivable right and assignable only to collecting society (sent. 2)

9 Authors cannot waive the remuneration right and can only assign it in advance to a collecting society. This is the regulation technique for statutory remuneration rights that has become customary, and it ensures that authors actually benefit from these claims.[37] This reflects the protective function of collecting societies in favour of authors.[38] It is questionable whether the remuneration right of a performer is also unassignable if the performance right as such is transferable. According to § 21 (1),

[29] Conrad/Nolte ZUM 2021, 111 (116); Metzger/Pravemann ZUM 2021, 288 (297 et seq.); Stieper ZUM 2021, 387 (390).
[30] Dreier/Schulze/Raue VGG § 39 mn. 7 et seqq.
[31] Dreier/Schulze/Raue VGG § 39 mn. 10.
[32] BT-Drs. 19/27426, 136; also → § 12 mn. 12.
[33] Dreier/Schulze/Raue VGG § 41 mn. 2.
[34] BT-Drs. 19/27426, 62.
[35] § 7 (2) sent. 2 RefE; → Introduction mn. 1.
[36] With criticism: Conrad/Nolte ZUM 2021, 111 (116).
[37] BT-Drs. 19/29894, 92.
[38] Dreier/Schulze/Raue VGG Vor § 1 mn. 5.

the provision is only applicable *mutatis mutandis* to the holders of related rights. Therefore, one can assume that the remuneration right is assignable as well.

### 6. Mandatory assertion by collecting society (sent. 3)

Only a collecting society, not the rightholder, can assert the remuneration right. This 10
reduces the transaction costs for the OCSSPs and ensures that the remuneration rights are enforced and that the revenue benefits the authors.

### 7. Participation of publisher (sent. 4)

Sent. 4 grants **publishers** a **statutory participation right** by referring to § 63a (2) 11
UrhG, which they can assign to a joint collecting society with authors. According to § 63a (2) UrhG, as a prerequisite for the right, the authors must have granted their publisher a licence, which is usually not the case, especially in the field of music.[39] In the absence of such a licence, **authors** may **agree to the participation of publishers** under § 27a VGG after the work has been published or when it is registered with the collecting society.[40] As long as the collecting society does not implement a different distribution plan, the **authors are entitled to two thirds of the revenues** according to § 27b VGG.[41] Due to the merit principle of collecting society law, a higher share for publishers must be objectively justified; this is generally only the case if they have to provide a special publishing service compared to other publishers.[42]

## IV. Information on statutory permissions in OCSSP's terms of service (sub. 3)

The OCSSPs must inform their users in their **terms of service** that the users are 12
legally entitled to communicate to the public copyright-protected content pursuant to sub. 1. The legislature did not follow suggestions in the legislative process to oblige OCSSPs to provide an easily accessible information sheet.[43] The **legal nature** of this information in the terms and conditions has not been conclusively determined. The question remains whether it is information about the legal situation and, thus, a mere **declaration of knowledge** (*Wissenserklärung*) by the OCSSP or whether it also constitutes a **contractual right** of the user against the OCSSP to provide such content on the platform. According to Art. 17 (9) subpara. 4 DSMD, OCSSPs must not only inform their users of the legal permissions, as in sub. 3, but must also inform them that they can use the protected subject matter within the scope of the copyright exceptions. Furthermore, the obligation to include this information in the general terms of service indicates a contractual right. Otherwise, the (Union) legislature would have opted for a general duty to inform without specific reference to the contractually relevant terms of service.

---

[39] Dreier/Schulze/Raue VGG § 27a mn. 2.

[40] Dreier/Schulze/Raue VGG § 27a mn. 7.

[41] BT-Drs. 19/29894, 93; Dreier/Schulze/Raue VGG § 27b mn. 3.

[42] BT-Drs. 19/27426, 120; Dreier/Schulze/Raue VGG § 27 mn. 3.

[43] Holznagel ZUM 2020, 1 (4); Gerpott MMR 2019, 420 (425).

## § 6 Extension of authorisations

**(1) If the service provider is authorised to communicate a work to the public, this authorisation shall also extend to the user, provided that the user does not act on a commercial basis or does not generate significant revenues.**

**(2) If the user has an authorisation to communicate a work to the public through a service provider, such authorisation shall also extend to the service provider.**

## § 6 Erstreckung von Erlaubnissen

**(1) Ist dem Diensteanbieter die öffentliche Wiedergabe eines Werkes erlaubt, so wirkt diese Erlaubnis auch zugunsten des Nutzers, sofern dieser nicht kommerziell handelt oder keine erheblichen Einnahmen erzielt.**

**(2) Verfügt der Nutzer über eine Erlaubnis, ein Werk über einen Diensteanbieter öffentlich wiederzugeben, so wirkt diese Erlaubnis auch zugunsten des Diensteanbieters.**

**Bibliography:** See the bibliography in the Introduction.

**Content**



# I. General

## 1. Objective

1 § 6 is an expression of the **interdependence** of **platform** and **user actions**. The liability of OCSSPs depends on users uploading copyright infringing content to the platform and making it accessible to the public (→ § 1 mn. 2). Therefore, **sub. 2** clarifies that the **authorisation of the users' acts** extends to the platform's act of communication to the public pursuant to § 1 (1). Conversely, with **sub. 1**, the legislature wanted to ensure that users also benefit from licences that OCSSPs conclude for the use of content on their platforms. This, too, is mostly a clarification of how the licence agreement between OCSSPs and rightholders would be interpreted anyway. Licenced content would be of limited economic value to an OCSSP if their user would still infringe copyright when making it accessible on the platform. Sub. 1, however, creates a statutory exemption from liability to provide legal certainty for users[1] who would have the burden of proof in individual legal disputes with rightholders and might not rely on the active support of the platform in every case. However, a prerequisite for the statutory extension is that they do not act commercially or do not generate significant income from the communication to the public.

[1] COM(2021) 288 final EN, 7.

### 2. EU law requirements

Sub. 1 implements **Art. 17 (2) DSMD**, which is specified in recital 69 DSMD. The extension of the statutory authorisation of the users' acts to the OCSSP in sub. 2 indirectly results from the requirements of **Art. 17 (9) subpara. 3 DSMD**, which are explained in recital 66 subpara. 1 sent. 6, 7 DSMD, and from the contractual authorisations in **recital 69 sent. 2, 3 DSMD**. 2

## II. Extension of the OCSSP's authorisations to the user (sub. 1)

### 1. Extension of licence to users

If the OCSSP obtains a licence or other **authorisation** from a rightholder to make copyright-protected content accessible on its platform, this authorisation extends to the communication to the public of its users if they do not act commercially (→ mn. 5) or only generate insignificant revenue from it (→ mn. 6). The exemption is intended to cover as many users as possible,[2] so it should be generously interpreted.[3] The provision contains **two independent requirements;** users are exempt if they fulfil one of the two requirements.[4] Thus, a non-commercial user can generate significant revenue in individual cases and still be covered by the statutory extension of the licence. Commercially acting users are exempted as long as they do not generate significant revenues from the communication to the public. The **burden of proof** that both conditions are not met lies with the rightholder.[5] 3

### 2. Legal nature

The extension of authorisation has a **dual nature** under contract law and liability law. In its capacity as a **contract law norm**, § 6 (1) stipulates in a binding manner for licence agreements under § 4 that the licenced use covers all uses of the platform's user mentioned in § 6 (1). It is thus a statutory extended **licence in favour of third parties.**[6] However, if the contract is not subject to German or correspondingly harmonised contract law of the Member States,[7] a provision with a contractual nature is not applicable. Therefore, the provision must also be interpreted as a **tort law provision**. Irrespective of the actual content of the contractual provision, it justifies the act of use regarding copyright law as a **statutory fiction of authorisation.**[8] As an exemption from liability, it is subject to the country of protection principle pursuant to Art. 8 (1), 15(b) Rome II Regulation[9] and exempts all acts of use covered by § 6 (1) under the UrhG. 4

### 3. Non-commercial

The statutory licence extension is limited to cases in which the user is not acting on a commercial basis or does not derive significant revenues from the communica- 5

---

[2] COM(2021) 288 final EN, 7.

[3] Würtenberger/Freischem GRUR 2019, 1140 (1157); Peters/Schmidt GRUR Int. 2019, 1006 (1008).

[4] COM(2021) 288 final EN, 7.

[5] Regarding Art. 17 (2) DSMD see, however: Spindler CR 2019, 277 (285); Würtenberger/Freischem GRUR 2019, 1140 (1157).

[6] Becker ZUM 2020, 681 (686); Wandtke/Hauck ZUM 2019, 627 (630 fn. 28).

[7] Cf. Dreier/Schulze/Raue UrhG Vor § 120 mn. 71 et seqq.

[8] Würtenberger/Freischem GRUR 2019, 1140 (1156).

[9] Dreier/Schulze/Raue UrhG Vor § 120 mn. 48.

tion to the public. Users do not act commercially if they act for **non-commercial purposes** and share the content without the intention of making a profit (recital 69 sent. 1 DSMD). In any case, this means private users who, for example, include background music in self-made videos or otherwise exchange information about sports, hobbies and other topics.[10] In the legislative process, there have been calls to limit the extension of licences to private uses. However, Art. 17 (2) DSMD provides for a binding extension to any user not acting on a commercial basis (German: *nicht auf der Grundlage einer gewerblichen Tätigkeit handeln*; French: *n'agissent pas à titre commerciale*). It is, therefore, questionable whether **public service broadcasters** *(öffentlicher Rundfunk)* can rely on the statutory extension of licence under § 6 (1).

### 4. No significant revenues

6 In addition, all uploads that do not generate significant revenues for the user are exempt. This licence extension also applies to users acting on a commercial basis.[11] Sub. 1 is intended to legalise small advertising revenues for users.[12] It seems too generous to set the threshold at revenues with which users can finance their livelihood.[13] It is not entirely clear what the **reference point** of non-significant revenues should be. The explanatory memorandum to the UrhDaG suggests that, in general, users must not generate substantial income from their (general) **commercial activities** to benefit from the licence extension.[14] However, recital 69 sent. 1 DSMD focuses on the **specifically exempted use.**[15] Accordingly, only the revenue generated by the uploaded content is relevant (German: *Gewinne, die die hochgeladenen Inhalte einbringen*; French: *les revenus générés par leurs contenus téléversés*). Whether a user does not generate significant revenues is to be assessed based on a comprehensive case-by-case analysis (→ § 10 mn. 14).[16] This primarily covers professional YouTubers, influencers and similar actors on other platforms.[17] Conversely, tutorials by companies, for example, are exempt if they do not generate significant revenue with the content itself.[18] Whether this distinction is appropriate can certainly be questioned. In the example of advertising spots from companies, the **advertising value** for the company using the content can go beyond the value that the content has for the OCSSP. If necessary, this advertising value can be taken into account as indirect revenue.[19]

### 5. Contractual extension to commercial users

7 Of course, OCSSPs and rightholders are free to **include commercial uses** in the licensing contract.[20] In that case, it can be presumed that commercial users can rely on the authorisation in any liability proceedings with the rightholder.

---

[10] COM(2021) 288 final EN, 7; Würtenberger/Freischem GRUR 2019, 1140 (1157).
[11] See, however: COM(2021) 288 final EN, 7.
[12] Becker ZUM 2020, 681 (686).
[13] See also Peters/Schmidt GRUR Int. 2019, 1006 (1008).
[14] BT-Drs. 19/27426, 136.
[15] Frey/Rudolph MMR 2021, 671 (674).
[16] COM(2021) 288 final EN, 7; also → § 10 mn. 14.
[17] Metzger/Pravemann ZUM 2021, 288 (292); Spindler CR 2019, 277 (285).
[18] COM(2021) 288 final EN, 7.
[19] Cf. Würtenberger/Freischem GRUR 2019, 1140 (1157); Frey/Rudolph MMR 2021, 671 (674).
[20] COM(2021) 288 final EN, 7.

## III. Extension of user's authorisations to the OCSSP (sub. 2)

### 1. Extension of authorisation to OCSSPs

The **extension of authorisation** from the user to the OCSSP is an expression of the 8
(limited) **accessory liability** of the OCSSP (→ § 1 mn. 2). The term 'authorisation' covers both contractual authorisations as well as statutory copyright exceptions.

### 2. Contractual authorisations

Sub. 2 covers contractual authorisations that the user has received from the right- 9
holder for use on the OCSSP's platform. The authorisation covers the entire **act of communication to the public.**[21] However, it may not be presumed in favour of the OCSSP that its users have acquired the necessary rights (recital 69 sent. 3 DSMD). The OCSSP must ascertain the existence of the authorisation.[22]

### 3. Statutory permission

According to § 6 (2), the copyright exceptions covering the user's acts on the 10
platform extend to the corresponding acts of communication to the public by the OCSSPs under § 1 (1).[23] According to the concept laid down in → § 1 mn. 5, 8, this is only a clarification: the UrhDaG regulates the act of communication to the public and, therefore, does not affect the copyright exceptions of the UrhG.[24] As the copyright exceptions of the UrhG apply to the act of communication by the OCSSP, these acts are not covered by the exclusive copyright of the rightholder, so that the OCSSP – contrary to the explanatory memorandum to the UrhDaG[25] – does not have to acquire a licence pursuant to § 4 (→ § 4 mn. 7).

---

[21] COM(2021) 288 final EN, 7.

[22] Dreier/Schulze/Specht-Riemenschneider UrhG § 97 mn. 78.

[23] BT-Drs. 19/27426, 45, 136 [on § 5 sub. 2]; however, see also p. 130; also in favour of an extension of the limitations: Hofmann NJW 2021, 1905 mn. 10; Husovec/Quintais GRUR Int. 2021, 325 (330); Wandtke/Hauck ZUM 2020, 671 (676); Grisse JIPLP 2019, 887 (891).

[24] See also Stieper ZUM 2021, 387 (389 et seq.); in more detail → § 1 mn. 5, 8.

[25] BT-Drs. 19/27426, 132.

# Part 3
# Unauthorised uses

## § 7
## Qualified blocking

**(1) In accordance with § 1 subsection 2, the service provider is obliged to make best efforts, by disabling access *[sperren]* or removal *[entfernen]* (blocking), to ensure that a work is not communicated to the public and is not available for this purpose in the future as soon as the rightholder so requests and provides the necessary information.**

**(2) [1]Measures taken pursuant to subsection 1 shall not result in the unavailability of content uploaded by users if the use is permitted by law or if the use does not infringe copyright. [2]§§ 9 to 11 shall apply to the use of automated procedures. [3]Sentence 2 shall not apply to uses of cinematographic works or moving images until the end of their first communication to the public, in particular, during the simultaneous transmission of sporting events, insofar as the rightholder so requests from the service provider and provides the necessary information for this purpose.**

**(3) The service provider shall immediately inform the user of the blocking of the uploaded content and inform him of the right to lodge a complaint pursuant to § 14.**

**(4) Start-up service providers (§ 2 subsection 2) shall not be subject to the provision in subsection 1 as long as the average monthly number of unique visitors to the internet pages of the service does not exceed five million.**

**(5) It shall be rebuttably presumed with regard to the principle of proportionality that small service providers (§ 2 subsection 3) shall not be subject to the provision in subsection 1.**

# Teil 3
# Unerlaubte Nutzungen

## § 7
## Qualifizierte Blockierung

**(1) Der Diensteanbieter ist nach Maßgabe von § 1 Absatz 2 verpflichtet, durch Sperrung oder Entfernung (Blockierung) bestmöglich sicherzustellen, dass ein Werk nicht öffentlich wiedergegeben wird und hierfür auch künftig nicht verfügbar ist, sobald der Rechtsinhaber dies verlangt und die hierfür erforderlichen Informationen zur Verfügung stellt.**

**(2) [1]Maßnahmen nach Absatz 1 dürfen nicht dazu führen, dass von Nutzern hochgeladene Inhalte, deren Nutzung gesetzlich erlaubt ist oder bei denen kein Verstoß gegen das Urheberrecht vorliegt, nicht verfügbar sind. [2]Beim Einsatz automatisierter Verfahren sind die §§ 9 bis 11 anzuwenden. [3]Satz 2 ist nicht anzuwenden auf Nutzungen von Filmwerken oder Laufbildern bis zum Abschluss ihrer erstmaligen öffentlichen Wiedergabe, insbesondere während der zeitgleichen Übertragung von Sportveranstaltungen, soweit der Rechtsinhaber dies vom Diensteanbieter verlangt und die hierfür erforderlichen Angaben macht.**

**(3) Der Diensteanbieter informiert den Nutzer sofort über die Blockierung des von ihm hochgeladenen Inhalts und weist ihn auf das Recht hin, nach § 14 Beschwerde einzulegen.**

**(4) Startup-Diensteanbieter (§ 2 Absatz 2) sind nicht nach Absatz 1 verpflichtet, solange die durchschnittliche monatliche Anzahl unterschiedlicher Besucher der Internetseiten des Dienstes 5 Millionen nicht übersteigt.**

**(5) Es wird widerleglich vermutet, dass kleine Diensteanbieter (§ 2 Absatz 3) im Hinblick auf den Grundsatz der Verhältnismäßigkeit nicht nach Absatz 1 verpflichtet sind.**

**Bibliography:** See the bibliography in the Introduction.

**Content**

# I. General remarks

## 1. Objective

If rightholders do not wish to licence their copyright-protected content to the OCSSP or the latter was allowed to reject a licensing offer (→ § 4 mn. 24 et seqq.), then §§ 7 and 8 oblige the OCSSP to **block** and thus make this content unavailable. According to the **legal definition** in § 7 (1), blocking is the disabling of access or removal of content. In the case of **disabling of access** for which more literal translation would be blocking, the OCSSP must prevent the content from being accessible on the platform; in the case of **removal**, the OCSSP must end the accessibility of the content that is already accessible on its platform. On a timeline, blocking prevents *ex ante* the content from being unlawfully made available; in the case of removal, the OCSSP acts *ex post* after the content has already been made available on the platform. The rightholder's blocking request creates a **legal obligation** between the OCSSP and the rightholder with duties of protection (*Schutzpflichten*) under § 241 (2) BGB. 1

## 2. Requirements under EU law

### a) EU law requirements

**§§ 7 and 8** basically follow the structure of **Art. 17 (4)(b) and (c) DSMD** (explained in recital 66 DSMD), whereby (b) is implemented by qualified blocking in § 7 (1) and (c) by simple blocking in § 8 (1), (3). For (b), under the Directive, the OCSSP has to 'ensure the unavailability' of the content (German: *sicherzustellen, dass … nicht verfügbar sind*; French: *garantir l'indisponibilité*), whereas according to (c), 2 the OCSSP has to 'disable access' to the protected subject matter (German: *sperren*; French: *bloquer l'accès*) or it must be 'removed' (German: *entfernen*; French: *retirer*) from the internet pages. Both required actions have been integrated in the legal definition in **§ 7 (1)**. This corresponds to the interpretation in recital 66 subpara. 5 DSMD; nevertheless, it will have to be observed whether the CJEU follows this integrated concept. When designing the best effort obligations, the principle of proportionality in **Art. 17 (5) DSMD** as well as the prohibition of general surveillance in **Art. 17 (8) subpara. 1 DSMD** (explained in recital 66 subpara. 2 sent. 1 DSMD) must be taken into account. **§ 7 (2)** transposes (together with §§ 9–11) **Art. 17 (7), (9) subpara. 3 DSMD** (explained in recital 66 subpara. 1 sent. 6–7, 70 DSMD). It is disputed whether this is contrary to EU law[1] or – conversely – necessary for compliance with EU fundamental law (→ mn. 3).[2] The information obligation in **sub. 3** is not explicitly required by Art. 17 DSMD, but it is a prerequisite for effective and expeditious complaint and redress procedures, which **Art. 17 (9) subpara. 1 DSMD** (explained in recital 70 DSMD) specifies. The relief for start-ups in **sub. 4** is an implementation of **Art. 17 (6) DSMD** (explained in recitals 66 subpara. 1 sent. 3, 67 DSMD). The rebuttable presumption in favour of small OCSSPs in **sub. 5** is a transposition of the principle of proportionality from **Art. 17 (5) DSMD** (→ § 2 mn. 27).[3]

**b) Conformity with fundamental rights**

3 The special liability procedure of Art. 17 DSMD is in **conformity with EU fundamental rights.**[4] Poland's action for annulment against Art. 17 (4)(b) and (c), last sentence, of the DSMD was unsuccessful. However, the blocking obligation interferes with the **right to freedom of expression** and **information** (Art. 11 CFR) because the obligation to block content is likely to restrict the usability of internet platforms as an important means of disseminating content.[5] Nevertheless, the Directive contains **sufficient safeguards** for the freedom of expression and information in Art. 17 (7), (9), specified in recitals 66, 70, so that the obligation interpreted in light of fundamental rights neither disproportionately interferes nor interferes with the essence of fundamental rights.[6] This is supported in particular by the fact that Art. 17 (7), (9) DSMD imposes the **obligation** on OCSSPs not to block or remove lawful content.[7] They may only block obvious copyright infringement in an automated manner.[8] These fundamental rights requirements must be taken into account when specifying best efforts (→ mn. 14 et seqq.), as also stipulated in sub. 2 (→ mn. 23). The automated filtering of content does not infringe the **prohibition of general monitoring obligations** (Art. 17 (8) subpara. 1 DSMD). OCSSPs are only obliged to block specific content for which the rightholders have provided the relevant information. There is no obligation to carry out an independent assessment of the content.[9]

---

[1] See Metzger/Pravemann ZUM 2021, 288 (295); Stieper ZUM 2021, 387 (389).

[2] Hofmann GRUR 2021, 895 (903); → mn. 3.

[3] BT-Drs. 19/27426, 138, → § 2 mn. 27.

[4] CJEU C-401/19, ECLI:EU:C:2022:297 – Poland/Parliament and Council; Raue ZUM 2022, 624.

[5] CJEU C-401/19, ECLI:EU:C:2022:297 mn. 55 et seq. – Poland/Parliament and Council.

[6] CJEU C-401/19, ECLI:EU:C:2022:297 mn 59–98 – Poland/Parliament and Council.

[7] CJEU C-401/19, ECLI:EU:C:2022:297 mn. 78, 85 – Poland/Parliament and Council; Raue ZUM 2022, 624.

[8] COM(2021) 288 final EN, 20; AG Saugmandsgaard Øe C-401/19, ECLI:EU:C:2021:613 mn. 198.

[9] CJEU C-401/19, ECLI:EU:C:2022:297 mn. 90 et seq. – Poland/Parliament and Council; AG Saugmandsgaard Øe C-401/19, ECLI:EU:C:2021:613 mn. 107 et seq.; Lennartz/Möllers GRUR 2021, 1109 (1112); see, however: Spindler, Gutachten zur Urheberrechtsrichtlinie, 2019, 22 et seq.

### 3. Overview of §§ 7 et seqq.

#### a) Simple blocking (§ 8)

In the case of simple blocking pursuant to § 8, the OCSSP reacts to a sufficiently substantiated notice from the rightholder that a **specifically designated work or subject matter** is already being communicated to the public on the platform without authorisation (*notice and take down*). The future blocking of such a work (*stay down*) can only be demanded if the rightholder provides the OCSSP with the necessary information (in this respect, clarifying § 8 (3)). 4

#### b) Qualified blocking (§ 7)

§ 7 addresses the qualified blocking of content. It differs from simple blocking under § 8 because the OCSSP must prevent or terminate the communication to the public of content uploaded by the user before it has received a corresponding individual notice from the rightholder. In return, the rightholder must provide the OCSSP with the necessary information to enable the OCSSP to **block content in the future** by proportionate means (especially by means of filtering software) (*notice and prevent*). Since manual control of large amounts of content uploaded by third parties (§ 2 (1) No. 1) is usually only possible with disproportionate costs, § 7 (1) *de facto* obliges OCSSPs to use filtering software ('**upload filter**').[10] Without corresponding information from the rightholder, there is no obligation to take action and also no obligation to monitor content without specific reason.[11] New in comparison to the liability system before the UrhDaG is primarily the notice and prevent part of the duty of care, which is the obligation to block content in a qualified manner without prior or imminent copyright infringement. Depending on the perspective, this is a 'paradigm shift'[12] or 'much ado about nothing'.[13] 5

#### c) Duty of care obligation

§§ 7 and 8 do **not** establish an **obligation of result** (recital 66 subpara. 2 sent. 4 DSMD)[14] because a complete and error-free blocking of unlawful content is practically impossible.[15] These sections only oblige OCSSPs to make best efforts to prevent the unlawful availability of copyright-protected content on their platforms. Violation of that obligation prevents exemption from liability under § 1 (2) No. 1. In that case, OCSSPs communicate to the public under § 1 (1) if the other requirements are met. Despite the wording ('obliged'), §§ 7 and 8 are not independent sources (*Anspruchsgrundlagen*) of the corresponding claims for removal and injunctive relief.[16] Their infringement entitles claims under §§ 97 et seqq. UrhG (→ § 1 mn. 10). Conversely, §§ 7 and 8 establish a **liability privilege** for OCSSPs because they are not liable for making content available on their platforms if they comply with the obligations set therein.[17] 6

---

[10] CJEU C-401/19, ECLI:EU:C:2022:297 mn. 54 – Poland/Parliament and Council; AG Saugmandsgaard Øe C-401/19, ECLI:EU:C:2021:613 mn. 62 – Poland/Parliament and Council; Spindler WRP 2021, 1111 mn. 23; Hofmann GRUR 2019, 1219 (1220); Grisse JIPLP 2019, 887 (894); Kaesling JZ 2019, 586 (588).

[11] Spindler, Gutachten zur Urheberrechtsrichtlinie, 2019, 16.

[12] Dreier GRUR 2019, 771 (775); Gerpott MMR 2019, 420 (421); Wandtke/Hauck ZUM 2020, 671).

[13] Hofmann ZUM 2019, 617 (629); see also Leistner ZGE 2020, 123 (186); Wagner GRUR 2020, 447 (450); Spindler WRP 2021, 1111 mn. 5.

[14] BT-Drs. 19/27426, 137; recital 66 subpara. 2 sent. 4 DSMD; CJEU C-401/19, ECLI:EU:C:2022:297 mn. 78 – Poland/Parliament and Council.

[15] Metzger/Pravemann ZUM 2021, 288 (291 et seq.); Hofmann NJW 2021, 1905 (1907).

[16] Cf. Metzger/Pravemann ZUM 2021, 288 (292).

[17] Spindler, Gutachten zur Urheberrechtsrichtlinie, 2019, 15.

#### d) Obligations of the rightholders

7 §§ 7 and 8 do not contain any obligations for the rightholders, but they create a burden to act and, therefore, to cooperate with the OCSSP.[18] In a first step, they must provide the information required for future blocking of the content (in particular, through the use of upload filters) pursuant to § 7 (1) or § 8 (3) before they can demand a corresponding blocking from the OCSSP. If they do not comply with this obligation, the OCSSP cannot force them to provide the information. In that case, the OCSSP is not obliged to block. This clear definition of the **burden of action** is one of the essential innovations of the UrhDaG.

#### e) Burden of proof

8 The burden of proof must be allocated along the lines of the burden of action. **Rightholders** must prove that they demanded that the OCSSP block the content in dispute and that they provided the necessary information to do so. According to general principles, rightholders must show that the content is protected by copyright and that they are entitled to exercise the right (→ § 1 mn. 17). **OCSSPs** must prove that qualified blocking was not possible despite best efforts[19] (recital 66 subpara. 3 DSMD) or that they are entitled to communicate the content to the public for other reasons (→ § 1 mn. 20). To assess the prospects of a claim, a rightholder is entitled to reasonable information on the functioning of the blocking procedures pursuant to § 19 (2) (on the scope of the claim → § 19 mn. 12).

## II. Qualified blocking (sub. 1)

### 1. Disable access or removal (blocking)

#### a) Legal definition

9 Sub. 1 requires the OCSSP to ensure with best efforts that content protected by copyright is **not accessible on its platform to the public without authorisation** (→ § 5 mn. 3). **Blocking** is legally defined as **disabling access** or **removal**. The Directive specifies the objective of best efforts as to 'ensure the unavailability of specific works'. This obligation begins immediately after the rightholder's blocking request and subsequently covers future uploads of identical content by users. The blocking obligation also includes **equivalent content**, which means **modifications of the content** that are still covered by copyright protection,[20] to the extent that this modified content can be detected with the help of the information provided and the available filtering technology (see → § 1 mn. 32).

#### b) Disable access

10 By disabling access (German: *sperren*; French: *bloquer l'accès*) to content, the OCSSP must ensure that **content** uploaded by the user – which is usually only initially accessible for the uploader in the internal user interface – is **not made available** to the public. The more literal – and in this context more suitable – translation of 'sperren' would be blocking. However, the OCSSP does not have to prevent the content from being uploaded to its (internal) servers. A user cannot be expected to upload the content

[18] BT-Drs. 19/27426, 137; Metzger/Pravemann ZUM 2021, 288 (292); Hofmann NJW 2021, 1905 (1907).

[19] Recital 66 subpara. 3 DSMD; Leistner ZUM 2020, 897 (900).

[20] Würtenberger/Freischem GRUR 2019, 1140 (1158).

again after a successful complaint procedure (§ 14). Moreover, uploading content that is not made available to the public does not fall within the scope of § 1 (1) and, thus, not within the scope of the UrhDaG.

**c) Removal**

**Removal** (German: *Entfernung*; French: *retirer*) means that the OCSSP must **stop making content available** that is currently accessible to the public on its platform (*take down*). Removal, however, does not mean that the OCSSP must permanently delete the content from its servers. If the public no longer has access to the content, neither the corresponding liability requirement of § 1 (1) nor the requirements for the liability exemption of § 1 (2) apply. The requirements of § 7 (1) depend on the fact that the OCSSP communicates to the public under § 1 (1) and, therefore, do not introduce any independent duties of care for the OCSSP. Moreover, user rights argue in favour of such an interpretation: A user should not be burdened with the necessity to re-upload the removed content after successfully challenging the removal in the complaint procedure (§ 14).[21] 11

**d) Prevention of future accessibility**

The OCSSP's obligation to block covers not only content that is on its platform at the 12 time of the blocking request but also all corresponding content that users try to upload and make accessible on the platform in the future (*stay down*). This primarily concerns the **disabling of access** to the content. However, if further developments in automated detection technology make it possible to detect the unlawful communication to the public of content that could not previously be detected or not reliably enough, then the blocking obligation also extends to the **removal** of content that already exists but has not yet been detected as unlawful.

**e) Expeditious action**

The OCSSP must **expeditiously initiate** blocking (German: *unverzüglich*; French: 13 *promptement*) after receiving a corresponding blocking request and the necessary information from the rightholder. This requirement is neither contained in § 7 nor in § 8. However, the corresponding requirement from Art. 17 (4)(c) DSMD can be generalised.[22]

## 2. Best efforts

**a) Best efforts**

The OCSSP has only an **obligation of means, not an obligation of result** (recital 66 14 subpara. 2 sent. 4 DSMD).[23] Thus, it does not have to ensure in every single case that copyright-protected content is not available on its platform without authorisation at any time. However, it must use best efforts towards that goal (→ § 1 mn. 24), which must be interpreted in light of the provisions of § 1 (2). According to the Explanatory Memorandum of the UrhDaG, the OCSSP can use manual, semi-automated or fully automated procedures.[24] In this context, OCSSPs must adhere to **high industry standards** (German: *hohe branchenübliche Standards*; French: *normes élevées du secteur en matière*; → § 1 mn. 21 et seqq.). This is a new standard of care to be autonomously determined

[21] Cf. also BGH 29.7.2021 – III ZR 179/20, GRUR 2021, 1433 mn. 85 – Hassrede (hate speech); Hofmann ZUM 2020, 665 (668).

[22] Cf. also Wandtke/Hauck ZUM 2020, 671 (678).

[23] Recital 66 subpara. 2 sent. 4 DSMD; BT-Drs. 19/27426, 137; Hofmann NJW 2021, 1905 (1907).

[24] BT-Drs. 19/27426, 137.

under EU law.[25] In any event, the OCSSP must comply with the standard duties of care expected from a reasonably diligent operator in its situation in order to counter copyright infringements on its platform in a credible and effective manner.[26] The OCSSP must also meet **high standards** (German: *hohe Standards*; French: *normes élevées*), that is, use **measures at the upper end of the applied standards** (for more details → § 1 mn. 23 et seq.). Thus, the OCSSP must use best industry practices (German: *bewährte Verfahren*; French: *meilleures pratiques du secteur*; recital 66 subpara. 2 sent. 2 DSMD). The German *bewährt* has the meaning of proven, established practices, while the English and French wording demands high or best standards. Accordingly, the OCSSP must use the best available, practically applicable technology.[27] An OCSSP cannot rely on the fact that other industry members do not use certain existing technologies, especially if they are not OCSSPs within the meaning of § 2. For novel services, if no common practice has yet developed or the provider is unique, the OCSSP must use the available technologies if they are sufficiently reliable. Of the various options available, the provider must choose the most effective means, even if these are more expensive than the next best solution. If necessary, it may also be reasonable for an OCSSP to support technical solutions with human oversight, for example, in cases in which rightholders are at risk of significant economic harm and flag their content accordingly.[28] To limit the OCSSP's effort, human oversight might only be necessary above certain thresholds that indicate that the possibly infringing content is frequently accessed by members of the public (→ § 1 mn. 30). The best efforts include banning users from the possibility of flagging (§ 11) for an appropriate time under § 18 (5) if they repeatedly and incorrectly flag content as permitted (→ § 18 mn. 2, 24).

### b) Proportionate efforts

15 According to § 1 (2), the scope of best efforts must be determined in light of the **proportionality principle** (→ § 1 mn. 25).[29] **No measures** may be imposed on OCSSPs that are '**excessively costly**' or '**unnecessarily complicated or costly**'.[30] They may not be required to take measures that '**economically jeopardise**' their legitimate business model or '**disproportionately complicate** their activities'.[31] The impossible cannot be demanded of OCSSPs; they are only obliged to block content to the extent that effective means are available (§ 1 (2) sent. 2 No. 3, → § 1 mn. 32). In addition, OCSSPs are only required to use resources that are available with **reasonable effort** and at **reasonable cost** (§ 1 (2) sent. 2 No. 4, → § 1 mn. 33). The size and economic capacity of the OCSSP must also be taken into account. Therefore, not all OCSSPs must use the same technical means.[32] The explanatory memorandum of the UrhDaG assumes that OCSSPs will usually use fully automated procedures to block content.[33]

### c) Consideration of user and third-party interests

16 Sub. 2 sent. 1 stipulates that best efforts do not include means that cause (considerable) blocking of **lawful content** (→ mn. 19 et seqq.). In particular, the fundamental

[25] Cf. COM(2021) 288 final EN, 8; Spindler CR 2020, 50 (54).

[26] On corresponding general obligations for platform service providers, cf. CJEU C-682/18 and C-683/18, ECLI:EU:C:2021:503 mn. 84 – YouTube and Cyando.

[27] Cf. Spindler CR 2019, 277 (286), who tends to be more generous.

[28] Cf. COM(2021) 288 final EN, 22.

[29] BT-Drs. 19/27426, 137.

[30] Generally for online services: CJEU C-324/09, ECLI:EU:C:2011:474 mn. 139 – L'Oréal/eBay et al.; C-360/10, ECLI:EU:C:2012:85 mn. 46 – SABAM/Netlog.

[31] BGH 12.7.2012 – I ZR 18/11, GRUR 2013, 370 mn. 22 – Alone in the Dark, with further references.

[32] BT-Drs. 19/27426, 137.

[33] BT-Drs. 19/27426, 137.

rights to freedom of expression and information as well as the protection of personal data must be taken into account[34], especially the **particular importance of the internet** for the freedoms of expression and information.[35] For OCSSPs, there is in principle an obligation of result because the blocking measures taken by the OCSSP 'must not have the effect' of making lawfully accessed user content 'unavailable'.[36] Therefore, OCSSPs may only prevent the accessibility of manifestly infringing content when using automated content recognition technology.[37] Content is manifestly infringing if there is no need for an independent assessment of the OCSSP with a detailed legal examination (see also Art. 16 (3) DSA).[38]

### 3. Obligation of the rightholder to cooperate

#### a) Blocking request

The OCSSP's duty of care and blocking obligation comes into effect only if a right- 17
holder demands the blocking and provides the necessary information (→ mn. 18).[39] The blocking request must be made in relation to **specific** copyright-protected **content** (recital 66 subpara. 5 DSMD). Unsubstantiated requests are not sufficient, for example, to block the rightholders 'entire repertoire' without specification of the included titles.

#### b) Provision of necessary information

Rightholders must provide all relevant and necessary information to enable the OCSSP 18
to block specified works and subject matter (recital 66 subpara. 5 DSMD). According to the Advocate General, the information must contain evidence that the claimant is entitled to enforce the rights.[40] The **type** and **scope** of the information required depends on the state of the art and the technology used by the OCSSP to block the content.[41] Rightholders must provide all information necessary for the automated technical recognition of a work by the OCSSP's filtering software.[42] In the absence of other established standards, this will usually be a **reference file** from which the OCSSP can extract the necessary information.[43] Insofar as the rightholders are in possession of the information in **digital form**, they must make it digitally available to the OCSSP.[44] The blocking request creates a statutory obligation between the OCSSP and rightholders pursuant to § 241 (2) BGB, which obliges each party to be considerate of the legitimate interests of the other party. However, the OCSSP may be expected to convert the provided files into the required format or to extract the necessary information if this is technically possible and statutorily permitted. If the OCSSP cannot rely on copyright exceptions for this, the rightholder

---

[34] Art. 8, 11 CFR; Art. 2 (1) in conjunction with Art. 1 (1) and Art. 5 GG.

[35] CJEU C-401/19, ECLI:EU:C:2022:297 mn. 45–47 – Poland/Parliament and Council; C-682/18 and C-683/18, ECLI:EU:C:2021:503 mn. 65 – YouTube and Cyando.

[36] AG Saugmandsgaard Øe C-401/19, ECLI:EU:C:2021:613 mn. 165 – Poland/Parliament and Council; COM(2021) 288 final EN, 2 et seq. Confirmed by CJEU C-401/19, ECLI:EU:C:2022:297 mn. 78 – Poland/Parliament and Council.

[37] COM(2021) 288 final EN, 20; AG Saugmandsgaard Øe C-401/19, ECLI:EU:C:2021:613 mn. 198, 205; Stieper JZ 2022, 682 (684); Raue ZUM 2022, 624 (630).

[38] Cf. CJEU C-401/19, ECLI:EU:C:2022:297 mn. 90 et seq. – Poland/Parliament and Council; Raue ZUM 2022, 624 (630).

[39] BT-Drs. 19/27426, 137; Spindler, Gutachten zur Urheberrechtsrichtlinie, 2019, 16.

[40] AG Saugmandsgaard Øe C-401/19, ECLI:EU:C:2021:613 mn. 148, 205 fn. 246; also Specht-Riemenschneider, Grundlegung einer verbrauchergerechten Regulierung interaktionsmittelnder Plattformfunktionalitäten, 2020, 36 et seq.

[41] BT-Drs. 19/27426, 137.

[42] Metzger/Pravemann ZUM 2021, 288 (292).

[43] Rauer/Bibi BB 2021, 1475 (1478); Conrad/Nolte ZUM 2021, 111 (118).

[44] See, however: Spindler, Gutachten zur Urheberrechtsrichtlinie, 2019, 16 et seq.

must give the necessary authorisation. If the rightholder provides no information, only insufficient information or information in unsuitable file formats, the blocking obligation is limited to the content that the OCSSP can technically block with the available information. To the extent that this is impossible **without information** from the rightholder, the OCSSP is **exempt from liability** (recital 66 subpara. 5 DSMD).

## III. No blocking of lawful content (sub. 2)

### 1. Principles

#### a) Conflict of objectives between the protection of copyrights and user freedoms

19 Sub. 2 sent. 1 requires the OCSSP not to block lawful content uploaded by its users. This leads to the difficult question of the relationship between sub. 1 and sub. 2, and, in turn, to the core of the hard-fought **conflict** of every platform regulation between the **effective protection of intellectual property rights** and **freedom of expression and information**. An effective protection of copyrights by automated content recognition technology will, in fact, reduce the users' freedom guaranteed by the copyright exception; however, the price to effectively safeguard those freedoms is that copyright-infringing content is initially accessible on the platform and only blocked afterwards upon notice by the rightholder. That leads to the very specific question: Should the parameters of the filtering software be set in such a way that it tends to produce false positives (classify lawful content as copyright-infringing and block it) or false negatives (classify copyright-infringing content as lawful and make it available)?[45] The basic problem of all currently existing filtering software is that it is – to a certain extent – able to recognise the use of specific content but is unable to take into account the context that makes the use lawful.[46] In particular, the copyright exceptions in favour of fundamental communication rights require a contextualisation of the use of copyright-protected content.[47] The initial Commission's draft of the then (much shorter) Art. 13 initially balanced the conflict of objectives clearly in favour of the rightholders.[48] However, this balancing of interests did not prevail in the legislative process.[49] In order to protect users' rights, Art. 17 (7) and Art. 17 (9) subpara. 3 DSMD require Member States to implement safeguards so that the measures used to protect rightholder interests do not result in the unavailability of lawful content.[50]

#### b) Protection of user rights through procedures

20 In the annulment proceedings, Poland/Council and Parliament, Spain and France took the position that this objective, and thus, the users' rights, can be sufficiently protected *ex post* by a subsequent complaint procedure.[51] Thus, OCSSPs would first be obliged to block all content reported by the rightholders within the scope of what is technically possible and reasonable. Only after a successful complaint procedure would

[45] See Raue/Steinbach ZUM 2020, 355 (361 et seq.).

[46] BT-Drs. 19/27426, 139; AG Saugmandsgaard Øe C-401/19, ECLI:EU:C:2021:613 mn. 148 – Poland/Parliament and Council; Senftleben ZUM 2019, 369 (372); Leistner ZUM 2020, 505 (507); Conrad/Nolte ZUM 2021, 111 (118).

[47] Becker ZUM 2019, 636 (644).

[48] COM(2016) 593 final.

[49] Cf. AG Saugmandsgaard Øe ECLI:EU:C:2021:613 mn. 176 – Poland/Parliament and Council.

[50] CJEU C-401/19, ECLI:EU:C:2022:297 mn. 80, 85 – Poland/Parliament and Council.

[51] Cf. AG Saugmandsgaard Øe C-401/19, ECLI:EU:C:2021:613 mn. 168 et seq. – Poland/Parliament and Council; also Lennartz/Möllers GRUR 2021, 1109 (1112 et seq.).

lawful uses of copyright-protected content be unblocked and made available on the platform. The burden of action would thus be placed on the users.

**c) Obligation of result**

This shift in the burden of action carries a considerable risk that users will not exercise their procedural rights, at least not in the majority of cases.[52] Furthermore, due to the dynamic attention curves on the internet, a delayed unblocking may come too late for the content to still attract attention.[53] Technical solutions can *de facto* prevent virtually all uses of copyright-protected content on a platform. Socially desirable transformative uses that are protected by fundamental rights would become invisible on the platform and all other platforms using the same automated recognition technology. Such a solution would disproportionately restrict user freedoms.[54] Therefore, Art. 17 (7) DSMD contains an obligation of result: User freedoms must be taken into account *ex ante* when specifying the extent of the OCSSPs' filtering obligations.[55] As a result, OCSSPs may only automatically block manifestly infringing content.[56] Ambiguous content may not automatically be blocked by qualified blocking (§ 7) but only by simple blocking (§ 8) after an assessment by the OCSSPs or independent courts. This interpretation is supported not only by the legislative history but also by the wording, the system and, above all, the fundamental rights of the Charta.[57] A legal obligation to use automated filtering systems that block lawful content to a considerable extent would **disproportionately restrict the freedom of expression and information**.[58] Conversely, user freedoms do not apply without restriction and must be balanced with the legitimate interests of the rightholders. This means that the safeguards for the user's rights have to be limited, too. Even if it cannot be ruled out that users may use copyrighted subject matter in its entirety under copyright exceptions, this is the rare exception.[59] Furthermore, when whole works are uploaded on an internet platform, the interests of the rightholder are particularly affected. As a fair balance of interests, the rightholders' interests should prevail and the users should be referred to complaint procedures.[60] As a result, OCSSPs may **only automatically block manifestly infringing content**, but not content for which (un)lawful use can only be assessed in context, such as short excerpts of a work incorporated into transformative works.[61] Content is manifestly infringing in any case if it is completely or essentially identical to content reported by the rightholder, for example, only an outside frame has been added, it has been mirrored or flipped by 180 degrees.[62] In this case, the 21

[52] Specht-Riemenschneider, Leitlinien zur nationalen Umsetzung des Art. 17 DSM-RL aus Verbrauchersicht, 2020, 12, 48 et seqq.; Kaesling/Knapp MMR 2020, 816 (819 et seq.).

[53] Leistner ZUM 2020, 505 (512).

[54] CJEU C-401/19, ECLI:EU:C:2022:297 mn. 44–98 – Poland/Parliament and Council; AG Saugmandsgaard Øe C-401/19, ECLI:EU:C:2021:613 mn. 187, 190 et seq. – Poland/Parliament and Council.

[55] AG Saugmandsgaard Øe C-401/19, ECLI:EU:C:2021:613 mn. 170 – Poland/Parliament and Council; COM(2021) 288 final EN, 20; Spindler WRP 2021, 1245 mn. 9; see, however: Lennartz/Möllers GRUR 2021, 1109 (1113 et seq.).

[56] Stieper JZ 2022, 682 (684); Raue ZUM 2022, 624 (630).

[57] CJEU C-401/19, ECLI:EU:C:2022:297 mn. 45–47 – Poland/Parliament and Council; AG Saugmandsgaard Øe C-401/19, ECLI:EU:C:2021:613 mn. 170–193 – Poland/Parliament and Council.

[58] CJEU C-401/19, ECLI:EU:C:2022:297 mn. 80, 85 – Poland/Parliament and Council; CJEU ECLI:EU:C:2011:771 mn 52 – Scarlet/SABAM; ECLI:EU:C:2012:85 mn 50 – SABAM/Netlog; AG Saugmandsgaard Øe C-401/19, ECLI:EU:C:2021:613 mn 186 – Poland/Parliament and Council.

[59] See also Schwartmann/Hentsch MMR 2020, 207 (211).

[60] AG Saugmandsgaard Øe C-401/19, ECLI:EU:C:2021:613 mn. 205 – Poland/Parliament and Council.

[61] AG Saugmandsgaard Øe C-401/19, ECLI:EU:C:2021:613 mn. 198, 206 – Poland/Parliament and Council; COM(2021) 288 final EN, 20; Stieper JZ 2022, 682 (684); Raue ZUM 2022, 624 (630). See also Leistner ZUM 2020, 505 (507).

[62] COM(2021) 288 final EN, 21.

OCSSPs would have to parameterise the threshold values of their filtering software in such a way that the automated content recognition only produces a few false positives.[63] User associations can enforce this parameterisation via § 18 (6) (→ § 18 mn. 26 et seqq.).

**d) Interplay of § 7 (2) and §§ 9–11**

22 § 7 (2) sent. 1 stipulates that lawful content may not be blocked by the platforms on the basis of the UrhDaG. However, in the practically relevant cases of **automated content filtering**, the necessary **balancing of interests** between the protection of copyrights and fundamental rights (→ mn. 19 et seq.) is regulated **conclusively in §§ 9–11** via the reference in **§ 7 (2) sent. 2**. To the extent technically possible and reasonable (→ mn. 4 et seq.), OCSSPs are required to automatically block protected subject matter reported by rightholders, unless the requirements of §§ 9–11 are met. In a first step, OCSSPs are required to block lawful content that does not meet these requirements.[64] The lawfulness of the specific use can only be asserted in a second step in the complaint procedure. Thus, users have to rely on an *ex post* consideration of their legitimate interests. This is problematic as the §§ 9–11, the result of a political compromise, do not limit the blocking obligation to obvious infringements. Consequently, OCSSPs seem to be obliged to block some forms of transformative uses, especially transformative uses that contain more than half of a work (§ 9 (2) sent. 1 No. 3). However, this result is irreconcilable with the requirements of the CJEU in Poland/Parliament and Council.[65] There are two possible alternatives to 'repair' the outcome: Either the provision is to be interpreted in conformity with fundamental rights and thus limiting the blocking obligations under § 7 (2) sent. 1 to manifestly infringing content.[66] Otherwise, § 7 (2) sent. 2 and § 9 are inapplicable due to a violation of Art. 11 CFR.[67]

## 2. Availability of lawful content (sent. 1)

23 Sub. 2 sent. 1 specifies the best effort obligation under sub. 1 and stipulates that such a measure may not result in the blocking of lawful (→ § 5 mn. 3) content. Therefore, in a **first step** to specify the best effort obligation, one must ask whether blocking the content reported by the rightholder is technically possible and otherwise reasonable (→ mn. 14 et seqq.). In a **second step**, content must be excluded from the blocking procedure if the infringement is not obvious and requires an independent assessment by the OCSSP (→ mn. 20 et seq.). If the blocking is carried out with the help of automated recognition technology, sub. 2 sent. 2 in conjunction with §§ 9–11 provides valuable guidelines. However, due to prevailing requirements of the user's fundamental rights, content may not be blocked even if it is not covered by § 9 (2) unless its use is manifestly infringing (→ mn. 22).

## 3. Use of automated procedures (sent. 2)

24 If contents are blocked by automated means, sentence 2 **restricts the obligation of result** under sentence 1. Until the conclusion of a possible complaint procedure (§ 14), the **OCSSP** may only make accessible under § 9 (1) user-generated content that meets

[63] For criteria see Raue/Steinebach ZUM 2020, 355 (362 et seqq.); Specht-Riemenschneider, Leitlinien zur nationalen Umsetzung des Art. 17 DSM-RL aus Verbrauchersicht, 2020, 92 et seq.

[64] BT-Drs. 19/27426, 139.

[65] CJEU C-401/19, ECLI:EU:C:2022:297 mn. 80, 85, 90 et seq. – Poland/Parliament and Council; Raue ZUM 2022, 624 (632 et seq.).

[66] Stieper JZ 2022, 682 (684); Raue ZUM 2022, 624 (633); see, however: Specht-Riemenschneider → § 9 mn. 3.

[67] Raue ZUM 2022, 624 (633).

the requirements of § 9 (2). All other content reported by rightholders must be blocked in accordance with sub. 1, insofar as this is technically possible for the OCSSP with reasonable means. In these cases, users are dependent on *ex post* enforcement of their rights in the complaint procedure.[68] According to § 9, images must be made accessible on the platform if they fulfil the requirement for minor use under § 10 or if the user has flagged the use as permitted under § 11. All other types of content may only be made accessible by the OCSSP under § 9 (2) if it – cumulatively – contains less than half of the works of third parties, combines parts of works with other content and makes only minor use of works of third parties (§ 10) or has been flagged as permitted by the user (§ 11). As a consequence, there will be transformative (and lawful) uses, which, according to the wording of the provision, the OCSSPs must automatically block in order to comply with the requirements of § 7 (1). However, this balancing of interests is **incompatible** with the **fundamental rights of the Union** (→ mn. 22).

### 4. Exceptions for cinematographic works and moving images (sent. 3)

OCSSPs must prevent the communication to the public of cinematographic works **25** and moving images before and during the first communication to the public in Germany if the rightholder so requests and provides the necessary information. The copyright exception for cinematographic works and moving images was inserted after a proposal by the Committee on Legal Affairs in sub. 2.[69] The aim of this provision is to protect particularly valuable uses of copyright-protected content, especially live broadcasts of sporting events[70] as well as the first broadcasting of TV series or movies in Germany.[71] Before and during the first broadcast, users should not be able to share small, copyright-protected excerpts on platforms, such as the goals of a football match or the key scene of a movie or a TV series. To **avoid over blocking**, the OCSSP may need to check transformative content with a human reviewer to see whether its use is possibly covered by a copyright exception.[72] With regard to the **type of works and other subject matter**, the increased best effort obligation is limited to cinematographic works (§ 88 UrhG) and moving pictures (§ 95 UrhG). The increased obligation is **limited to the time** until the conclusion of the first communication to the public in Germany. Therefore, the rightholder must inform the OCSSP, in addition to the information already required under sub. 1, of whether certain cinematographic works or moving pictures have not yet been communicated to the public for the first time in Germany, when the first act of communication is about to begin and, in any case, when it will end. After completion of the first act of communication, the automatic blocking must be terminated if the user upload meets the other requirements of §§ 9–11 or § 7 (2) sent. 1.

## IV. Information to users (sub. 3)

The OCSSP must inform the user that it will block the uploaded content and not make **26** it accessible to the public. This notice must be given **immediately** and, therefore, as a rule, automatically. The OCSSP must also inform the users of their **right to complain** under § 14 as well as the copyrights they are allegedly infringing with the upload of the content

---

[68] BT-Drs. 19/27426, 139.
[69] See Metzger/Pravemann ZUM 2021, 755 (758 et seq.).
[70] Bischof/Brost MMR 2021, 303.
[71] BT-Drs. 19/29894, 93.
[72] COM(2021) 288 final EN, 23; cf. also Spindler WRP 2021, 1111 mn. 32.

and the identity of the rightholder. The information must enable them to substantiate their complaint under § 14 (2) (→ § 14 mn. 7).[73]

## V. Start-up privilege (sub. 4)

27 Start-ups (§ 2 (2), → § 2 mn. 25) are **exempt from** the **obligation of qualified blocking** as long as the monthly number of unique visitors does not exceed 5 million.

## VI. Small OCSSPs privilege (sub. 5)

28 In the case of small OCSSPs (§ 2 (3), → § 2 mn. 28), it is rebuttably presumed that they cannot be expected to make the technical and organisational efforts required for the qualified blocking of content. This aims to enable independent service providers to operate small **niche platforms** (→ § 2 mn. 26). However, the rebuttable nature of the presumption means that they may be required to make such efforts if, for example, cost-effective automated filtering solutions are available that can be operated by small OCSSPs with reasonable effort. Unlike the start-up privilege under sub. 4, as the privilege for small OCSSPs is designed as a rebuttable presumption it can be qualified as an **interpretation of the proportionality requirement** in Art. 17 (5) DSMD and, therefore, **complies with EU law** (→ § 2 mn. 27).

# § 8 Simple blocking

**(1) In accordance with § 1 subsection 2, the service provider shall terminate the communication to the public of a work by blocking it as soon as the rightholder so requests and provides a sufficiently substantiated notice of the unauthorised communication to the public of the work.**

**(2) § 7 subsection 2 sentence 1 and subsection 3 shall apply accordingly.**

**(3) The service provider shall only be obliged to block future unauthorised uses of the work in accordance with § 7 after the rightholder has provided the necessary information required for this purpose.**

# § 8 Einfache Blockierung

**(1) Der Diensteanbieter ist nach Maßgabe von § 1 Absatz 2 verpflichtet, die öffentliche Wiedergabe eines Werkes durch Blockierung zu beenden, sobald der Rechtsinhaber dies verlangt und einen hinreichend begründeten Hinweis auf die unerlaubte öffentliche Wiedergabe des Werkes gibt.**

**(2) § 7 Absatz 2 Satz 1 und Absatz 3 ist entsprechend anzuwenden.**

**(3) Zur Blockierung künftiger unerlaubter Nutzungen des Werkes ist der Diensteanbieter nach Maßgabe von § 7 erst verpflichtet, nachdem der Rechtsinhaber die hierfür erforderlichen Informationen zur Verfügung stellt.**

**Bibliography:** See the bibliography in the Introduction.

**Content**



[73] Specht-Riemenschneider, Leitlinien zur nationalen Umsetzung des Art. 17 DSM-RL aus Verbrauchersicht, 2020, 87 et seq.

# I. General remarks

## 1. Objective

Under **sub. 1**, OCSSPs are required to **terminate** the unauthorised communication to the public of a specific copyright-protected content after a duly substantiated notice. Simple blocking is particularly important in two cases: first, if the rightholder does not wish to provide the OCSSP with the required information under § 7 (1); second, if qualified blocking of the content is not possible despite this information and despite the best efforts of the OCSSP.[1] This obligation corresponds in principle to the previous concept of *notice and take down*. The blocking obligation is to be specified according to the principles of § 1 (2). The OCSSP is obliged to **comply with high industry standards of professional diligence**, which are, however, subject to **proportionality**. The simple blocking under sub. 1 only requires the OCSSP to remove the specifically named content from its platform. This blocking does not require the use of automated content recognition software.[2] Its use is only necessary to comply with the *stay down* obligation of sub. 3 which refers to § 7. Through the reference to § 7 (2) sent. 1, (3), **user rights** must also be observed in the case of simple blocking. The rightholder's blocking request creates a **legal obligation** with duties of care under § 241 (2) BGB. 1

## 2. EU law requirements

§ 8 implements **Art. 17 (4)(c) DSMD** (explained in recital 66 DSMD). In specifying the best efforts obligation, the principle of proportionality in **Art. 17 (5) DSMD** and the prohibition of general surveillance in **Art. 17 (8) subpara. 1 DSMD** (explained in recital 66 subpara. 2 sent. 1 DSMD) must be taken into account. The reference to the protection of users' interests in § 7 (2) sent. 1 is based on **Art. 17 (7) and (9) subpara. 3 DSMD** (explained in recital 66 subpara. 1 sent. 6–7, 70 DSMD). The obligation to inform users about the blocking via the reference to § 7 (3) is not directly provided by Art. 17 DSMD, but it is a necessary precondition for effective and expeditious appeal and redress procedures, which **Art. 17 (9) subpara. 1 DSMD** (explained in recital 70 DSMD) provides. 2

---

[1] COM(2021) 288 final EN, 15.
[2] Metzger/Pravemann ZUM 2021, 288 (292).

### 3. Burden of proof

3 The burden of proof is to be allocated along the lines of the burden of action. Therefore, **rightholders** must prove that they demanded that the OCSSP block the content in dispute and that they gave a sufficiently substantiated notice of the unauthorised communication to the public. According to general principles, rightholders must show that the content is protected by copyright and that they are entitled to act (→ § 1 mn. 17). The **OCSSP** must then prove that it could not possibly block the content despite its best efforts[3] or that it is authorised to use the content for other reasons (→ § 1 mn. 20).

## II. Simple blocking (sub. 1)

### 1. Blocking

#### a) Obligation to block

4 After a duly substantiated notice from the rightholder, the OCSSP must block content that is communicated without authorisation to the public on its platform. The blocking request may be based on the distortion of the work under § 14 UrhG (§ 13 (3) UrhDaG). Even though § 7 (1) defines blocking as disabling access (German: *sperren)* or removal (German: *entfernen),* in the context of simple blocking under sub. 1, only the removal (French: *retirer*) of content that has already been made accessible comes into consideration. The prevention of future uploads by means of blocking is governed by sub. 3. The OCSSP must therefore put an end to **the availability of the reported content** on its platform. However, it does not have to permanently delete the content from its servers. If the public no longer has access to the copyright-infringing content, the corresponding liability requirement of § 1 (1), and thus, the duty of care causing the liability exemption of § 1 (2), no longer applies; § 8 (1) does not introduce any independent duties for the OCSSP. Moreover, user rights argue in favour of such an interpretation: Users should not be burdened with the necessity to upload the removed content again after they successfully challenged the removal in the complaint procedure (§ 14).[4] The obligation to block under sub. 1 applies only to the specific infringement(s) that are the subject of the rightholder's notice. The removal of **identical** or **equivalent content** already on its platform but not the subject of the rightholder's notice is governed by § 7 (1) (→ § 7 mn. 9).[5] The same applies to the blocking of future uploads according to sub. 3.

#### b) Expeditious action

5 The OCSSP must block the reported content 'as soon as' (German: *sobald*) the rightholder so requests and provides the necessary information. The OCSSP must then expeditiously initiate the blocking (Art. 17 (4)(c) DSMD; German: *unverzüglich*; French: *promptement*) after receiving a corresponding blocking request and the necessary information from the rightholder. The required reaction time must take into account that the cessation of making content available is not delayed in such a way as to cause

---

[3] Recital 66 subpara. 3 DSMD; Leistner ZUM 2020, 897 (900).

[4] Cf. also BGH 29.7.2021 – III ZR 179/20, GRUR 2021, 1433 mn. 85 – Hassrede (hate speech); Hofmann ZUM 2020, 665 (668).

[5] Metzger/Pravemann ZUM 2021, 288 (292); see, however: Hofmann GRUR 2019, 1219 (1220); Würtenberger/Freischem GRUR 2019, 1140 (1158).

disproportionate damage to the rightholder.[6] The faster and more (geographically) widespread the accessed content is, the faster the OCSSP must react.

#### c) Unauthorised communication to the public

The content must be protected by copyright and communicated to the public without authorisation. According to sub. 2 in conjunction with § 7 (1) sent. 1, the OCSSP must ensure that it does not block content that has been lawfully used. According to the Advocate General in Poland/Parliament and Council, the OCSSPs may only block manifestly illegal content and otherwise only comply with a court decision (see also → § 7 mn. 21).[7] **6**

### 2. In accordance with high industry standards

#### a) High industry standards

In blocking content pursuant to sub. 1, the OCSSP must comply with high industry standards (§ 1 (2) No. 1). Art. 17 (4) DSMD only requires OCSSPs to comply with high industry standards for qualified blocking in (b). The extension of this obligation to simple blocking in § 8 is in conformity with the aim of the Directive and, therefore, is a permissible specification by the German legislature (→ § 1 mn. 3). The requirement of high industry standards is relevant in the context of simple blocking in three aspects. First, OCSSPs must provide the rightholders with an easily accessible procedure to provide them with the necessary notices of specific infringements. This is now specified in Art. 16 DSA. Second, OCSSPs are required to take the **necessary organisational precautions** that enable them to carry out expeditious blocking after receiving a notice Third, OCSSPs must implement sufficient safeguards to ensure that no lawful content is blocked despite corresponding requests from an (alleged) rightholder (sub. 2). **7**

#### b) Proportionality

The obligation of simple blocking is subject to the proportionality requirement.[8] Thus, the organisational arrangements listed in → mn. 7 are subject to the reservation that **suitable** and **effective means are available at reasonable cost**.[9] According to § 1(2) No. 2, the reasonableness of the requirements varies according to the size and economic capacity of the OCSSP (→ § 1 mn. 28, 33); the type, audience and scope of the service (→ § 1 mn. 28); and the type of copyright-protected content downloaded by users (→ § 1 mn. 29). **8**

### 3. Obligation of the rightholder to cooperate

The OCSSP is only obliged to block under sub. 1 if the rightholder so requests by a **sufficiently substantiated notice** (German: *hinreichend begründeter Hinweis*; French: *notification suffisamment motivée*)[10]: The notice must enable the OCSSP to immediately block the content and without further assessment. As a rule, this requires the precise **indication of the location** (e.g., the URL). General information, such as that there is **9**

---

[6] See CJEU C-682/18 and C-683/18, ECLI:EU:C:2021:503 mn. 141 – YouTube and Cyando (on Art. 8 InfoSoc Directive).

[7] AG Saugmandsgaard Øe C-401/19, ECLI:EU:C:2021:613 mn. 197 et seq. – Poland/Parliament and Council, insofar not subject of the CJEU decision.

[8] COM(2021) 288 final EN, 8.

[9] BT-Drs. 19/27426, 138.

[10] CJEU C-401/19, ECLI:EU:C:2022:297 mn. 89 et seq. – Poland/Parliament and Council; see also AG Saugmandsgaard Øe C-682/18 and C-683/18, ECLI:EU:C:2020:586 mn. 187 – YouTube and Cyando; Spindler WRP 2021, 1111 mn. 33.

illegal content on the platform, is not sufficient.[11] In addition, the notice must provide the OCSSP with 'sufficient information to enable the [OCSSP] to satisfy itself, **without a detailed legal examination**, that the communication of the content at issue is illegal and that removing that content is compatible with freedom of expression and information'.[12] The rightholder must identify the work or the subject matter, describe the infringement and, if applicable, explain why the user cannot rely on a copyright exception.[13] If the notice of the rightholder is insufficient, the OCSSP must inform the rightholder in good faith (§ 242 BGB) and ask for further information to the extent reasonable according to the circumstances.[14] The notice and the blocking request must come from the rightholder or an entitled third party. Corresponding notices by an independent third party do not trigger the blocking obligation.[15] Without such notice, the service provider is not required to take action.[16]

## III. Availability of lawful content (sub. 2)

### 1. Safeguards for user's interests

10 In any case of blocking, including simple blocking under § 8, the OCSSP must ensure that it does not remove lawfully uploaded content. This is an **obligation of result** (→ § 7 mn. 20 et seq.). An OCSSP is **only** obliged to block **content** that is **manifestly infringing** or if the infringement has been confirmed by a court ruling. If the OCSSP does not block content that requires a substantive legal examination of the context and a difficult legal balancing of interests to determine infringement, it is not in breach of best efforts under §§ 1 (2), 8 (1).

### 2. Information

11 Due to the reference to § 7 (3), the OCSSP must inform users that it has blocked content that was uploaded by them. This notice must be given **immediately** and, therefore, as a rule, automatically. The OCSSP must also inform users of their **right to complain** under § 14. In order for users to substantiate their complaint under § 14 (2), the OCSSP must provide information about which copyrights have been infringed with the upload of the content and the identity of the rightholder.

## IV. Blocking of future unauthorised uses (sub. 3)

### 1. Future unauthorised use

12 Sub. 1 only obliges the OCSSP to block the specifically reported content. Accordingly, another upload of the same content must only be blocked under § 8 (1) after a new notice by the rightholder (→ mn. 4). The obligation to block future unauthorised uses of

---

[11] Spindler GRUR 2020, 253 (256).

[12] CJEU C-401/19, ECLI:EU:C:2022:297 mn. 91 – Poland/Parliament and Council. See also CJEU C-682/18 and C-683/18, ECLI:EU:C:2021:503 mn. 116 – YouTube and Cyando (Art. 14 E-Commerce Directive).

[13] See AG Saugmandsgaard Øe C-682/18 and C-683/18, ECLI:EU:C:2020:586 mn. 190 – YouTube and Cyando.

[14] Cf. BGH 17.8.2011 – I ZR 57/09, GRUR 2011, 1038 mn. 32.

[15] Hofmann GRUR 2019, 1219 (1220); Pravemann GRUR 2019, 783 (786).

[16] CJEU C-401/19, ECLI:EU:C:2022:297 mn. 89 – Poland/Parliament and Council.

the same content is regulated in sub. 3. Consequently, the OCSSP is **only** obliged to block future uploads of the copyright-infringing content (*stay down* obligation) if the rightholder has provided the **necessary information under § 7 (1)** (→ § 7 mn. 18). The same applies to equivalent **content.**[17] However, the requirement of providing the necessary information should not be handled in an overly formalistic way. The decisive factor here is the element of **necessity**. Insofar as the OCSSP is able to prevent the future upload and the removal of this and comparable content with the information given in the substantiated notice under sub. 1 in conjunction with the content uploaded by the user, it is obliged to do so even without separate information.[18] In this case, the OCSSP may not invoke the fact that the rightholder did not provide additional information. Because sub. 3 also does not impose any obligation of result on the OCSSP, its best efforts – especially in the case of equivalent content – are limited to the extent that qualified blocking with the information available is **technically possible with reasonable efforts** and does **not disproportionately restrict the user's rights.**

### 2. Blocking in accordance with § 7

The scope, requirements and limits as well as the safeguards for user interests of the 13 *stay down* obligation in sub. 3 are governed by § 7. Reference can be made to this commentary for its requirements and limitations.

### 3. Exemptions for start-ups and small OCSSPs

By reference to § 7, the exceptions for start-ups and small OCSSPs in § 7 (4) and (5) 14 also apply to the *stay down* obligation in § 8 (3).[19] Therefore, even after a simple blocking request, OCSSPs are generally not obliged to engage in a subsequent qualified blocking.

---

[17] AG Saugmandsgaard Øe C-401/19, ECLI:EU:C:2021:613 mn. 200 – Poland/Parliament and Council. See, however: Spindler GRUR 2020, 253 (256); Schonhofen/Kimmich WRP 2019, 1415 (1419).

[18] Cf. Hofmann NJW 2021, 1905 mn. 12.

[19] BT-Drs. 19/27426, 138.

# Part 4
# Uses presumably authorised by law

## § 9
## Communication to the public of presumably legitimate uses

**(1) In order to avoid disproportionate blocking in the use of automated procedures, presumably legitimate uses shall be communicated to the public until the conclusion of a complaint procedure (§ 14).**

**(2) [1]In respect of user-generated content that**

1. **contains less than half of a work by a third party or several works by third parties,**
2. **combines parts of works according to number 1 with other content, and**
3. **makes only minor use of works of third parties (§ 10) or is marked as statutorily permitted (§ 11),**

**it shall be rebuttably presumed that its use is permitted by law in accordance with § 5 (presumably legitimate uses). [2]Images may be used in their entirety in accordance with §§ 10 and 11.**

# Teil 4
# Mutmaßlich erlaubte Nutzungen

## § 9
## Öffentliche Wiedergabe mutmaßlich erlaubter Nutzungen

**(1) Um unverhältnismäßige Blockierungen beim Einsatz automatisierter Verfahren zu vermeiden, sind mutmaßlich erlaubte Nutzungen bis zum Abschluss eines Beschwerdeverfahrens (§ 14) öffentlich wiederzugeben.**

**(2) [1]Für nutzergenerierte Inhalte, die**

1. **weniger als die Hälfte eines Werkes eines Dritten oder mehrerer Werke Dritter enthalten,**
2. **die Werkteile nach Nummer 1 mit anderem Inhalt kombinieren und**
3. **Werke Dritter nur geringfügig nutzen (§ 10) oder als gesetzlich erlaubt gekennzeichnet sind (§ 11),**

**wird widerleglich vermutet, dass ihre Nutzung nach § 5 gesetzlich erlaubt ist (mutmaßlich erlaubte Nutzungen). [2]Abbildungen dürfen nach Maßgabe von §§ 10 und 11 vollständig verwendet werden.**

**Bibliography:** Akester, 'Technological accommodation of conflicts between freedom of expression and DRM: the first empirical assessment', 2009, available at <https://papers.ssrn.com/sol3/papers.cfm?abstract_id=1469412> (last accessed 22.1.2024); Bernzen/Kehrberger, 'Rechtsdurchsetzung durch Informationstechnik', RW 2019, 374; Blythe, 'Freedom of speech and the DMCA: abuse of the notification and takedown process', 41 EIPR (2019), 70; Chen/Durkee/Friend/Urban, 'Updating 17 U.S.C. § 512's Notice and Takedown Procedure for Innovators, Creators, and Consumers' (2011), available at <https://www.law.berkeley.edu/wp-content/uploads/2015/04/cranoticetakedown.pdf> (last accessed 12.3.2024); Conrad/Nolte, 'Schrankenbestimmungen im Anwendungsbereich des UrhDaG', ZUM 2021, 111; Müller-Terpitz, 'Filter als Gefahr für die Meinungspluralität? – Verfassungsrechtliche Erwägungen zum Einsatz von Filtertechnologien', ZUM 2020, 365; Raue/Steinebach, 'Upload Filter – Funktionsweisen, Einsatzmöglichkeiten und Parametrisierung', ZUM 2020, 355; Seltzer, 'Free Speech Unmoored in Copyright's Safe Harbor: Chilling Effects of the DMCA on the First Amendment', 24 Harv. J. L. & Tech (2010), 171; Specht-Riemenschneider, 'Plattformbetreiberhaftung auf dem Prüfstand – Mit gemeinsamen Leitlinien in die Zukunft?', MMR 2020, 137; Specht-Riemenschneider, 'Das Beste, was dem Urheberrecht passieren konnte', WRP Editorial 8/2021, I; Specht-Riemenschneider, Stellungnahme zum Urheberrechtsdiensteanbietergesetz (UrhDaG), available at <https://www.bundestag.de/resource/blob/833240/f19a65ef05e1668864b77a8688948af2/stellungnahme-specht-riemenschneider-data.pdf> (last accessed 12.3.2024); Urban/Quilter, 'Efficient Process or Chilling Effects – Takedown Notices under Section 512 of the Digital Millennium Copyright Act', 22 Santa Clara Computer & High Tech. L.J. (2006), 621. – See also the bibliography in the Introduction.

**Content**



# I. General remarks

## 1. Objective

§§ 9–12 are intended to contribute to creating a balance of interests between rightholders, OCSSPs and users prescribed by (EU) constitutional law and to be implemented by copyright law. They are intended to counter the dangers for users arising from the fact that large OCSSPs often use automated procedures for qualified blocking pursuant to § 7 (so-called upload filters). These upload filters can lead to **over blocking** of permissible content, inter alia, because they cannot reliably identify contextual uses, such as parodies and quotations, as statutorily permissible.[1] However, behind the provisions in copyright law that exempt certain actions of users from authorisation, there are often (EU) constitutional values that conflict with the protection of intellectual property. There **is no automatic priority of the right to protection of intellectual property** over other fundamental rights.[2] This was most recently made clear by the Advocate General in his opinion on Poland's action for annulment against Art. 17 DSMD: 'In the current state of forms of communication, the right to freedom of expression […] entails, in particular, the freedom to access those [large] platforms and express oneself on them, in principle, without interference by public authority'.[3] However, the provisions on the public reproduction of presumably legitimate uses do not only take into account the user's **freedom of expression**, which requires, especially in current debates, that statements in social media are published online in a timely manner,[4] but above all provide protection for the user's **artistic freedom**, which also guarantees the possibility to creatively deal with protected works of third parties in the context of, for example, quotations and parodies. If statutorily permissible uses are prevented, the burden of enforcing the law significantly changes. It is initially up to the rightholders to make efforts to enforce their rights; however, automated filtering obligations **shift this enforcement burden** to the users. It is no longer the rightholders 1

[1] BT-Drs. 19/27426, 139.

[2] AG Saugmandsgaard Øe C-401/19, ECLI:EU:C:2021:613 mn. 129 – Poland/Parliament and Council.

[3] AG Saugmandsgaard Øe C-401/19, ECLI:EU:C:2021:613 mn 103 – Poland/Parliament and Council.

[4] Gielen/Tiessen EuZW 2019, 639 (645); Kaesling/Knapp MMR 2020, 816 (821); Leistner ZUM 2020, 505 (511 et seq.); Raue/Steinebach ZUM 2020, 355 (363).

who must seek to enforce their legal positions, but the users who must enforce the user rights to which they are entitled. Evidence from the United States and the United Kingdom shows that this is extremely disadvantageous for the user.[5] After all, users often have neither the financial means nor the knowledge to effectively enforce their rights.[6] The disadvantage to users that results from the shifting of the burden of law enforcement to them through the use of upload filters is aimed to be compensated by the obligation to reproduce presumably legitimate uses. In this respect, § 9 first establishes a subjective user right of communication to the public of presumably legitimate uses and, second, contains a rebuttable presumption of such presumably legitimate uses.[7]

## 2. EU law requirements

2 §§ 9–12 serve to **implement Art. 17 (7) and (9) subpara. 3 DSMD**, which require an effective guarantee of user rights.[8] This provision underwent various amendments during the legislative process at the EU level.[9]

## 3. Conformity with EU law

3 Providing for user rights in the use of automated filtering obligations is prescribed both by Art. 17 DSMD and by the case law of the CJEU,[10] and thus, it is mandatory in order to ensure that the UrhDaG does not violate (EU) constitutional law (on this, also → § 7 mn. 19 et seqq.;[11]). This applies to both the *ex ante* measures of § 10 and the *ex post* measures of § 11.[12] In this respect, Art. 17 (7), (9) DSMD determines the **essential content of the safeguards** necessary to minimise the risks to freedom of expression posed by the contested provisions, while it is left to the Member States and the Commission to specify the **modalities** for doing so.[13] In his opinion on Poland's action for annulment, the Advocate General considered it necessary that the filtering techniques take into account match rates of works uploaded and works to be blocked and that thresholds be set such that automatic blocking of content is justified above the threshold, while below the threshold, a copyright exception, such as the quotation exception, can reasonably be used.[14] This speaks in favour of the compatibility of § 10 with EU law, which provides for precisely such a rule. The Advocate General also considered it possible to link such a solution to a mechanism that allows users to signal at the time of uploading or immediately thereafter (flagging) whether they consider that a copyright exception or limitation applies to them, whereupon the provider concerned would have to manually

---

[5] Akester, 'Technological accommodation of conflicts between freedom of expression and DRM', 104 et seq.; Blythe 41 EIPR (2019), 70 (77, 86); Chen/Durkee/Friend/Urban, 'Updating 17 U.S.C. § 512's Notice and Takedown Procedure for Innovators, Creators, and Consumers'; Seltzer 24 Harv. J. L. & Tech (2010), 171 (229); Urban/Quilter 22 Santa Clara Computer & High Tech. L.J. (2006), 621 (636 et seqq.).

[6] Bernzen/Kehrberger RW 2019, 374 (399 et seq.); Kaesling/Knapp MMR 2020, 816 (819 et seq.); Specht-Riemenschneider, Leitlinien zur nationalen Umsetzung des Art. 17 DSM-RL aus Verbrauchersicht, 48 et seqq.

[7] Specht-Riemenschneider MMR 2020, 137 (138).

[8] BT-Drs. 19/27426, 46.

[9] For more on these changes, see Specht-Riemenschneider, Leitlinien zur Umsetzung des Art. 17 DSM-RL aus Verbrauchersicht, 24 et seqq.

[10] CJEU C-70/10, ECLI:EU:C:2011:771 mn. 43 et seqq. – Scarlet Extended; CJEU C-360/10, ECLI:EU:C:2012:85 mn. 41 et seqq. – SABAM/Netlog; CJEU C-314/12, ECLI:EU:C:2014:192 mn. 46 et seqq. – UPC Telekabel/Constantin Film et al.

[11] Cf. also on the conflicting constitutional positions in general: Müller-Terpitz ZUM 2020, 365 et seqq.

[12] Specht-Riemenschneider WRP Editorial 8/2021, I.

[13] AG Saugmandsgaard Øe C-401/19, ECLI:EU:C:2021:613 mn. 210 – Poland/Parliament and Council.

[14] AG Saugmandsgaard Øe C-401/19, ECLI:EU:C:2021:613 mn 211 – Poland/Parliament and Council.

check the content in question.[15] This clearly speaks in favour of the admissibility of § 11 under EU law. The provisions of §§ 9–12 seem too far-reaching in not limiting the rights of rightholders in this respect. However, in his opinion on Poland's action for annulment against Art. 17 DSMD, the Advocate General, on the contrary, raised doubts as to whether the provisions of §§ 9–12 grant users sufficient powers. He explicitly advocated that only content that is manifestly unlawful, meaning that its unlawfulness is obvious without having to be specifically assessed in its context, may be blocked through pre-filtering. This refers to content that is identical in wording or meaning, i.e. identical reproductions of works and other subject matter named by the rightholders without additions as well as reproductions with insignificant changes so that the public would not distinguish them from the original subject matter.[16] However, transformative uses 'which may be covered by exceptions and limitations to copyright' may not be blocked according to the Advocate General.[17] A similar conclusion can be drawn from the Commission's guidelines. While in its consultation paper on these guidelines, the Commission had proposed that likely infringing content may also be automatically blocked *ex ante*,[18] in the final guidelines, the Commission advocates that such blocking should only be provided for manifestly infringing content.[19] The provisions of §§ 7, 9–12 take the opposite approach: they require blocking unless a use is highly likely to be subject to an exemption.[20] Although the legislature intended the provisions of §§ 7, 9–12 UrhDaG to **implement** Art. 17 DSMD, an interpretation of §§ 7, 9–12 UrhDaG in conformity with EU law or a further development of the law in accordance with the Quelle case law[21] must fail because the basic concept underlying §§ 7, 9–12 UrhDaG already assumes a different starting position (blocking if the content is not subject to an exception provision with a high degree of probability instead of blocking only manifestly unlawful content). In this respect, the legislature will have to make adjustments if the CJEU follows the opinion of the Advocate General and the Commission (also → § 7 mn. 22).

## 4. Origin

In their current version, §§ 9–12 were only introduced in the RegE to the UrhDaG. 4
They are based, inter alia, on **suggestions made by the Commission**, which published a consultation paper on Art. 17 DSMD within the framework of the stakeholder dialogue pursuant to Art. 17 (10) DSMD.[22] In this paper, the Commission proposed to exclude presumably legitimate uses from automated blocking.[23] Although the previous drafts of the UrhDaG also contained individual provisions to protect user rights, these were **not part of a comparably differentiated system**. The permissibility of minor uses was provided for in an independent exemption provision in § 6 of the discussion draft/ministerial draft (for more details → § 10 mn. 4). The possibility of labelling statutorily

[15] AG Saugmandsgaard Øe C-401/19, ECLI:EU:C:2021:613 mn. 211 – Poland/Parliament and Council.

[16] E.g., in the case of purely technical changes to circumvent the filtering system, such as a change of format, reversal or change of image speed; AG Saugmandsgaard Øe C-401/19, ECLI:EU:C:2021:613 mn. 198 et seq. – Poland/Parliament and Council.

[17] AG Saugmandsgaard Øe C-401/19, ECLI:EU:C:2021:613 mn. 203 – Poland/Parliament and Council.

[18] Commission, Targeted consultation addressed to the participants to the stakeholder dialogue on Article 17 of the Directive on Copyright in the Digital Single Market, 15 et seq.

[19] COM(2021) 288 final EN, 20 et seqq.

[20] Specht-Riemenschneider, Stellungnahme zum Urheberrechtsdiensteanbietergesetz (UrhDaG), 15.

[21] CJEU C-404/06, ECLI:EU:C:2008:231 – Quelle AG.

[22] BT-Drs. 19/27426, 46.

[23] Commission, Targeted consultation addressed to the participants to the stakeholder dialogue on Article 17 of the Directive on Copyright in the Digital Single Market, 15; see, however, → mn. 3 on the Commission's proposal in the Guidelines, which deviated from this position.

permitted uses, which led to a temporary obligation of the OCSSP to communicate to the public, was provided for in § 8 discussion draft/ministerial draft (in detail → § 11 mn. 4). A liability privilege for the OCSSP for the period of such reproduction was contained in § 16 (1) discussion draft/ministerial draft (see → § 12 mn. 5). Accompanying statutory claims for remuneration of the rightholders were provided for in § 7 (2) discussion draft/ministerial draft and § 16 (2) ministerial draft (for details → § 12 mn. 4).

### 5. Systematics

5 § 9 should be read in conjunction with §§ 10 and 11, to which it refers. It applies to **automated blocking**, that is, both *ex ante* automated blocking and automated blocking of equivalent content after a notice and takedown procedure has been carried out in accordance with § 8. (→ § 8 mn. 12 et seq.). Measures against repeated blocking of authorised uses are found in § 18 (6). § 9 will also have to be read in context with the requirements of the Digital Services Act (DSA). The DSA provides that 'very large online platforms' should use the necessary tools to carefully mitigate systemic risks. This also, and especially, includes impairments of a user's freedom of expression, cf. recitals 80 et seqq., Art. 35 DSA.

## II. Duty of communication to the public (sub. 1)

### 1. Subjective user right

6 Presumably legitimate uses must first be communicated to the public by the OCSSP. In addition, the wording of § 9 (1) sent. 1 already contains a separate basis for the user's claim to communication to the public of presumably legitimate uses under sub. 2 (→ § 5 mn. 4).[24] This interpretation is also required by the objective of §§ 9–12: If the user can in the extreme case **take legal action against the OCSSP for communication to the public**, this effectively counteracts the threat of over blocking when using upload filters.[25] This gives practical effect to (EU) fundamental rights, which the user rights in Art. 17 (7) DSMD, as implemented by §§ 9–12, serve to protect.[26] Without a statutory right to public communication of presumably legitimate uses, users would ultimately have only corresponding contractual claims against the OCSSP. The experience with deletions and re-uploads under the NetzDG shows that such claims are not equally effective.[27] The subjective user right under sub. 1 is directed at the non-blocking of presumably legitimate uses due to possible copyright infringement. However, it appears that it cannot be directed against a blocking decision based on permissible terms of use of the OCSSP. § 9 is only applicable to **automated blocking procedures.**[28] In the case of non-automated blocking, however, such a subjective user right results from an interpretation of § 7 (2) sent. 1 in conformity with the Directive. The concept of communication to the public is based on Art. 3 (1) of the InfoSoc Directive since the UrhDaG is not based on an independent right of communication to the public (→ Introduction mn. 7, 12).[29]

---

[24] Metzger/Pravemann ZUM 2021, 288 (294); cf. also Hofmann GRUR 2019, 1219 (1227); Schwartmann/Hentsch MMR 2020, 207 (212); Spindler CR 2020, 50 (57).

[25] Schwartmann/Hentsch MMR 2020, 207 (212).

[26] Spindler CR 2019, 277 (289).

[27] Spindler CR 2019, 277 (289); Spindler CR 2020, 50 (57); see, however: Volkmann CR 2019, 376 (382 et seq.).

[28] BT-Drs. 19/27426, 47, 139.

[29] See: 'Anmerkungen von Louise Specht-Riemenschneider' on CJEU GRUR 2021, 1054 et seqq. – YouTube and Cyando.

### 2. Response possibilities of the rightholder

The rightholder can lodge a complaint against the communication to the public under § 14. The rightholder can also initiate a complaint procedure before an external complaints body because the external complaints body under § 15 can be called upon to fulfil the obligations under § 14. For the duration of the complaint procedure, the OCSSP must continue to publicly communicate the content. This also applies if the duration of the procedure exceeds the one week period prescribed by § 14 (3) No. 3[30] as failures by the OCSSP to conduct the complaints procedure should not be to the detriment of the users. If the complaint procedure is concluded with a **decision in** favour of the rightholder, the OCSSP's duty of communication to the public according to sub. 1 ends. It can then block the content according to §§ 7 and 8. If, on the other hand, the complaint procedure ends with a decision in favour of the user, that is, if the user can actually invoke a legal authorisation within the meaning of § 5, the content must continue to be communicated to the public. **7**

## III. Presumably legitimate uses (sub. 2)

### 1. Presumptive effect

Sub. 2 contains a **statutory presumption** that certain transformative uses fall under the copyright exception provision of § 5. The presumption is designed to be rebuttable. The user who has the burden of proof for the authorisation of use must first state and, if necessary, prove the actual conditions of sub. 2. Pursuant to § 292 (1) ZPO, it is then up to the rightholder to provide (full) evidence to the contrary – that is, the lack of authorisation to use – to rebut the presumption. However, in his opinion on Poland's action for annulment against Art. 17 DSMD, the Advocate General stated that the OCSSP cannot normally be required to examine the legality or illegality of the content placed online by the user. He, therefore, argued that only manifestly unlawful content should be subject to the automated blocking decision[31] (→ mn. 3). If the CJEU follows this, the presumption of sub. 2 can also only be rebutted if the rightholder demonstrates and proves that there has been a manifest **infringement** (on manifest unlawfulness → mn. 3). In the law on statements, the BGH has just abandoned such a criterion for the assessment of an infringement by a search engine operator.[32] **8**

### 2. Requirements

#### a) Extent of use of the work (sub. 2 sent. 1 No. 1, sent. 2)

The content uploaded by the user must contain less than half of the work of a third party or several works of different third parties. Here, reference is made to the concept of a work under copyright law. However, this requirement only applies to works that do not constitute **illustrations**, i.e. works that are not photographic works within the meaning of § 2 (1) No. 5 UrhG and are not photographs within the meaning of § 72 (1) UrhG.[33] The user may use more than half of the illustration and even the entire illustration because, **9**

---

[30] BT-Drs. 19/27426, 139.

[31] AG Saugmandsgaard Øe C-401/19, ECLI:EU:C:2021:613 mn. 194 et seq. – Poland/Parliament and Council.

[32] BGH NJW 2018, 2324.

[33] Cf. for the same term in the context of the quotation exception: Dreier/Schulze UrhG § 51 mn. 26 et seqq.

from the legislature's point of view, it is not feasible to make a partial use of illustrations in a meaningful way.[34] The explanatory memorandum to the UrhDaG only explicitly mentions 'photographs or graphics'.[35] Thus, the legislature probably did not want to include motion pictures and cinematographic work in the term illustration.

**b) Combination (sub. 2 sent. 1 No. 2)**

10 The part of the work used may not be used in isolation but must be combined with at least one other piece of content. This can be the user's **own content** as well as the **content of a third party**. Whether this content is itself **protected by copyright** is **irrelevant**. This follows from a reversal of sub. 2 sent. 1 No. 1 that speaks of works, whereas sub. 2 sent. 1 No. 2 uses the more general term of content. The concept of content is broader than that of works, but the former includes the latter. Therefore, the use of the term 'content' with which the works or parts of works must be combined under sub. 1 means that a combination should also be possible with content that is not protected by copyright. A restriction to the combination with content not eligible for protection does not result from this. This interpretation is also supported by the objective of the provision. It is intended to cover uses that cannot be recognised as permitted by automated systems due to their typical contextual nature, such as quotations or parodies.[36] However, these uses may precisely require the combination of copyright-protected works of third parties, for example, for mashups or collages.

**c) Minor use or labelling as permitted by law (sub. 2 sent. 1 No. 3)**

11 The use must fulfil one of two requirements that are to be understood in the alternative: It must either be **minor** within the meaning of § 10 (→ § 10 mn. 9 et seqq.) or it must have been **labelled as statutorily permitted** in accordance with § 11 (→ § 11 mn. 9 et seqq.).

**d) No re-exception for manifestly unlawful labelling**

12 If the user has labelled his or her content as lawful pursuant to sub. 2 sent. 1 No. 3 in conjunction with § 11, it is irrelevant for the establishment of the rebuttable presumption whether his or her labelling is accurate. The requirements of sub. 2 are also met if the communication of the content to the public is **manifestly unlawful**. While the previous provisions contained an exception from the obligation to communicate to the public in the event that the user was manifestly incorrect in labelling content as authorised,[37] such provisions no longer exist.[38] However, in these cases the rightholders can rebut the presumption according to sub. 2 in the complaint procedure, so that the content is then no longer to be communicated to the public. Rightholders are also sufficiently protected by the red button solution, which can also be used to prevent the temporary communication to the public of presumably legitimate uses (→ § 14 mn. 14 et seqq.).

## IV. Information and notice obligations (sub. 3)

13 If an OCSSP is obliged under sub. 1 to communicate to the public presumably legitimate content, it has two obligations under sub. 3 towards the rightholder concerned. First, it must inform the rightholder that the content is being **communicated to**

[34] BT-Drs. 19/27426, 140.
[35] BT-Drs. 19/27426, 140.
[36] BT-Drs. 19/27426, 47.
[37] Cf. § 12 sent. 1 DiskE/§ 12 (1) sent. 1 RefE.
[38] With criticism: Conrad/Nolte ZUM 2021, 111 (120).

**the public;** and second, it must inform the rightholder of his or her right to initiate a **complaint procedure** against this communication to the public pursuant to § 14. This enables the rightholder to verify the permissibility of the use and, if necessary, to challenge it in the complaint procedure to rebut the presumption of legal authorisation to use under § 5 and to enable the blocking of the content after all.[39] The OCSSP must fulfil its duties to **immediately** inform and notify. It must, therefore, inform the rightholder in the immediate temporal context of the user's presumably legitimate upload. The rightholder does not have to be informed of the alternative possibility of appealing to an external complaints body pursuant to § 15 (1), but such a notice is also not detrimental. The way in which the information is provided is left to the OCSSP, but in view of the telos of the provision, it must be assumed that a conventional communication channel must be chosen, which the rightholder has opened and through which receipt of the information can therefore be expected.

## § 10
## Minor uses

**The following uses of third-party works shall be deemed to be minor within the meaning of § 9 subsection 2 sentence 1 number 3 provided that they do not serve commercial purposes or only serve to generate insignificant income:**

1. **uses of up to 15 seconds of a cinematographic work or motion picture,**
2. **uses of up to 15 seconds of an audio track,**
3. **uses of up to 160 characters of a text, and**
4. **uses of up to 125 kilobytes of a photographic work, photograph or graphic.**

## § 10
## Geringfügige Nutzungen

**Die folgenden Nutzungen von Werken Dritter gelten als geringfügig im Sinne des § 9 Absatz 2 Satz 1 Nummer 3, sofern sie nicht zu kommerziellen Zwecken oder nur zur Erzielung unerheblicher Einnahmen dienen:**

1. **Nutzungen bis zu 15 Sekunden je eines Filmwerkes oder Laufbildes,**
2. **Nutzungen bis zu 15 Sekunden je einer Tonspur,**
3. **Nutzungen bis zu 160 Zeichen je eines Textes und**
4. **Nutzungen bis zu 125 Kilobyte je eines Lichtbildwerkes, Lichtbildes oder einer Grafik.**

**Bibliography:** Becker, 'Automatisierte Rechtsdurchsetzung im Umsetzungsentwurf zu Art. 17 DSM-RL', ZUM 2020, 681; CDU, 'Kompromiss zum Urheberrecht: Keine Uploadfilter!', 15.3.2019, available at <https://archiv.cdu.de/artikel/kompromiss-zum-urheberrecht-keine-uploadfilter> (last accessed on 12.3.2024); Conrad/Nolte, 'Schrankenbestimmungen im Anwendungsbereich des UrhDaG', ZUM 2021, 111; Gerpott, 'Artikel 17 der neuen EU-Urheberrechtsrichtlinie: Fluch oder Segen? – Einordnung des Streites um "Upload-Filter" auf Online-Sharing-Plattformen', MMR 2019, 420; Hentsch, 'Verbesserungsvorschläge für den Gesetzesentwurf zur Anpassung des Urheberrechts', MMR-Aktuell 2021, 438119; Hofmann, 'Das neue Urheberrechtsdiensteanbieter-Gesetz', NJW 2021, 1905; Holznagel, 'Verfassungsrechtliche Fragen der Umsetzung von Art. 17 DSM-RL', ZUM 2020, 1; Husovec/Quintais, 'How to License Article 17? Exploring the Implementation Options for the New EU Rules on Content-Sharing-Platforms', GRUR Int. 2021, 325; Klass, 'Der Kampf ums Urheberrecht – Die Neuregelung der urheberrechtlichen Verantwortlichkeit von Upload-Plattformen', ZRP 2021, 74; Nordemann/Waiblinger, 'Art. 17 DSM-RL – Spannungsverhältnis zum bisherigen Recht? – Zur systematischen Einordnung von Art. 17 DSM-RL', GRUR 2020, 569; Peters/Schmidt, 'Das Ringen um Upload-Filter geht in die 2. Runde', GRUR Int. 2019, 1006. – See also the bibliography in the Introduction.

---

[39] BT-Drs. 19/27426, 149.

**Content**



## I. General remarks

### 1. Objective

1 § 10 defines the requirements under which a use is deemed to be minor under § 9 (2) sent. 1 No. 3. If works are used to an extremely small extent and combined with other works, it is likely that the use is a statutorily permitted use under § 5 (1), such as a **quotation or pastiche**, and, therefore, that the communication to the public is lawful anyway.[1] This justifies the obligation of communication to the public for such micro uses that are combined with other content. The provision thus contributes to the protection of user rights without unreasonably prejudicing the interests of the rightholders. This is because the exploitation of the entire work on the primary market can hardly be impaired by micro uses[2] and, moreover, per § 12 (1), the rightholders are to be remunerated even in the case of communication to the public of content pursuant to §§ 9–11 (see also the comments on → § 9 mn. 1).

### 2. EU law requirements

2 § 10 is based on Art. 17 (7) and (9) DSMD. Art. 17 (7) and (9) determine the **essential content of the safeguards** necessary to minimise the risks to freedom of expression, while it is for the Member States and the Commission to specify the **modalities** for doing so.[3] In his opinion on Poland's action for annulment against Art. 17 DSMD, the Advocate General considered it necessary that the filtering techniques take into account match rates of works uploaded and works to be blocked and that thresholds be set such that automatic blocking of content is justified above the threshold, while below the threshold, the application of a copyright exception, such as the quotation exception, can reasonably be used.[4] The same is also proposed by the Commission in its guidelines on the implementation of Art. 17 DSMD.[5] § 10 provides for just such a regulation.

[1] BT-Drs. 19/27426, 140.
[2] BT-Drs. 19/27426, 145.
[3] AG Saugmandsgaard Øe C-401/19, ECLI:EU:C:2021:613 mn. 210 – Poland/Parliament and Council.
[4] AG Saugmandsgaard Øe C-401/19, ECLI:EU:C:2021:613 mn. 211 – Poland/Parliament and Council.
[5] COM(2021) 288 final EN, 21.

### 3. Conformity with EU law

§ 10 can essentially be justified by **considerations of proportionality**. It reduces the otherwise boundless **forecasting risk** of the OCSSP with regard to the examination of the lawfulness of an act of use in that the provision allows the OCSSP to assume for an extremely limited period of time, namely solely until the decision in the complaint procedure of a maximum of one week, that a use that fulfils the cumulative requirements of §§ 9 and 10 is generally covered by an exemption in § 5.[6] Furthermore, according to Art. 17 (7) DSMD, measures taken by platforms must not have the effect of preventing the availability of works that do not infringe copyright. Without a reduction in the risk of forecasting, there is a risk of strategic automated over blocking of content. This is to the detriment of users' freedoms of communication, which the CJEU has already found to be affected on several occasions when content is automatically blocked on platforms.[7] Therefore, § 10 is also an expression of the **obligation under Art. 17 (7) DSMD**[8] (also → § 7 mn. 21). In this respect, it is not only compatible with the provisions of the Directive but is even necessary in order to implement the provisions of Art. 17 DSMD.[9] 3

### 4. Origin

§ 10 was only introduced in its current form in the RegE to the UrhDaG. Its predecessor provisions were fundamentally different. The absolute limits on the use of third-party works were (in part, considerably) more generous: Up to 20 seconds from cinematographic works, motion pictures and audio tracks, a maximum of 1,000 characters from texts and up to 250 kilobytes from photographic works, photographs and graphics (§ 6 (1) RefE; almost identical already § 6 (1) DiskE). However, the predecessor norms of § 10 differed even more in that they constituted an independent exception for minor uses and did not merely create the presumption that such an exception would apply. The CDU had proposed such a **minor use exception** in a position paper to prevent the introduction of upload filters.[10] In the explanatory memorandum to the RefE, the legislature explained in detail why § 6 DiskE/RefE should not conflict with the case law of the CJEU, according to which the **catalogue of exceptions in Art. 5 InfSoc Directive** is **exhaustive:**[11] Art. 17 DSMD would constitute a new *sui generis* legal regime for OCSSPs that took precedence over the provisions of the InfoSoc Directive as *lex specialis*.[12] This reasoning, however, did not convince most copyright scholars.[13] In response to this criticism, the exception for minor use was deleted from the UrhDaG. In its place, § 10 was introduced as part of 4

---

[6] Specht-Riemenschneider, Stellungnahme zum Urheberrechtsdiensteanbietergesetz (UrhDaG), 21.

[7] CJEU C-70/10, ECLI:EU:C:2011:771 mn. 50, 52 – Scarlet Extended; CJEU C-360/10, ECLI:EU:C:2012:85 mn. 40 – SABAM/Netlog; CJEU C-314/12, ECLI:EU:C:2014:192 mn. 47 – UPC Telekabel/Constantin Film et al.

[8] Hofmann ZUM 2020, 665 (670); Hofmann GRUR 2021, 895 (903); Hofmann NJW 2021, 1905 (1908).

[9] However, with criticism: Conrad/Nolte ZUM 2021, 111 (120); Metzger/Pravemann ZUM 2021, 288 (295).

[10] CDU, 'Kompromiss zum Urheberrecht: Keine Uploadfilter!'.

[11] CJEU C-310/15, ECLI:EU:C:2016:878 mn. 34 – Soulier and Doke; CJEU C-161/17, ECLI:EU:C:2018:634 mn. 17 – Cordoba; CJEU C-476/17, ECLI:EU:C:2019:624 mn. 56 et seqq. – Pelham.

[12] BT-Drs. 19/27426, 44 et seq.; for the classification as *lex specialis* see also COM(2021) 288 final, 2.

[13] Becker ZUM 2020, 681 (685); Hofmann ZUM 2020, 665 (669 et seq.); Leistner ZUM 2020, 897 (910 et seq.); Rauer/Bibi WRP 2020, 1533 (1540); Wandtke/Hauck ZUM 2020, 671 (677); Würtenberger/Freischem GRUR 2020, 1063 (1067). With criticism: Dreier GRUR 2019, 771 (776); Hofmann GRUR 2019, 1219 (1221); Holznagel ZUM 2020, 1 (4); Nordemann/Waiblinger GRUR 2020, 569 (575); Peters/

the system of presumptively permitted uses. In doing so, the German legislature followed a proposal made by the Commission in its **consultation paper** within the framework of the stakeholder dialogue: In particular, minor uses in the context of which a work is combined with user content should be treated as presumably legitimate because there is a high probability that the user can invoke a copyright exception.[14]

### 5. Legal nature

5 According to the explanatory memorandum to the UrhDaG, it is a procedural instrument and not (any longer) an independent exception.[15] There is some evidence to suggest that unlike the provision in the RefE, § 10 actually lacks the character of an independent exception provision and that the provision is even necessary in order to comply with the requirements of the DSMD (→ mn. 2, → mn. 3). § 10 in conjunction with § 9(2) is a time-limited presumption that certain uses are subject to the exception provision of § 5.[16] It is, therefore, by no means the case that a minor use must always be compulsorily communicated to the public. On the contrary, minor uses within the meaning of § 10 are only relevant within the meaning of § 9.[17]

### 6. Systematics

6 § 10 is to be read, in particular, in conjunction with **§§ 9 and 11.**

## II. Prerequisites

### 1. Relative limit of use

#### a) Material scope of application

7 § 10 is only applicable to **automated procedures** for blocking user content.[18]

#### b) Extent of the work used

8 The absolute limits set out in § 10 are only of practical relevance if the third-party protected work used by the user is **more than twice as large as** the excerpt used. After all, the user can only invoke the presumption in § 9(2) if he uses less than half of another's work (→ § 9 mn. 9). If this half is already smaller than the limits specified in § 10, the absolute limits of § 10 are no longer relevant. An example of this is a poem that is 300 characters long: § 9(2) No. 1 allows a maximum of 149 characters to be used. The 160-character limit of § 10 No. 3 has no independent meaning apart from this.[19]

---

Schmidt GRUR Int. 2019, 1006 (1012); Spindler CR 2019, 277 (290); Spindler CR 2020, 50 (56 et seq.); see, however: Gerpott MMR 2019, 420 (424); Husovec/Quintais GRUR Int. 2021, 325 (334 et seqq.).

[14] Commission, Targeted consultation addressed to the participants to the stakeholder dialogue on Article 17 of the Directive on Copyright in the Digital Single Market, 16. For a rebuttable presumption see also: Hofmann ZUM 2020, 665 (670).

[15] See also Hofmann ZUM 2020, 665 (670); Hofmann NJW 2021, 1905 (1908); Klass ZRP 2021, 74 (76); see, however: Hentsch MMR-Aktuell 2021, 438119; Metzger/Pravemann ZUM 2021, 288 (295).

[16] Cf., for instance, Hofmann NJW 2021, 1905 (1909).

[17] Specht-Riemenschneider, Stellungnahme zum Urheberrechtsdiensteanbietergesetz (UrhDaG), 20.

[18] BT-Drs. 19/27426, 46.

[19] BT-Drs. 19/27426, 140.

## 2. Absolute limits of use

### a) Cinematographic work and motion picture (No. 1)

**A maximum of 15 seconds** may be taken from cinematographic works within the meaning of § 2 (1) No. 6 UrhG and motion pictures within the meaning of § 95 UrhG. Based on the typical length of a feature film of 90 minutes, this corresponds to 0.3 per cent of the film. If such a small part is used, it is obvious that this constitutes a statutorily permitted use, such as a quotation, a parody or a pastiche.[20] 9

### b) Audio track (No. 2)

Similarly, **a maximum of 15 seconds** may be extracted from audio tracks. The provision does not specify which categories of works are to be covered by the term audio track. What is meant are probably musical works within the meaning of § 2 (1) No. 2 UrhG and sound carriers within the meaning of § 85 (1) sent. 1 UrhG. With an average song length of three and a half minutes, a 15-second excerpt represents seven per cent of this. In this case, too, it is obvious that it is a statutorily permitted use.[21] 10

### c) Text (No. 3)

**A maximum of 160 characters** may be used from linguistic works within the meaning of § 2 (1) No. 1 UrhG. This corresponds to 27 words, that is, one to two sentences, based on the average length of all word forms in the Duden[22] corpus. This is intended to cover, in particular, classical quotations that are indispensable for the formation of opinion in a democratically constituted society.[23] However, the provision does not clarify whether the 160 characters should also include the **spaces** between words.[24] The historical interpretation indicates that the spaces should not be counted, as the explanatory memorandum to the UrhDaG focuses solely on the length of the words. 11

### d) Photographic work, photograph and graphic (No. 4)

**A maximum of 125 kilobytes** may be taken from photographic works within the meaning of § 2 (1) No. 5 UrhG, photographs within the meaning of § 72 (1) UrhG and graphics that may, for example, represent scientific or technical works within the meaning of § 2 (1) No. 7 UrhG or works of applied art within the meaning of § 2 (1) No. 4 UrhG. It should be permissible to use excerpts from these works as well as to use the works as a whole, as the use of excerpts from these works would often lead to distortions of their meaning.[25] It is unclear whether the maximum value of 125 kilobytes should only apply to **uncompressed** or also to compressed **data sets** (e.g., for JPG). The historical interpretation speaks in favour of the former: the legislature assumed that this was a value at the lower end of the typical file size for user-generated content.[26] The exploitation of high-resolution images should continue to be reserved for the primary market.[27] However, such an interpretation is contradicted by both the wording and the purpose of the law: In No. 4, the legislature did not specify a particular resolution but a file size. If, for example, JPG-files had to be converted first, this would be detrimental to legal certainty because it would be difficult for users to foresee whether the provision applies. 12

---

[20] BT-Drs. 19/27426, 140.
[21] BT-Drs. 19/27426, 140.
[22] For general information about the Duden, cf. https://en.wikipedia.org/wiki/Duden.
[23] BT-Drs. 19/27426, 140.
[24] Wandtke/Hauck ZUM 2020, 671 (677).
[25] BT-Drs. 19/27426, 140.
[26] BT-Drs. 19/27426, 140.
[27] BT-Drs. 19/27426, 145.

#### e) Hybrid works

13 § 10 does not contain any provisions on the extent to which works that cannot be assigned to any of the categories of works mentioned may not be used because they are hybrid works.[28] In this case, a **focal point approach** should be taken: The absolute limits of the work category that predominates – qualitatively or quantitatively – are applicable.

### 3. Purpose of use

14 The minor use of third-party protected works **may not serve commercial purposes** (see also → § 6, mn. 5). If it does, the use only falls within the scope of application of § 10 if the user intends to generate **only insignificant income** (see also → § 6 mn. 6). Uses made with the **intention of making a profit** serve commercial purposes.[29] If this intention is lacking, the user may in any case invoke § 10. Users who act with the intention of making a profit, however, can only rely on this if they only intend to generate very little income. In their opinion, the income must be so low that it can be rated as equivalent to non-commercial use. This would be the case, for example, if the income insignificantly exceeded the costs of use (e.g., the production costs). As a result, a ***de minimis* threshold is** established.[30] It is irrelevant if the revenues actually turn out to be greater than forecast. According to the wording of the standard ('serve'), it is solely the intention of the user at the time of the act of use that matters.

## § 11
## Flagging as permitted use

**(1) If user-generated content is to be automatically blocked when uploaded and if it is not a minor use pursuant to § 10, the service provider shall be obliged,**

1. **to inform the user of the rightholder's blocking request,**
2. **to inform the user at the same time when providing the information under number 1 of the necessity of a legal authorisation under § 5 for a communication to the public and**
3. **to enable the user to flag the use as statutorily permitted under § 5.**

**(2) If user-generated content is to be automatically blocked after it has been uploaded, subsection 1 shall apply with the proviso that the content shall be deemed to be presumed legitimate for 48 hours even without the presence of a flagging under subsection 1 number 3.**

## § 11
## Kennzeichnung als erlaubte Nutzung

**(1) Soll ein nutzergenerierter Inhalt beim Hochladen automatisiert blockiert werden und handelt es sich nicht um eine geringfügige Nutzung nach § 10, so ist der Diensteanbieter verpflichtet,**

1. **den Nutzer über das Blockierverlangen des Rechtsinhabers zu informieren,**
2. **den Nutzer zugleich mit der Information nach Nummer 1 auf die Erforderlichkeit einer gesetzlichen Erlaubnis nach § 5 für eine öffentliche Wiedergabe hinzuweisen und**
3. **es dem Nutzer zu ermöglichen, die Nutzung als nach § 5 gesetzlich erlaubt zu kennzeichnen.**

**(2) Soll ein nutzergenerierter Inhalt erst nach dem Hochladen automatisiert blockiert werden, so findet Absatz 1 mit der Maßgabe Anwendung, dass der Inhalt auch ohne Vorliegen einer Kennzeichnung nach Absatz 1 Nummer 3 für 48 Stunden als mutmaßlich erlaubt gilt.**

---

[28] Wandtke/Hauck ZUM 2020, 671 (677).
[29] Cf. recital 69 DSMD.
[30] Wandtke/Hauck ZUM 2020, 671 (677).

**Bibliography:** ARD/ZDF, 'Zum Referentenentwurf eines Zweiten Gesetzes zur Anpassung des Urheberrechts an die Erfordernisse des digitalen Binnenmarktes des BMJV', 2.9.2020, available at <https://www.bmj.de/SharedDocs/Downloads/DE/Gesetzgebung/Stellungnahmen/2020/110920_Stellungnahme_ARD-ZDF_RefE_Urheberrecht-ges.pdf?__blob=publicationFile&v=3> (last accessed 12.3.2024); Holznagel, 'Verfassungsrechtliche Fragen der Umsetzung von Art. 17 DSM-RL', ZUM 2020, 1; Müller-Terpitz, 'Filter als Gefahr für die Meinungspluralität? – Verfassungsrechtliche Erwägungen zum Einsatz von Filtertechnologien', ZUM 2020, 365; Raue/Steinbach, 'Uploadfilter – Funktionsweisen, Einsatzmöglichkeiten und Parametrisierung', ZUM 2020, 355; SVRV, 'Gutachten zur Lage der Verbraucherinnen und Verbraucher in Deutschland', 2021, available at <https://www.svr-verbraucherfragen.de/wp-content/uploads/SVRV_Gutachten_2020.pdf> (last accessed 1.9.2021). – See also the bibliography in the Introduction.

**Content**



# I. General remarks

## 1. Objective

§ 11 supplements § 9 by providing for the possibility of marking a use as lawful (so-called flagging) and, thus, specifying the conditions under which the presumption of lawful authorisation to use comes into play pursuant to § 9 (2) sent. 1 No. 3. This ensures the **precedence of the copyright exceptions**[1] (see also the comments on → § 9 mn. 1). 1

[1] Cf. Dreier GRUR 2019, 771 (777).

### 2. EU law requirements

2 As part of the differentiated provisions of §§ 9–12, § 11 **implements** the requirements of **Art. 17 (7) DSMD.**[2] However, the legislature makes use of the **Member States' leeway** (→ Introduction mn. 9) in the implementation, as a flagging mechanism is not expressly provided for in the DSMD.[3]

### 3. Conformity with EU law

3 Pre-flagging mechanisms are necessary to implement the requirements of Art. 17 (7) DSMD.[4] The obligation to provide information to the user in the event of a blocking or even a request to block is admittedly not prescribed in the DSMD. However, despite its fully harmonising character, it is harmless to establish corresponding procedural information obligations in favour of the user by way of **interpretation in conformity with EU fundamental law** using Art. 17 DSMD. Recital 71 DSMD provides that user organisations shall have certain information rights, but it does not express a mandatory restriction to solely user organisations.

### 4. Origin

4 In its current version, the provision of § 11 was only introduced in the RegE of the UrhDaG. However, the previous drafts also contained labelling provisions that took user interests into account to an even greater extent in one respect: § 8 (1) of the DiskE/RefE provided for obligations of the OCSSP that largely corresponded to the obligations of the OCSSP under the current § 1. Among other things, the OCSSP was to be obliged to enable users to mark a use as statutorily or contractually permitted.[5]According to § 8 (2) sent. 1 DiskE/RefE, if the user made use of this, it should result in the **marked content not being** allowed to be **blocked** without further preconditions. The labelling should not lead to an obligation of the OCSSP to communicate publicly **only** if it was obviously incorrect. In another respect, however, § 8 DiskE/RefE lagged behind today's § 11: In the previous drafts, there was no possibility for the user to mark permitted uses as such even after they had been uploaded.

### 5. Legal nature

5 Considered together with § 9 (2), § 11 establishes a time-limited presumption that certain uses are subject to the provisions of § 5. However, it is **not** to be classified as **an independent exception provision**. Accordingly, content that a user has flagged as lawful does not always have to be communicated to the public; rather, user flagging as defined in § 11 is to be considered solely within the framework of § 9 and has no independent relevance.

### 6. Systematics

6 § 11 is to be read, in particular, in conjunction with **§§ 9 and 10.**

---

[2] BT-Drs. 19/27426, 141.

[3] AG Saugmandsgaard Øe C-401/19, ECLI:EU:C:2021:613 mn. 210 – Poland/Parliament and Council; see also Metzger/Pravemann ZUM 2021, 288 (296).

[4] AG Saugmandsgaard Øe C-401/19, ECLI:EU:C:2021:613 mn. 210 – Poland/Parliament and Council.

[5] § 8 (1) No. 2 DiskE/§ 8 (1) No. 3 RefE.

# II. Pre-flagging (sub. 1)

## 1. Material scope of application

### a) Material scope of application

An OCSSP only has to enable marking under § 11 if it uses **automated systems** to comply with its obligations to block under §§ 7 and 8.[6] Moreover, it can only prevent the blocking of content for copyright reasons. The OCSSP is free to refuse the communication to the public of marked content for other reasons. In particular, the OCSSP does not have to communicate content that is punishable by law or content that violates its terms and conditions to the public.[7] § 11 also does not establish a user claim for the communication to the public of content for which the OCSSP does not open a platform from the outset according to the contract of use. For example, a platform for audio and video content may refuse to publish a caricaturistic image.[8] After all, there can be **no general claim to online publication** of content given the private autonomy of the OCSSP.[9] **7**

### b) Criticism

Unlike its predecessor provisions, § 11 (1) no longer permits the labelling of a use as being **in the public domain or contractually permitted**. The explanatory memorandum to these predecessor provisions referred, in particular, to uses permitted by Creative Commons licences.[10] If the copyright term has expired or a licence has been granted, there is no apparent reason the content should not be made publicly available. Therefore, § 11 should be extended to these cases, even if Art. 17 (7) DSMD does not explicitly stipulate this.[11] **8**

## 2. Requirements

### a) User generated content

The marked content must first be user-generated content within the meaning of § 9 (2) Nos 1, 2. **9**

### b) No minor use

Furthermore, flagging under sub. 1 can only be considered if there is no minor use under § 10. The two ways in which the presumption under § 9 (2) can be invoked are in an alternative relationship to each other. On the one hand, § 11 can be applied when the extent of the use of the work **exceeds the absolute limits of § 10** (→ § 10 mn. 9 et seqq.). On the other hand, it is applicable when the use of small parts of a work serves **commercial purposes** or is intended to generate income that is not insignificant (→ § 10 mn. 14). **10**

---

[6] BT-Drs. 19/27426, 46, 141.

[7] BT-Drs. 19/27426, 141; BGH GRUR-RS 2021, 2397 mn. 78 – Facebook.

[8] BT-Drs. 19/27426, 149.

[9] Against such a general claim, see also Hofmann GRUR 2019, 1219 (1227); Müller-Terpitz ZUM 2020, 365 (373 et seq.); Spindler CR 2020, 50 (57); cf. also Leistner ZGE 2020, 123 (169 et seq.); Leistner ZUM 2020, 505 (511).

[10] Explanatory memorandum to DiskE, 90 et seq.; BT-Drs. 19/27426, 148.

[11] ARD/ZDF, 'Zum Referentenentwurf eines Zweiten Gesetzes zur Anpassung des Urheberrechts an die Erfordernisse des digitalen Binnenmarktes des BMJV', 23 et seq.; Specht-Riemenschneider, Stellungnahme zum Urheberrechtsdiensteanbietergesetz (UrhDaG), 26.

**c) Blocking request**

11 In addition, the rightholder must have requested (→ § 7 mn. 17) that the upload of the user content be blocked. In contrast to sub. 2, sub. 1 only applies if the **uploading of content** is to be **prevented** and not if content has already been uploaded and subsequently needs to be removed (→ mn. 16 et seqq.).

**d) No further requirements**

12 The possibility of flagging is open to all users to the same extent. Some literature has suggested that – in parallel to the red button procedure for trusted rightholders in § 14 (4) (→ § 14 mn. 14 et seqq.) – only **trusted users** should be allowed to flag.[12] However, the legislature rightly refrained from such a restriction. The granting of user rights only to a specific group of users would not meet the requirements of a fair balance of rights and interests that copyright law is required to establish by the constitution.

### 3. Obligations of the OCSSP

**a) Duty to notify (sub. 1 No. 1)**

13 If the user attempts to upload content that the rightholder has previously requested to be blocked, the OCSSP must **notify the user** that a **blocking request** has been made. This is intended to make the user aware – possibly for the first time – that he or she is using a protected work and must comply with the requirements of copyright law.[13] The information medium is not specified in more detail. However, according to the meaning and purpose of the duty to inform, it must be assumed that a conventional communication channel must be chosen, which the rightholder has opened and through which receipt of the information can therefore be expected.

**b) Duty to inform (sub. 1 No. 2)**

14 At the same time the user is notified of the blocking request, the OCSSP must **inform** the user that he/she requires a **legal authorisation pursuant to § 5** for the upload he or she is attempting to carry out. Unlike what was provided for in the predecessor provisions, the service provider does not have to inform the user of the possibility of obtaining a contractual authorisation for the planned upload. The question arises as to how the information is to be conveyed. It is sufficiently known from consumer law that more information does not necessarily lead to the user being more informed, and too much information can even lead to a reduction or even an abortion of the information intake. Information can even be detrimental above a certain amount.[14] Given the meaning and purpose of the standard (raising awareness of the copyright infringement), only the absolutely necessary information should be allowed to be provided without any unnecessary additions. This increases the likelihood of information success.

**c) Duty to offer a flagging option (sub. 1 No. 3)**

15 Finally, the OCSSP must enable users to mark their content as a statutorily permitted use (so-called **pre-flagging**[15]). Unlike what was provided for in the predecessor provi-

---

[12] Schwartmann/Hentsch MMR 2020, 207 (212); for the introduction of the category of 'trusted user' or 'trusted uploader', see also Holznagel ZUM 2020, 1 (5); Leistner ZGE 2020, 123 (201 et seqq.), Leistner ZUM 2020, 505 (512); Müller-Terpitz ZUM 2020, 365 (373); Raue/Steinbach ZUM 2020, 355 (363); Spindler CR 2020, 50 (53).

[13] BT-Drs. 19/27426, 141.

[14] In detail and with further sources: SVRV 'Gutachten zur Lage der Verbraucherinnen und Verbraucher in Deutschland', 370 et seqq.

[15] See BT-Drs. 19/27426, 141.

sions, it does not have to be possible to mark the use as contractually permitted. The legislature assumes that in the case of contractually permitted uses, the rightholder's request to block will already be lacking.[16] In terms of time, sub. 1 No. 3 – unlike sub. 1 No. 2 ('at the same time') – does not clarify when the OCSSP must enable the user to flag. However, the objective of the provision to protect user rights requires that the possibility be made available in **close temporal connection** with the information and the notice under sub. 1 No. 1 and sub. 1 No. 2. After all, the information and notice provide users with all the knowledge they need to examine the content for a possible copyright infringement. If users then had to wait until they could make the communication to the public, they would possibly refrain from doing so again, despite its lawfulness. In view of the telos of the provision, the labelling option should be easily accessible and feasible.

## III. Post-flagging (sub. 2)

### 1. Requirements

In principle, labelling under sub. 2 has the same requirements **as labelling under** 16
**sub. 1**, as the comprehensive reference to the latter shows. Therefore, it is possible for the user to upload user-generated content (→ mn. 9) that does not already meet the requirements of § 10 for minor use (→ mn. 10). On the other hand, the rightholder must have expressed a request to block this content (→ mn. 11). In contrast to sub. 1, this request must relate to **user content that has already been uploaded**. This may be relevant, for example, if the conditions for qualified blocking under § 7 did not exist at the time the content was uploaded because the rightholder had not provided the necessary information at that time. It is also conceivable, for example, that a licence for use existed at the time of the upload but has since expired.[17]

### 2. Obligations of the OCSSP

#### a) Reference to the obligations under sub. 1

Even in the case of a subsequent blocking request, the OCSSP is obliged to notify the 17
user whose content the rightholder has referenced, to inform him or her of the necessity of a legal authorisation for the use and to grant him or her the possibility to flag this use as statutorily permitted (so-called **post-flagging;**[18] → mn. 13 et seqq.). In this respect, there are no changes to the obligations under sub. 1.

#### b) 48-hour period

Pre- and post-flagging lead – if the other requirements of § 9 (2) are met (→ § 9 18
mn. 9 et seqq.) – to the use in question being presumed to be permitted and, therefore, to the content being initially communicated to the public pursuant to § 9 (1) (→ § 9 mn. 6 et seq.). However, even **without such flagging**, user content is presumed to be permitted for 48 hours after a subsequent blocking request pursuant to sub. 2 and must be communicated to the public by the OCSSP during this period. According to the explanatory memorandum to the UrhDaG, the 48-hour period begins as soon as the OCSSP has sent the information pursuant to sub. 1 to the user.[19] Correctly, however,

[16] BT-Drs. 19/27426, 141.
[17] BT-Drs. 19/27426, 141.
[18] BT-Drs. 19/27426, 141.
[19] BT-Drs. 19/27426, 141.

the time limit should only begin with the time of receipt of the information because the objective of the 48-hour time limit is to allow the user to react to a subsequent request by the rightholder to block the information.[20] This possibility is not guaranteed by the provision of information alone, but by its receipt by the user. In addition, the correct way of providing information should be added (→ mn. 13 et seq.), without which the time period should not start to run. The legislature must make improvements here. If the 48-hour period ends without the user having flagged the content as a statutorily permitted use, the **fiction** of presumably legitimate use under sub. 2 **no longer applies**. The OCSSP is then no longer obliged to communicate the content to the public; the OCSSP can now block it under §§ 7 and 8 and is liable for unlawful communication to the public. However, the user is free to **flag the content as statutorily permitted use even after** the deadline has expired and, if applicable, **after blocking**, thus again triggering the effect of § 9 (1). Alternatively, he or she can appeal against the blocking under § 14.[21]

## § 12 Remuneration by service providers; liability

**(1) [1]The service provider shall pay the author reasonable remuneration for the communication to the public of presumably legitimate uses in accordance with §§ 9 to 11. [2]§ 5 subsection 2 sentence 2 to 4 shall apply mutatis mutandis.**

**(2) [1]The service provider shall not be liable under copyright law for the communication to the public of presumably legitimate uses under §§ 9 to 11 until the conclusion of a complaint procedure, but at the latest, until the expiry of the time limit for the decision on the complaint (§ 14 subsection 3 number 3). [2]After the decision on the complaint, the service provider shall only be liable for damages under copyright law if it has culpably infringed the obligations under § 14 in carrying out the complaint procedure; claims for injunctive relief and removal shall remain unaffected.**

**(3) In the case of minor use (§ 10), the user shall not be liable under copyright law for the communication to the public of presumably legitimate uses until the conclusion of a complaint procedure under § 14.**

## § 12 Vergütung durch Diensteanbieter; Verantwortlichkeit

**(1) [1]Für die öffentliche Wiedergabe mutmaßlich erlaubter Nutzungen nach den §§ 9 bis 11 hat der Diensteanbieter dem Urheber eine angemessene Vergütung zu zahlen. [2]§ 5 Absatz 2 Satz 2 bis 4 ist entsprechend anzuwenden.**

**(2) [1]Für die öffentliche Wiedergabe mutmaßlich erlaubter Nutzungen nach den §§ 9 bis 11 ist der Diensteanbieter bis zum Abschluss eines Beschwerdeverfahrens, längstens aber bis zum Ablauf der Frist zur Entscheidung über die Beschwerde (§ 14 Absatz 3 Nummer 3) urheberrechtlich nicht verantwortlich. [2]Nach der Entscheidung über die Beschwerde haftet der Diensteanbieter nur dann urheberrechtlich auf Schadensersatz, wenn er bei der Durchführung des Beschwerdeverfahrens schuldhaft gegen die Pflichten nach § 14 verstoßen hat; Ansprüche auf Unterlassung und Beseitigung bleiben unberührt.**

**(3) Im Falle einer geringfügigen Nutzung (§ 10) ist der Nutzer für die öffentliche Wiedergabe mutmaßlich erlaubter Nutzungen bis zum Abschluss eines Beschwerdeverfahrens nach § 14 urheberrechtlich nicht verantwortlich.**

**Bibliography:** Conrad/Nolte, 'Schrankenbestimmungen im Anwendungsbereich des UrhDaG', ZUM 2021, 111; Frey/Rudolph, 'Das Urheberrechts-Diensteanbieter-Gesetz', MMR 2021, 671; Hentsch, Verbesserungsvorschläge für den Gesetzesentwurf zur Anpassung des Urheberrechts', MMR-Aktuell 2021, 438119; Hilty/Kaiser/Moscon/Richter/Stumpf/Sutterer, 'Stellungnahme zum Referentenentwurf

[20] BT-Drs. 19/27426, 141.
[21] BT-Drs. 19/27426, 141.

vom 2. September 2020', available at <https://pure.mpg.de/rest/items/item_3263936_1/component/file_3263937/content> (last accessed 12.3.2024); Pappi, 'Neue Möglichkeiten der Rechtewahrnehmungen bei Plattformnutzungen', ZUM 2020, 11; Positionspapier der Urheberrechtswissenschaft: Zitate und Parodien müssen vergütungsfrei bleiben!, available at <https://www.zar.kit.edu/downloads/News/Positionspapier%20der%20Urheberrechtswissens.pdf> (last accessed 12.3.2024); Senftleben, 'Filter obligations after the reform of European copyright law – The end of free net culture?', ZUM 2019, 369. – See also the bibliography in the Introduction.

**Content**



# I. General remarks

## 1. Objectives of sub. 1

The remuneration obligation under sub. 1 pursues two objectives. First, it ensures 1
that rightholders receive **fair remuneration** for the use of their works within the scope of §§ 9–11. After all, when the presumption under § 9 (2) applies, it is most likely that the uses in question are statutorily permitted uses. The reasons for which a remuneration obligation is provided for these uses under § 5 (2) (→ § 5 mn. 1) also apply to the uses covered by the presumption. On the one hand, this is intended to improve the position of rightholders in that they also receive remuneration for such minor uses of their works that could not be monetised up to now due to a lack of technical registrability. On the other hand, the intention is to give rightholders the choice to go through the complaint procedure under § 14 or not. Even if they decide not to do so, for example, because the effort required seems too great, they should at least be compensated for the use. The second aim of the provision is to provide **flat-rate damage** (within the meaning of Art. 13 (2) Var. 2 of the Enforcement Directive)

for cases in which the presumably legitimate uses turn out to be unlawful during the complaint procedure.[1]

### 2. Objectives of sub. 2 and sub. 3

2 Subs. 2 contains a **special provision** which, in deviation from § 1 (2) sent. 1, allows the copyright **liability of the OCSSP** to lapse during the complaint procedure. The maximum time limit in sub. 2, sent. 1, second half of the sentence in conjunction with § 14 (3) No. 3 (one week after filing the complaint) is intended to be an incentive for the OCSSP to bring these proceedings to a speedy conclusion.[2] The fact that the copyright liability of the user pursuant to sub. 3 ceases during the complaint procedure serves to **protect social communication practices** on upload platforms by creating legal certainty. The creative engagement with existing content that takes place on the platforms ultimately contributes to a lively social debate culture. If the users were held fully liable for even the smallest use of third-party protected works thereon the platforms, there would be a **chilling effect** on their freedom of expression and artistic freedom.[3]

### 3. EU law requirements

3 § 12 implements[4] – together with §§ 9–11 – **Art. 17 (7) DSMD**, which contains provisions for the protection of user rights.

#### a) Origin of sub. 1

4 Large parts of § 12 were proposed for the first time in the draft of the UrhDaG in a form similar or identical to the current version. However, corresponding approaches were already partly found in the previous drafts. A statutory claim to remuneration was provided for therein for **minor uses.**[5] For content flagged as authorised by the user, however, such a claim was only to exist if the **marking subsequently turned out to be incorrect.**[6] While sub. 1 initially only provided for the assertion of the statutory right to remuneration by collecting societies, the requirements for its enforcement were further specified by the corresponding application of § 5 (2) sent. 2–4, now regulated in sub. 1 sent. 2 as a result of the corresponding resolution recommendation of the Committee on Legal Affairs in the Bundestag.[7]

#### b) Origin of sub. 2 and sub. 3

5 The exemption of the OCSSP from copyright liability, which is now found in sub. 2, was already partially regulated in the previous drafts. According to § 16 (1) DiskE or § 16 (1) sent. 1 RefE, the OCSSP should not be responsible for the communication to the public of content that users had marked as permissible if the marking was not obviously incorrect. The **privilege** should apply either until the end of the complaint procedure or until the expiry of the one-week decision period on the complaint.[8] However, the privileging of the OCSSP for the period after the decision on the complaint was only introduced as a result of the resolution recommendation of the

---

[1] BT-Drs. 19/27426, 142.

[2] BT-Drs. 19/27426, 142.

[3] BT-Drs. 19/27426, 142; with criticism for the liability privilege for users, see however, Hofmann GRUR 2021, 895 (903); Hofmann NJW 2021, 1905 (1909); Metzger/Pravemann ZUM 2021, 288 (295).

[4] At least in sub. 3; BT-Drs. 19/27426, 142.

[5] § 7 (2) DiskE/RefE.

[6] § 16 (2) RefE.

[7] BT-Drs. 19/29894, 93.

[8] § 16 sent. 2 DiskE/§ 16 (1) sent. 2 RefE.

Committee on Legal Affairs in the Bundestag.[9] It was a reaction to the criticism by various experts of the OCSSP's liability in this phase, which was considered too strict:[10] Without this addition, its liability under § 1 (2) sent. 1 would have been independent of how carefully it examined the legal situation in the complaint procedure. For example, without the provision of § 1 (2) sent 2, if the OCSSP decided after a thorough examination to continue to publicly communicate content because it viewed the use as covered by a copyright exception, it could still have been held liable in the subsequent court proceedings if the court took a different view.[11] This would have created a **substantial liability risk** for the OCSSP in the event of a wrong prognosis of the lawfulness of a use. Even an OCSSP that would have met all the requirements imposed on it by the legislature with regard to filtering obligations and complaint procedures would have been liable for damages to the rightholder if the **prognosis decision** to be made by it on the lawfulness of content had ultimately been viewed differently by a court, that is, an act of use considered lawful by the OCSSP had ultimately been qualified as unlawful by the court –possibly through the chain of instances years later. Due to the possibility of a triple damage calculation, this liability risk would have been considerably higher than the risk of liability towards the user in the event that the OCSSP had initially blocked content and a court had ultimately come to the conclusion that this content was lawful. Therefore, there would have been an incentive for **strategic over blocking.**[12] A provision on the **exemption of users from liability**, which is now found in sub. 3, was not yet envisaged in the draft legislation.

## 4. Criticism

The obligation to pay remuneration for presumably statutorily permitted uses 6
in sub. 1 is to be rejected, as is the obligation to pay remuneration for (actually) statutorily permitted uses according to § 5 (2) (→ § 5 mn. 7). The legislature risks a dam burst here. Caricatures and parodies, like quotations (for which there is no longer a remuneration obligation under § 5 (2) UrhDaG – in contrast to what was still envisaged in the draft bill), are created through the exercise of powers protected under (EU) fundamental law and should remain **free of remuneration** due to the very considerable importance of these fundamental communication rights for the opinion-forming process. Any remuneration inhibits the exercise of these fundamental rights. In particular, if the **freedom of parody** on platforms is made subject to remuneration, claims will quickly be voiced to require remuneration from other intermediaries in the offline area as well (press, film, broadcasting) – with incalculable risks for the freedom of the press, art and opinion. In addition, exceptions provisions are made subject to remuneration, particularly if they impair the exploitation of a work on the primary market. This is not to be feared from caricatures, parodies and quotations, and, therefore, a remuneration obligation is not justified either. In any case, parodies and quotations should also continue to be remuneration free in the case of micro uses.[13] For a micro use by way of quotations, at least an alignment of sub. 1 with the principle of non-compensation under § 5 is to be carried out.

---

[9] BT-Drs. 19/29894, 93 et seq.

[10] BT-Drs. 19/29894, 93 et seq.

[11] Conrad/Nolte ZUM 2021, 111 (122).

[12] Specht-Riemenschneider, Stellungnahme zum Urheberrechtsdiensteanbietergesetz (UrhDaG), 27 et seq.; now also BT-Drs. 19/29894, 93.

[13] Cf.: Positionspapier der Urheberrechtswissenschaft: Zitate und Parodien müssen vergütungsfrei bleiben!

### 5. Systematics

7 § 12 **supplements** the provisions of **§§ 9–11** by stipulating certain legal consequences – remuneration right, liability privilege – of their application. By referring to § 5 (2) sent. 2–4, sub. 1 sent. 2 creates a parallelism for the claim to remuneration with the regulation of statutory remuneration for (actually) statutorily permitted uses. Sub. 2 is a ***lex specialis* to § 1 (2) sent. 1** (→ mn. 1), which supersedes the general provisions for the copyright liability of OCSSPs in its scope of application. It must also be regarded in the context of the regulation of the complaint procedure in **§ 14**, as the application of the liability privilege is closely connected to the OCSSP's compliance with its requirements for the procedure in terms of timing and design.

## II. Statutory remuneration obligation (sub. 1)

### 1. Scope of application

8 § 12 is only applicable to **automated blocking procedures.**[14]

### 2. Prerequisite

9 The obligation to pay remuneration is triggered when an OCSSP communicates to the public a **use that is presumably legitimate** in accordance with §§ 9–11. The concept of communication to the public is based on Art. 3 (1) of the InfoSoc Directive since the UrhDaG is not based on an independent right of communication to the public (→ Introduction mn. 7, 12).[15]

### 3. Capacity to sue

10 According to the wording of sub. 1 sent. 1, only **authors are entitled** to remuneration. However, the **holders of related rights** also have capacity to sue. This follows from the fact that § 21 orders the application of the (entire) UrhDaG to related rights and their owners. Although the explanatory memorandum to the UrhDaG does not expressly state that the right to remuneration under sub. 1 is also available to the owners of related rights, it is not evident why § 21, which according to its wording, meaning and purpose aims at a comprehensive equality of the holders of related rights with the authors, should not also refer to the right to remuneration pursuant to sub. 1. In any case, this applies *de lege lata.* However, § 21 extends the scope of application of the UrhDaG to all related rights, contrary to the wording of Art. 17 (1) subpara. 2 DSMD. This is contrary to the Directive and, therefore, must be corrected (but also → § 21 mn. 2). The extension of the scope of application is to be limited to the rightholders mentioned in Art. 3 (1) and (2) of the InfoSoc Directive.[16]

### 4. Capacity to be sued

11 The party obliged to satisfy the claim is the **OCSSP** that makes the communication to the public. The user who uploaded the content in question, however, is not capable of being sued. This is to take account of the fact that it is primarily the OCSSP that

[14] BT-Drs. 19/27426, 47.

[15] See: 'Anmerkungen von Louise Specht-Riemenschneider' on CJEU GRUR 2021, 1054 et seqq. – YouTube and Cyando.

[16] Specht-Riemenschneider, Stellungnahme zum Urheberrechtsdiensteanbietergesetz (UrhDaG), 29 et seq.

economically benefits from the presumably legitimate use, which secures for the OCSSP the attention of the public.[17] However, the **user** will often be an **'indirect debtor'**,[18] since the service provider will presumably pass on to this user the remuneration that he has to pay to the rightholder. The CJEU has classified this practice as permissible with regard to statutory remuneration rights in the field of copyright exceptions.[19]

### 5. Extent of the claim

According to the wording of sub. 1 sent. 1, the remuneration must be **reasonable.** **12**
The extent of the claim that meets this requirement can be determined in the same way as for the claim to reasonable remuneration for statutorily permitted uses under § 5 (2) sent. 1 (→ § 5 mn. 8). After all, the statutory obligation to pay remuneration under sub. 1 sent. 1 is justified by the same considerations (→ mn. 1). The extent of the remuneration shall thereafter be based on the **fictitious market price**. This can be determined in a two-step procedure: First, the hypothetical licence fee for a single licencing can be determined, and second, the fee can then be increased or decreased in proportion to the extent of actual use. If a work is strongly alienated or only small excerpts from it are used, the remuneration may subsequently be lower than the licence fee. If extracts with a particularly high recognition value are used or extracts that attract particular attention (e.g., the chorus of a song), the remuneration may be higher.[20] It is **not** possible, however, to apply a **flat rate** for the calculation or to take a representative sample of users as a basis.[21] The draft bill still referred to this simplification, which § 60h (3) sent. 1 UrhG provides for uses within the scope of certain copyright exceptions.[22] However, the reference is now no longer included in the wording of the law. The practicability of the now proposed calculation method remains to be seen.[23]

### 6. Collecting society obligation

The rightholder cannot assert the claim for remuneration against the OCSSP itself. **13**
The assertion of the claim is **reserved for the respective collecting society** pursuant to sub. 1 sent. 2 in conjunction with § 5 (2) sent. 3. If the author has granted a right to his or her work to a publisher, this must be a joint collecting society of authors and publishers (cf. sub. 2 in conjunction with § 5 (2) sent. 4 in conjunction with § 63a (2) sent. 2 UrhG; for details on publisher participation, see → mn. 16).

### 7. Non-waivability of the claim

The rightholder may **not waive** his or her statutory claim to remuneration pursuant **14**
to sub. 1 sent. 2 in conjunction with § 5 (2) sent. 2. This applies both to the period before the claim arose and afterwards. If the legislature had wanted to allow a waiver after the arising of the claim, it would have excluded the waiver of the claim only 'in advance' This is the case, for example, in § 63a (1) sent. 1 UrhG for certain statutory claims to remuneration under the UrhG, which the holder may, therefore, waive after the claim has arisen. From the fact that § 5 (2) sent. 2 deviates from this and only

---

[17] BT-Drs. 19/27426, 142.

[18] Conrad/Nolte ZUM 2021, 111 (115).

[19] CJEU C-462/09, ECLI:EU:C:2011:397 mn. 29 – Stichting/Opus; CJEU Joined Cases C-457/11 to C-460/11, ECLI:EU:C:2013:426 mn. 77 et seq. – VG Wort/Kyocera and Others.

[20] BT-Drs. 19/27426, 136; on the calculation under § 5(2) → § 5 mn. 8.

[21] With criticism: Conrad/Nolte ZUM 2021, 111 (116).

[22] §§ 7 (2) sent. 2, 16 (2) sent. 2 RefE.

[23] With criticism: Spindler WRP 2021, 1111 (1118).

restricts the assignability of the claim in advance of the arising of the claim and that there is no such restriction on waivability, it follows by implication that waivability is to be excluded at any time. This interpretation is also taken into account by § 22, which provides that the provisions of this Act cannot be deviated from by contract. This also precludes the contractual agreement of a waiver of a claim.

### 8. Assignability of the claim

15 Rightholders may only assign their statutory claims to remuneration **in advance to a collecting society** (sub. 1 sent. 2 in conjunction with § 5 (2) sent. 2). In the period after the claim arises, the claim can be assigned without restriction.[24] § 22, according to which the provisions of the UrhDaG cannot be deviated from by contract, does not prevent this because an assignment does not constitute such a deviation from the statutory provisions. Statutory claims to remuneration are, in principle, assignable without restriction.[25] If something else is to apply, the legislature must provide for this. This is not the case for the present claim.

### 9. Publisher's share

16 Authors may or must share the income to which they are entitled under the remuneration claim pursuant to sub. 1 sent. 1 with their publishers. If the author has **granted the publisher a right to his or her work**, it follows from the reference in sub. 1 sent. 2 to § 5 (2) sent. 4 in conjunction with § 63a (2) sent. 1 UrhG that he or she must give the publisher a reasonable share in the revenue generated within the scope of the remuneration right under sub. 1 sent. 1. The publisher is thereafter entitled to a statutory participation claim that it can bring into the collecting society.[26] The reference in sub. 1 sent. 2 to § 5 (2) sent. 4 in conjunction with § 27a (1) VGG also means that authors can subsequently – meaning after the publication of his or her work or its registration with a collecting society – agree with the latter that his or her publisher shall have a share in the revenue from the statutory remuneration claim.[27] While § 63a (2) UrhG comes into play if a (not necessarily exclusive) right to use has been granted, § 27a VGG becomes relevant if such a right has not been granted.[28] The collecting society determines the amount of the publisher's share (sub. 1 sent. 2 in conjunction with§ 5 (2) sent. 4 in conjunction with § 27a (2) VGG). If the collecting society does not determine a different distribution, the author is entitled to at least two-thirds of the revenue pursuant to § 27b VGG.[29] Even if this provision is not expressly referred to in the UrhDaG, the legislature considers it to be applicable to the remuneration right under sub. 1 sent. 1 because § 27b VGG, in turn, expressly refers to § 63a (2) UrhG and § 27a VGG.[30] In detail on the publisher's share in statutory remuneration rights.[31]

---

[24] Left open in Conrad/Nolte ZUM 2021, 111 (116) fn. 58; see, however: Spindler WRP 2021, 1111 (1118).

[25] Cf. Dreier/Schulze/Raue VGG§ 29 mn. 23.

[26] Cf. Dreier/Schulze/Raue VGG § 27 mn. 21 et seqq.

[27] Cf. Dreier/Schulze/Raue VGG § 27a mn. 7.

[28] Hofmann GRUR 2021, 895 (899); Dreier/Schulze/Raue VGG § 27a mn. 2.

[29] Cf. Dreier/Schulze/Raue VGG § 27b mn. 3.

[30] BT-Drs. 19/29894, 93.

[31] Cf. Dreier/Schulze/Schulze UrhG § 63a mn. 15 et seqq.; Dreier/Schulze/Raue VGG § 27 mn. 21 et seqq.

### 10. Relationship to other remuneration obligations

The relationship of the remuneration right under sub. 1 to other statutory remuneration rights of the rightholder is left open.[32] This concerns not only the relationship to the claim under § 5 (2) but also to the copyright exception provisions subject to remuneration under the UrhG. With regard to the obligation to pay remuneration for incorrectly flagged uses, which was still envisaged in the draft bill, the explanatory memorandum to the bill provided that **no additional remuneration claim** should arise if remuneration was already payable due to a copyright exception provision.[33] A corresponding restriction is missing in the explanatory memorandum to the UrhDaG. However, from a teleological point of view, it must also apply to the obligation to pay remuneration under sub. 1. This obligation is ultimately intended to ensure that the rightholder receives an appropriate remuneration for the use of his or her works. However, this is already ensured if the rightholder has (any) legal claim to remuneration. Granting the rightholder several claims would not remunerate him appropriately but unduly favour him. **17**

## III. Liability of the OCSSP (sub. 2)

### 1. Legal nature

Sub. 2 provides that the OCSSP is not liable under copyright law for the communication to the public of a presumably legitimate use or is liable only under certain circumstances. Dogmatically, the provision represents a **liability privilege** according to the legislature's intention.[34] **18**

### 2. Prerequisite for and scope of the privilege

The liability privilege applies as soon as an OCSSP communicates to the public a presumably legitimate use under §§ 9–11. If the rightholder does not lodge a complaint under § 14 against this, the OCSSP may invoke sub. 2 sent. 1 for the entire **duration of the communication to the public**. However, there is no time limit for lodging a complaint under § 14, so that it can be lodged at any time. If the rightholder lodges a complaint, the service provider may only unrestrictedly rely on the privilege for the duration of the complaint procedure, and for a maximum period of **one week from the lodging of this complaint** (cf. § 14 (3) No. 3). If the OCSSP does not decide on the complaint, it is liable according to the general rules, that is, under the conditions of § 1 (2) No. 1 (→ § 1 mn. 11 et seqq., 18 et seqq.). If the OCSSP has decided on the complaint within this period, the liability privilege pursuant to sub. 2 sent. 2 continues to apply in principle, unless the OCSSP has, first, breached its obligations under § 14 in carrying out the complaint procedure and, second, is at fault with regard to this. However, according to sub. 2 sent. 2, the OCSSP is only protected from a claim for damages by the rightholder pursuant to § 97 (2) UrhG. Claims for injunctive relief and removal under § 97 (1) UrhG remain unaffected by the privilege and can therefore still be asserted. This essentially corresponds to the principles of today's *Störerhaftung* (breach of duty of care).[35] **19**

---

[32] Conrad/Nolte ZUM 2021, 111 (116) fn. 58.
[33] BT-Drs. 19/27426, 154.
[34] BT-Drs. 19/27426, 139.
[35] Cf. Dreier/Schulze UrhG § 97 mn. 28 et seqq.

## IV. Liability of the user (sub. 3)

### 1. Legal nature

20 Sub. 3 provides that the user is not liable under copyright law for the communication to the public of certain presumably legitimate uses until the conclusion of the complaint procedure. Like sub. 2, sub. 3 also contains a **liability privilege**. This follows from the identical wording of the two provisions and their close systematic connection.

### 2. Prerequisite for the privilege

21 The liability privilege is only applicable if a presumably legitimate **minor use within the meaning of § 10** is concerned. For uses that are presumably legitimate because the user has flagged them according to § 11, the user is liable according to the general provisions of §§ 97 et seqq. UrhG. Therefore, the user is exposed to a greater liability risk than the OCSSP, which can invoke its liability privilege under sub. 2 for these presumably legitimate uses too.[36]

### 3. Scope of the privilege

22 The liability privilege applies as soon as the user communicates to the public the presumably legitimate use as defined in Art. 3 (1) InfoSoc Directive. If the rightholder does not complain, the user can invoke the privilege for the **entire duration of the communication to the public**. If the rightholder lodges a complaint, this only applies to the user for the duration of the complaint procedure. Unlike for the OCSSP (→ mn. 19), however, the liability privilege does not cease for the user one week at the latest after filing the complaint. Even if a decision on the complaint is made only after the expiry of this period, the user can invoke sub. 3 until the time of the decision. Afterwards, the user is liable unrestrictedly according to §§ 97 et seqq. UrhG.

---

[36] Metzger/Pravemann ZUM 2021, 288 (295).

# Part 5
# Legal remedies

## § 13
## Remedies; protection against distortion; access to the courts

**(1) For users and rightholders, participation in complaint procedures under §§ 14 and 15 shall be voluntary.**

**(2) For users, rightholders and service providers, participation in out-of-court dispute resolution pursuant to §§ 16 and 17 shall be voluntary.**

**(3) [1]The protection of the author against distortion of his work under § 14 of the Copyright Act shall remain unaffected. [2]For this purpose, within the scope of application of §§ 9 to 11, the author may also demand simple blocking under § 8.**

**(4) The right to appeal to the courts shall remain unaffected.**

# Teil 5
# Rechtsbehelfe

## § 13
## Rechtsbehelfe; Schutz vor Entstellung; Zugang zu den Gerichten

**(1) Für Nutzer und Rechtsinhaber ist die Teilnahme an Beschwerdeverfahren nach den §§ 14 und 15 freiwillig.**

**(2) Für Nutzer, Rechtsinhaber und Diensteanbieter ist die Teilnahme an außergerichtlichen Streitbeilegungen nach den §§ 16 und 17 freiwillig.**

**(3) [1]Der Schutz des Urhebers vor Entstellung seines Werkes nach § 14 des Urheberrechtsgesetzes bleibt unberührt. [2]Der Urheber kann hierzu auch im Anwendungsbereich der §§ 9 bis 11 die einfache Blockierung nach § 8 verlangen.**

**(4) Das Recht, die Gerichte anzurufen, bleibt unberührt.**

**Bibliography:** Gerpott, 'Art. 17 der neuen EU-Urheberrechtslinie: Fluch oder Segen? – Einordnung des Streits um "Upload-Filter" auf Online-Sharing-Plattformen', MMR 2019, 420; Müller-Terpitz, 'Filter als Gefahr für die Meinungspluralität? – Verfassungsrechtliche Erwägungen zum Einsatz von Filtertechnologien', ZUM 2020, 365. – See also the bibliography in the Introduction.

**Content**



## I. General remarks

### 1. Objective

§ 13 provides an **overview** in subs 1–2 and 4 **of the remedies** that are available to the 1
various parties – users, rightholders, OCSSPs – in the event of a conflict.[1] It does not, however, contain detailed rules for their implementation, which can be found instead in the following §§ 14–17. The provision of sub. 3 refers to the moral right of the

[1] BT-Drs. 19/27426, 143.

rightholder, which is not affected by the provisions of §§ 9–11. The protection of the **integrity interest** in the context of the statutorily permitted uses is (of course) guaranteed.[2] Sub. 3 sent. 1 is merely of a clarifying nature in this respect since the protection of the author's moral right against distortions already results from § 14 UrhG (→ mn. 7). The possibility provided for in sub. 3 sent. 2 to simple blocking of content that infringes moral rights even in the case of its presumably legitimate use is merely intended to underline the importance of personality protection in the digital context.[3]

### 2. EU law requirements

2 Sub. 4 serves to implement **Art. 17 (9) subpara. 1, subpara. 2 DSMD.**[4] However, the legal remedies provided for therein were not envisaged from the beginning of the European legislative process.[5]

### 3. Systematics

3 § 13 should be read, in particular, in connection with the provisions on the complaint procedure, **§§ 14 and 15**, and the provisions on out-of-court dispute resolution, **§§ 16 and 17**.

## II. Appeal procedure (sub. 1)

4 Sub. 1 refers to the complaint procedure pursuant to §§ 14 and 15. It stipulates that **users and rightholders** are **not legally obliged** to participate in this procedure. However, such an obligation de facto exists for rightholders in certain constellations.[6] After all, according to § 12 (2) sent. 1, OCSSPs may invoke a liability privilege until the conclusion of the complaint procedure or the expiry of the decision period on the complaint with regard to presumably legitimate uses. After the decision on the complaint, the OCSSP is only liable for damages under copyright law if it has culpably breached the obligations under § 14 in carrying out the complaint procedure (→ § 12 mn. 19). Users are also exempt from liability under § 12 (3) until the complaint procedure has been completed if they make a minor use as defined in § 10 (→ § 12 mn. 21 et seq.). In these situations, if a rightholder wants to take action against the OCSSP or the user, he or she must first file a complaint in order for the privilege of liability to lapse. In contrast, the **OCSSP has a legal obligation** to carry out the complaint procedure. On the one hand, this follows from an *argumentum e contrario* from sub. 1, which prescribes voluntariness only for users and rightholders. On the other hand, it follows from the reverse of sub. 2, which also provides that the participation of OCSSPs in out-of-court dispute resolution procedures is voluntary. The OCSSP is therefore obliged to have an (internal or external) complaint procedure in place. If users or rightholders lodge a complaint, it is also mandatory for the OCSSP to decide on this.[7]

---

[2] BT-Drs. 19/27426, 42.

[3] BT-Drs. 19/29894, 94.

[4] See, however, BT-Drs. 19/27426, 143, which only mentions subpara. 1.

[5] For details on this process, see Specht-Riemenschneider, Leitlinien zur nationalen Umsetzung des Art. 17 DSM-RL aus Verbrauchersicht, 24 et seqq.

[6] Cf. BT-Drs. 19/27426, 152.

[7] BT-Drs. 19/27426, 143.

## III. Out-of-court dispute resolution (sub. 2)

With regard to the out-of-court dispute resolution procedures under §§ 16 and 17, sub. 2 provides for the **voluntariness of participation for all parties involved**. Neither users nor rightholders or OCSSPs are obliged to participate in such proceedings. However, it may be expedient for users and rightholders to conduct the procedure: If they request legal protection in court instead, this does not result in the (current) inadmissibility of their action but may trigger the **negative costs consequence under § 93 ZPO**. **5**

## IV. Judicial legal protection (sub. 4)

Pursuant to sub. 4, the possibility of recourse to the courts remains unaffected. The judicial remedy is not displaced or even impaired if a complaint procedure first conducted or an out-of-court settlement of the dispute was sought.[8] Conversely, going through one of the two procedures is also not a procedural prerequisite for subsequent court proceedings.[9] These legal remedies only **expand the possibilities for legal protection**. Judicial legal protection is open to **all parties**. For users, this results from the fact that Art. 17(9) subpara. 2 sent. 5 DSMD makes their access to court mandatory in order for them to be able to enforce the interference of a copyright exception provision. For reasons of equality of arms, this possibility must also exist in the same way for the rightholders who want to assert that a copyright exception does not apply or that the use is unlawful for other reasons.[10] Lastly, legal recourse must also be open to OCSSPs, especially against decisions in out-of-court dispute resolution proceedings. After all, according to the liability concept of the UrhDaG, they no longer have a purely intermediary position.[11] If they are now threatened with perpetrator liability if their users upload infringing content, they must also be able to create legal clarity by resorting to the courts. **6**

## V. Moral rights (sub. 3)

### 1. Distortion of the work

Sub. 3 sent. 1 is **foreign matter** in the system of § 13. It does not deal with the remedies available to the parties but focuses on substantive copyright law. The protection of the author against the distortion of his or her work under § 14 UrhG remains unaffected under sub. 3 sent. 1. Therefore, the statutory authorisation of use under § 5 does not include the power to distort the work used or otherwise impair it in a way that is likely to jeopardise the author's legitimate intellectual or personal interests in the work.[12] If the user uses the work in this way, the author may **prohibit** him or her from using it, irrespective of whether the user has otherwise been permitted to do so.[13] The **7**

---

[8] Cf. Müller-Terpitz ZUM 2020, 365 (373).

[9] Rauer/Bibi BB 2021, 1475 (1479).

[10] Cf. also Gerpott MMR 2019, 420 (425); Hofmann GRUR 2019, 1219 (1223); Leistner ZGE 2020, 123 (143).

[11] See, however: Leistner ZGE 2020, 123 (143).

[12] BT-Drs. 19/27426, 143.

[13] BT-Drs. 19/27426, 42.

provision is **purely declaratory in nature** since the prohibition of distortion always exists in principle even if users can invoke a copyright exception provision.[14] Beyond the wording of sub. 3 sent. 1, they must also take into account the other expressions of moral rights in **§§ 12 and 13 UrhG**.

### 2. Simple blocking

8 From the point of view of the legislature, sub. 3 sent. 2 is also only clarifying. According to this provision, in the case of distortion under § 14 UrhG, **simple blocking of a work under § 8 can be demanded** even in the case of a presumably legitimate use under §§ 9–11.[15] According to the wording, only the author falls within the personal scope of application of this provision. However, it follows from § 21 (1) that the **holder of a related right** may also make use of this mechanism, provided that protection under personality rights also exists for his or her subject matter.[16] Conversely, it follows from sub. 3 sent. 2 that the rightholder cannot demand qualified blocking under § 7 on the basis of the distortion of a work. It remains to be seen to what extent rightholders will make use of the possibility of simple blocking in order to prevent the communication to the public of a presumably legitimate use after all. A central role in preventing such circumvention of §§ 9–11 is likely to be played by § 18 (3) No. 2, which is intended to counter abusive blocking on grounds of moral rights.[17] The reason the legislature explicitly provides for the possibility of simple blocking only for the distortion of a work remains unclear. Other uses of a work that infringe moral rights must also continue to be blocked according to the general requirements of the notice and stay-down procedure.

## § 14
## Internal complaints procedure

**(1) The service provider shall make available to users and rightholders an effective, free of charge and expeditious complaints procedure on blocking and on communication to the public of protected works.**

**(2) Complaints shall be substantiated.**

**(3) The service provider shall be obliged to immediately:**

**1. communicate the complaint to all parties involved;**
**2. give all interested parties the opportunity to comment; and**
**3. decide on the complaint, at latest within one week after it has been lodged.**

**(4) If, after examination by a natural person, a trustworthy rightholder declares that the presumption under § 9 subsection 2 is to be rebutted and that the continued communication to the public substantially impairs the economic exploitation of the work, the**

## § 14
## Internes Beschwerdeverfahren

**(1) Der Diensteanbieter muss den Nutzern und den Rechtsinhabern ein wirksames, kostenfreies und zügiges Beschwerdeverfahren über die Blockierung und über die öffentliche Wiedergabe von geschützten Werken zur Verfügung stellen.**

**(2) Beschwerden sind zu begründen.**

**(3) Der Diensteanbieter ist verpflichtet, unverzüglich**

**1. die Beschwerde allen Beteiligten mitzuteilen,**
**2. allen Beteiligten Gelegenheit zur Stellungnahme zu geben und**
**3. über die Beschwerde zu entscheiden; spätestens innerhalb einer Woche nach deren Einlegung.**

**(4) Erklärt ein vertrauenswürdiger Rechtsinhaber nach Prüfung durch eine natürliche Person, dass die Vermutung nach § 9 Absatz 2 zu widerlegen ist und die fortdauernde öffentliche Wiedergabe die wirtschaftliche Verwertung des Werkes erheblich beeinträchtigt, so**

[14] Cf. Dreier/Schulze UrhG § 14 mn. 2)
[15] BT-Drs. 19/29894, 94.
[16] BT-Drs. 19/29894, 94.
[17] Spindler WRP 2021, 1111 (1116).

**service provider shall, in derogation of § 9 subsection 1, be obliged to immediately block until the complaint procedure has been concluded.**

**(5) Decisions on complaints must be taken by natural persons who are impartial.**

**ist der Diensteanbieter in Abweichung von § 9 Absatz 1 zur sofortigen Blockierung bis zum Abschluss des Beschwerdeverfahrens verpflichtet.**

**(5) Entscheidungen über Beschwerden müssen von natürlichen Personen getroffen werden, die unparteiisch sind.**

**Bibliography:** Bischoff/Brost, 'Internetpiraterie bei Sportübertragungen – Plädoyer für einen besseren Rechtsschutz der Sportveranstalter', MMR 2021, 303; Conrad/Nolte, 'Schrankenbestimmungen im Anwendungsbereich des UrhDaG', ZUM 2021, 111; Grisse, 'After the storm – examining the final version of Art. 17 of the new Directive (EU) 2019/790', 14 JIPLP (2019), 887; Holznagel, 'Verfassungsrechtliche Fragen der Umsetzung von Art. 17 DSM-RL', ZUM 2020, 1; Raue/Steinebach, 'Uploadfilter – Funktionsweisen, Einsatzmöglichkeiten und Parametrisierung', ZUM 2020, 355. – See also the bibliography in the Introduction.

**Content**



# I. General remarks

## 1. Objective

§ 14 gives users and rightholders access to an internal complaint procedure. This 1
also and especially contributes to the **protection of the rightholder**, since according to § 9 (1), the OCSSP is obliged in the case of a presumably legitimate use to first communicate to the public the content concerned. By way of the complaints procedure, the rightholder can rebut the presumption of legal permissibility under § 9 (2) and thus still achieve a blocking of the content.[1] The so-called **red button solution**[2] in

[1] BT-Drs. 19/27426, 47.

[2] Also called 'kill switch', see Metzger/Pravemann ZUM 2021, 288 (298).

sub. 4 also particularly serves to protect the rightholder. It gains significance for such presumably legitimate uses when the presumption under § 9 (2) would be easily rebutted in the case of a human review of the use, and it is intended to cover, in particular, the unlawful use of premium content which would significantly disrupt its exploitation on the primary market.[3] This is intended to counter abuse by users who falsely invoke statutory permission.[4] Analogous applicability is excluded due to the exceptional nature of the provision. To protect user rights at the same time, the red button solution is only established for trustworthy rightholders. This protection against abuse is flanked by § 18 (3) No. 1, according to which abusive rightholders are temporarily excluded from the red button procedure.[5] The design of the complaint procedure in sub. 2 and sub. 3 is intended to take into account the procedural principles of the **right to be heard** and **to a speedy decision**.[6] This is in line with the requirements of CJEU case law,[7] according to which the right to be heard is a central requirement for safeguarding users' fundamental rights.[8]

### 2. EU law requirements

2 The obligation to introduce an internal complaints procedure serves to implement **Art. 17 (9) subpara. 1, 2 DSMD**, which prescribe an effective and expeditious complaints procedure of OCSSPs.[9] In § 14, these requirements are **overreachingly implemented** insofar as Art. 17 (9) subpara. 1 DSMD only stipulates the obligation to provide a complaints procedure for users. There is no comparable provision for rightholders. The obligation to state reasons for complaints was also standardised in an overreaching manner. Art. 17 (9) subpara. 2 sent. 1 DSMD only provides that rightholders must give reasons for their complaints; there is no comparable requirement for users.

### 3. Origin

3 § 14 in its current version is **largely congruent** with its predecessor provisions. However, the predecessor provisions lacked the red button solution for trusted rightholders now provided for in sub. 4. The introduction of a category of '**trusted flaggers**' among rightholders, however, had already been proposed by the German government in its protocol declaration, which it made when the DSMD was adopted in order to make clear its aim of preventing upload filters as far as possible.[10] This idea was also welcomed in the literature[11] and was finally adopted for the first time in the RegE. On the parallel proposal to introduce a category of 'trusted users' → § 10 mn. 12.

---

[3] BT-Drs. 19/27426, 143.

[4] Hofmann GRUR 2019, 1219 (1228).

[5] BT-Drs. 19/27426, 144.

[6] BT-Drs. 19/27426, 143.

[7] CJEU C-314/12, ECLI:EU:C:2014:192 mn. 54 – UPC Telekabel/Constantin Film et al.

[8] Spindler CR 2020, 50 (58).

[9] BT-Drs. 19/27426, 143 et seq.

[10] Statement by Germany dated 15.4.2019, 2016/0280 (COD) 7986/19, ADD 1 REV 2, 5.

[11] Hofmann GRUR 2019, 1219 (1228); Leistner ZGE 2020, 123 (201, 204 et seq.); Leistner ZUM 2020, 505 (512); Raue/Steinebach ZUM 2020, 355 (363); Spindler CR 2020, 50 (55); Würtenberger/Freischem GRUR 2019, 1140 (1161).

## II. Establishment of a complaints procedure (sub. 1)

### 1. Obligation to establish

According to sub. 1, the OCSSP must compulsorily provide an internal complaints procedure that can be used by users and rightholders alike. Such procedures were in place on many platforms in the past.[12] Now, however, they are **mandatory for all OCSSPs**. There are no exceptions for start-up OCSSPs or small OCSSPs. Furthermore, an OCSSP is not exempt from its obligation to set up an internal complaints procedure if it has opened the possibility of going through an out-of-court dispute resolution procedure under §§ 16 and 17. These procedures independently coexist. 4

### 2. Scope of the procedure

Within the framework of the complaint procedure, it should be possible to deal with **all copyright issues** regarding the challenged use. In particular, it shall be possible to examine whether the use of uploaded content is covered by a licence or legal permission. However, the procedure should also serve to clarify general copyright issues, such as the protectability or term of protection of the work. It should also be possible to solve issues with moral rights within this framework.[13] 5

### 3. Design of the procedure

The complaints procedure must be **effective, free of charge and expeditious**. The effectiveness of the procedure requires **user-friendly** accessibility and delivery options for documents and legal titles within the country. It is conceivable, for example, that all communication should take place electronically through the mechanism provided by the OCSSP rather than by email or other external means.[14] After all, the mechanism can only achieve its objective of enabling users to exercise their rights in practice if access to it is made as easy as possible for them.[15] Free of charge means that the user must not be exposed to **any financial claims**. This includes contributions that serve solely to cover costs. The burdens of the complaint procedure must be borne by the OCSSP in order to remove further obstacles that could prevent the user from enforcing his or her rights.[16] In terms of time, Art. 17(9) subpara. 2 sent. 2 DSMD specifies that complaints must be processed **immediately**. In this context, the concept of immediacy must be autonomously interpreted under EU law and it is not possible to refer to previous case law – for example, on the blog entry procedure.[17] In the absence of concrete indications in the recitals, the principle of proportionality requires the consideration of the capacity of the respective OCSSP concerned. However, the procedure may take a maximum of one week. This time limit for the decision on the complaint is set by sub. 3 No. 3. 6

---

[12] Grisse 14 JIPLP (2019), 887 (898).

[13] BT-Drs. 19/27426, 143.

[14] COM(2021) 288 final, 25.

[15] Grisse 14 JIPLP (2019), 887 (899).

[16] Grisse 14 JIPLP (2019), 887 (898 et seq.).

[17] BGH GRUR 2012, 311 mn. 27 – Blog-Eintrag; OLG Köln ZUM-RD 2016, 249; LG Nürnberg-Fürth ZUM 2013, 70; cf. on this in detail and with further references: Dreier/Schulze/Specht-Riemenschneider KUG §§ 33–50 mn. 5i).

## III. Reasoning of complaints (sub. 2)

7 Both users and rightholders are obliged to give reasons for complaints they raise under the internal complaint procedure. As regards the content and scope of the reasoning, Art. 19(9) subpara. 2 sent. 1 DSMD provides that it must be given in an appropriate manner. Recital 70 DSMD requires due reasoning. However, the **degree of detail** required is not specified. However, on the one hand, it can be demanded that it be high enough that the rightholder and the work can be identified with legal certainty so that there are no misunderstandings. Information must be provided on the term of protection and it must be possible to hold the rightholder responsible in the event of an unjustified reference to his or her rightholder status.[18] In the context of the stakeholder dialogue, the Commission proposed with regard to the **wording** that rightholders, in particular, be encouraged to provide reasoning that is simple enough in terms of language and content to be comprehensible to the average internet user.[19] It is not sufficient if the rightholder merely reiterates the information he or she has already provided to the OCSSP in the context of his or her blocking request.[20] On the other hand, complainants must not be required to provide a level of detail that, in fact, prevents them from exercising their rights.[21] To make this possible, the OCSSP could, for example, provide forms with predefined answer options.[22]

## IV. Obligations of the OCSSP in the complaints procedure (sub. 3, sub. 5)

### 1. Notification (sub. 3 No. 1)

8 If a complaint is raised, the OCSSP must **immediately** inform all parties involved (→ mn. 6) according to sub. 3 No. 1. The duty to inform does not only refer to the **fact that a complaint has been made**. The OCSSP must also inform the parties involved about the **content** of the complaint. This follows from the wording of sub. 3 No. 1, according to which it is not the raising of the complaint that must be communicated but the complaint itself. Only in this way is the right to a fair hearing taken into account (→ mn. 1) because only knowledge of the content of the complaint enables the other party to take a position on it within the framework of the complaints procedure.

### 2. Enabling a statement (sub. 3 No. 2)

9 Pursuant to sub. 3 No. 2, the OCSSP must give all parties involved the opportunity to immediately make a statement (→ mn. 6) after the complaint has been raised. It is important that both parties are given the opportunity to make a statement as only on an informed basis can an appropriate decision be made by the OCSSP.[23] However, it is not

[18] Specht-Riemenschneider, Leitlinien zur nationalen Umsetzung des Art. 17 DSM-RL aus Verbrauchersicht, 87 et seq.

[19] Commission, Targeted consultation addressed to the participants to the stakeholder dialogue on Article 17 of the Directive on Copyright in the Digital Single Market, 17.

[20] See COM(2021) 288 final EN, 24.

[21] Specht-Riemenschneider, Leitlinien zur nationalen Umsetzung des Art. 17 DSM-RL aus Verbrauchersicht, 88.

[22] COM(2021) 288 final EN, 24 et seq.; Kaesling/Knapp MMR 2021, 11 (14).

[23] BeckOGK/Specht-Riemenschneider, 01.12.2023, BGB § 823 mn. 1519 et seqq.

a prerequisite that the parties involved actually (promptly) submit a statement.[24] The statement procedure can be **automated**,[25] since, according to sub. 5, the obligation to involve a natural person only exists for the decision on the complaint itself. Conversely, the upstream procedural steps do not require human involvement.

### 3. Decision (sub. 3 No. 3, sub. 5)

#### a) One-week period

Pursuant to sub. 3 No. 3, the OCSSP must make an **immediate** decision on a complaint **10** (→ mn. 6), but within **one week at the latest**.[26] This applies irrespective of the complexity of the decision.[27] The OCSSP is not released from the obligation to decide on the complaint if it exceeds the one-week deadline. According to § 12 (2) sent. 1, the consequence of the expiry of the time limit is only that the OCSSP's liability privilege for the communication of the content to the public under this section ceases to apply (→ § 12 mn. 19). An extension of the time limit by agreement of the parties is not possible. It is a matter of **mandatory law**. Otherwise, the OCSSP would be free to extend the duration of its liability privilege by party agreement. However, this specific duration is precisely an expression of the balance of interests undertaken by the legislature and thus not disposable.

#### b) Natural person

The decision on the complaint must be made by a natural person in accordance with **11** sub. 5. This precludes the use of automated systems for the complaint procedure. At this point, at the latest, a human being must check the use in question for the first time. The person must be **impartial** according to sub. 5. This must also and especially be ensured in relation to the OCSSP, as this is intended to counteract the latter's possible 'over-enforcement bias'.[28] Under § 15 (1) (→ § 15 mn. 1), the OCSSP can make use of an external complaints body to fulfil this obligation.

#### c) Requirements for the examination

§ 14 does not contain any requirements regarding the standard to be applied when **12** deciding on the **merits** of an appeal.[29] In part, it is proposed that the requirements for the issuance of a judicial interim injunction be taken as a basis.[30] Accordingly, both a substantive claim for an injunction and a ground for an injunction in the sense of urgency must be established (§§ 935, 940 ZPO). However, the additional requirement of such a ground for injunction is contrary to the objective of the standard, which is to contribute to the practical enforcement of user rights. After all, not every upload may be urgent so that the complaint of some users is likely to remain unsuccessful, even though they could invoke a statutory authorisation for the use. However, the **blog entry procedure** that was developed for infringements of personality rights[31] can provide

---

[24] So for the rightholders: COM(2021) 288 final EN, 24.

[25] Leistner ZGE 2020, 123 (208); Leistner ZUM 2020, 505 (512 et seq.).

[26] With criticism regarding the shortness of the time period: Conrad/Nolte ZUM 2021, 111 (121); Rauer/Bibi BB 2021, 1475 (1479); Frey MMR 2021, 671 (675); however, the criticism overlooks the fact that the obligations of the UrhDaG only apply to service providers who can be expected to fulfil them within one week, see § 2 UrhDaG.

[27] See, however: COM(2021) 288 final EN, 24.

[28] Kaesling/Knapp MMR 2021, 11 (14).

[29] Cf. Holznagel ZUM 2020, 1 (5).

[30] Conrad/Nolte ZUM 2021, 111 (122).

[31] For its (modified) adoption, see also Conrad/Nolte ZUM 2021, 111 (122); Leistner ZGE 2020, 123 (204 et seqq.); Leistner ZUM 2020, 505 (512); Schwartmann/Hentsch MMR 2020, 207 (211 et seq.); Spindler CR 2020, 50 (58); see also Dreier/Schulze/Specht-Riemenschneider UrhG § 97 mn. 28 et seqq.).

orientation. A similar approach was also proposed by the Commission in the context of the stakeholder dialogue.[32] Translated to copyright law, the procedure is as follows: Upon request of the user, the rightholder's claim to the content must be forwarded to the user for comment. If no statement is received within a reasonable time based on the circumstances, the content complained of must be deleted. On the other hand, if the user substantiates his or her claim to exceptions and limitations of copyright, the rightholder shall be required to submit a statement and, if necessary, evidence substantiating the alleged infringement. If the rightholder does not submit a statement or does not provide the required evidence, further examination is not required. If, however, the rightholder's statement or the evidence submitted shows an unlawful infringement of copyright law, the content complained of must be deleted. The BGH specified and supplemented these procedural requirements to the effect that the OCSSP's duty is not limited to requesting a short statement ('in two sentences') from the user. The OCSSP may also be required to obtain **further evidence** to substantiate the facts presented.[33] An orientation towards the similarly structured **cross-appeal procedure *(Gegenvorstellungsverfahren)* of the NetzDG** can also be considered, although the requirements can ultimately be conclusively determined only by the CJEU.

#### 4. Practical design

13 With the specifications for the design of the internal complaints procedure according to subs 3 and 5, the legislature has only made the core points of this procedure mandatory. In all other respects, the OCSSP has a **great deal of leeway** in designing its complaints procedure.[34]

## V. Red button solution (sub. 4)

### 1. Requirements

#### a) Trusted rightholder

14 The red button solution is only available to trustworthy rightholders. The assessment of trustworthiness is **not static**, but can vary from notification to notification.[35] In favour of the rightholder, reference can be made, for example, to the extent of its valuable repertoire deposited with the OCSSP, the associated deployment of particularly qualified personnel or the fact that the rightholder has successfully conducted a large number of complaint proceedings in the past.[36] In the practical application of these criteria, however, it must be borne in mind that the economic size of the rightholder must not automatically be taken as an indication of its trustworthiness.[37] For example, it can be taken into account to the disadvantage of the rightholder if the latter has already falsely marked a certain number of uploads as unlawful.[38] The assessment of trustworthiness is the **responsibility of the OCSSP**. The OCSSP can carry out this assessment automatically.[39] This follows from the fact that sub. 5 prescribes examination by a

---

[32] Commission, Targeted consultation addressed to the participants to the stakeholder dialogue on Article 17 of the Directive on Copyright in the Digital Single Market, 17.

[33] BGH GRUR 2016, 855 – www.jameda.de.

[34] BT-Drs. 19/27426, 143.

[35] Leistner ZGE 2020, 123 (201); Leistner ZUM 2020, 505 (512).

[36] BT-Drs. 19/27426, 144; see also Raue/Steinebach ZUM 2020, 355 (363).

[37] Metzger/Pravemann ZUM 2021, 288 (298).

[38] Leistner ZGE 2020, 123 (201); Leistner ZUM 2020, 505 (512).

[39] Critically, Metzger/Pravemann ZUM 2021, 288 (298 et seq.).

natural person only for the decision on the complaint. Therefore, all upstream procedural steps can be done without human intervention. Moreover, sub. 4 itself speaks for this, as it only requires the use of a natural person for the rightholder in the context of the red button solution. Per *argumentum e contrario* the same does not apply to the OCSSP. This does not leave the rightholder without protection, as the assessment of trustworthiness is fully open to **judicial review**.[40] It would have been desirable to define the requirements for a trustworthy rightholder by law in order to provide a uniform and reliable legal framework. The legislature has failed to do this.

#### b) Examination by a natural person

The rightholder must have verified the use for which he or she is making the complaint in advance by a natural person. Thus, he or she may not use an automated procedure to make the statement under sub. 3.[41] If the rightholder does use such a procedure to report what he or she considers to be unauthorised uses, the rightholder's classification as trustworthy *ex ante* is ruled out.[42] **15**

#### c) Statement of the rightholder

The rightholder must make a statement to the OCSSP on **two points**. First, he or she must declare that the **presumption** of lawful use under § 9 (2) **is to be rebutted** in the specific case. In doing so, he or she only has to state that there is actually no legal authorisation for the use in question. More detailed reasons for this assessment do not have to be given by the rightholder. According to sub. 2, such reasoning is only mandatory in the context of the complaints procedure (→ mn. 7). Second, the rightholder must declare that the continued communication to the public of the presumably legitimate use would **significantly impair the economic exploitation of his or her work**. An example of this is when a user cuts a recent cinema film in half, combines it with his or her own content and labels it as lawful content to meet the requirements of § 9 (1). According to § 9 (1), such content is to be made publicly available until the conclusion of the complaint procedure, but in the case described, it can significantly impair the exploitation of the film in the crucial first phase after release. If such an impairment exists, it is unreasonable to expect the rightholder to tolerate the public communication of the content until the decision on the complaint.[43] The situation would be similar, for example, in the case of the prior publication of a musical work or a summary of the highlights of a current sports event by users.[44] **16**

### 2. Legal consequence

If a trustworthy rightholder makes use of the red button in accordance with sub. 1, the OCSSP must **deviate from § 9 (1)** (→ § 9 mn. 6 et seq.) and **block** the challenged user content. The OCSSP may neither check the facts of the case nor involve the user concerned before doing so, nor may the OCSSP exercise discretion in deciding on the legal consequences.[45] The blocking must be **automated** and **immediately** carried out.[46] Only technical delays resulting from the use of automated procedures are harmless.[47] The blocking must be maintained until the conclusion of the complaint procedure. **17**

---

[40] BT-Drs. 19/27426, 144.
[41] With criticism: Bischoff/Brost MMR 2021, 303 (307).
[42] BT-Drs. 19/27426, 144.
[43] BT-Drs. 19/27426, 143.
[44] COM(2021) 288 final EN, 22.
[45] BT-Drs. 19/27426, 144.
[46] For a rapid *ex ante* human review in comparable cases: COM(2021) 288 final EN, 22.
[47] BT-Drs. 19/27426, 144.

## § 15
## External complaints body

**(1) The service provider may make use of a recognised external complaints body to fulfil its obligations under § 14.**

**(2) [1]The decision on the recognition of an external appeal body shall be taken by the Federal Office of Justice in agreement with the German Patent and Trademark Office. [2]In all other respects, the provisions of the Network Enforcement Act concerning the recognition of an institution of regulated self-regulation shall apply mutatis mutandis to the requirements and the procedure for recognition.**

## § 15
## Externe Beschwerdestelle

**(1) Der Diensteanbieter kann sich zur Erfüllung seiner Pflichten nach § 14 einer anerkannten externen Beschwerdestelle bedienen.**

**(2) [1]Die Entscheidung über die Anerkennung einer externen Beschwerdestelle trifft das Bundesamt für Justiz im Einvernehmen mit dem Deutschen Patent- und Markenamt. [2]Für die Voraussetzungen sowie für das Verfahren der Anerkennung gelten im Übrigen die Vorschriften des Netzwerkdurchsetzungsgesetzes über die Anerkennung einer Einrichtung der Regulierten Selbstregulierung entsprechend.**

**Bibliography:** FSM, 'Tätigkeitsbericht als Einrichtung der Regulierten Selbstregulierung nach dem Netzwerkdurchsetzungsgesetz', available at <https://www.fsm.de/files/2022/03/netzdg_taetigkeitsbericht_2020-2021.pdf> (last accessed 12.3.2024); Grisse, 'After the storm – examining the final version of Art. 17 of the new Directive (EU)' 2019/790, 14 JIPLP (2019), 887; Kaesling, 'Die EU-Urheberrechtsnovelle – der Untergang des Internets?', JZ 2019, 586. – See also the bibliography in the Introduction.

**Content**

# I. General remarks

## 1. Objective

§ 15 gives OCSSPs the option of transferring the complaints procedure that they are obliged to set up under § 14 (1) to an external complaints body.[1] A specialised complaints body has two advantages: First, the complaints body can become more professional and develop **specialist expertise.**[2] This can lead to a reduction in the costs of complaint decisions due to economies of scale and scope in the long term. In addition, the quality of appeal decisions may increase.[3] Second, the advantage of such an external body is that it is not integrated into the organisation of the OCSSP. The fear that the decisive persons in an internal complaints procedure might not be sufficiently independent[4] can thus be countered to a certain extent. Admittedly, external complaint bodies also work on behalf of the OCSSPs, so that complete neutrality cannot be expected.[5] However, their **independence** is at least greater than that of internal decision makers, especially if the external complaints body – as envisaged by the legislature[6] – acts for several OCSSPs at the same time. 1

## 2. EU law requirements

The introduction of the external complaints procedure has its legal basis in **Art. 17(9) subpara. 1 and 2 DSMD**. This article stipulates that Member States shall require OCSSPs to establish effective and expeditious complaints procedures for their users. However, the DSMD does not specify the body that is to handle these procedures. The possibility for service providers to outsource complaint procedures to external complaint bodies, in addition to carrying them out themselves, was established by the German legislature within the scope of its leeway in implementation. On the background to the complaints procedure under EU law → § 13 mn. 2. 2

## 3. Origin

§ 15 is one of the few sections of the UrhDaG that has **not undergone any changes in content** in the course of the legislative process. 3

## 4. Systematics

§ 15 itself does not contain any requirements for the execution of the complaints procedure before an external complaints body. However, the same requirements apply as for the complaints procedure before an internal complaints body. This follows from the fact that § 15 (1) **refers to the entire § 14**, that is, also to its statements on procedural organisation.[7] Also relevant are **§ 13 (1)**, according to which participation in a complaints procedure, even before an external complaints body, is voluntary for users and rightholders (→ § 13 mn. 4), and § **13 (4)**, according to which the option to 4

---

[1] BT-Drs. 19/27426, 47.
[2] BT-Drs. 19/27426, 144.
[3] Kaesling/Knapp MMR 2021, 11 (14).
[4] Kaesling JZ 2019, 586 (589); Kaesling/Knapp MMR 2021, 11 (14).
[5] Kaesling/Knapp MMR 2021, 11 (14).
[6] BT-Drs. 19/27426, 144.
[7] BT-Drs. 19/27426, 144.

participate in such a complaints procedure does not affect the possibility of seeking judicial redress (→ § 13 mn. 6).

## II. Complaints procedure (sub. 1)

### 1. Procedural design

5 The same guidelines apply to the process and the design of a procedure before an external complaints body as for the internal complaints procedure with the OCSSP (→ mn. 4). Therefore, the procedure must be **effective, free of charge and expeditious** (sub. 1 in conjunction with § 14 (1); → § 14 mn. 6). Both users and rightholders must **justify** their complaints to the external complaints body (sub. 1 in conjunction with § 14 (2); → § 14 mn. 7). After receiving a complaint, the external complaints body is obliged to **notify** all parties involved of the complaint to give them the opportunity to **comment** and then to **decide** within one week at the latest (sub. 1 in conjunction with § 14 (3); → § 14 mn. 8 et seqq.). It must always be ensured that the complaint is **impartially** decided by a **natural person** (sub. 1 in conjunction with § 14 (5); → § 14 mn. 11). There are no special features compared to the internal complaints procedure. In particular, the reference to the provisions of the NetzDG does not result in a different procedural design.

### 2. Red button solution

6 Even if an external complaints body is involved, the OCSSP itself must ensure that the so-called red button solution is implemented. Although § 15 (1) refers to the entire § 14, the obligation to immediately block content according to the red button solution cannot be covered by the reference, as it does not depend on whether an internal or external complaint procedure is implemented. In both cases, the OCSSP itself must ensure that it complies with its obligation under § 14 (4). The possibility of involving an external complaints body is not intended to relieve the OCSSP of this obligation. Therefore, § 15 (1) must according to its objective correctly refer only to § 14 (1)–(3) and (5). This is probably a drafting error on the part of the legislature. The declaration that there is content that must immediately be blocked under § 14 (4) must always be made to the OCSSP itself. If the declaration is made to the external complaints body, the external complaints body is obliged to pass on this declaration. This results from the contractual relationship existing between the OCSSP and the external complaints body, which obliges both parties to show mutual consideration of respective interests in accordance with § 241 (2) BGB. If the complaints body violates this obligation, it is liable pursuant to §§ 280 (1), 241 (2) BGB if the OCSSP for this reason fails to block content that should be blocked.

## III. Recognition of the complaints body (sub. 2)

### 1. Relevant provisions

7 For the procedure to recognise an institution as an external complaints body, the requirements of the NetzDG on the recognition of an institution of regulated self-regulation are to be applied *mutatis mutandis* in addition to the requirements of § 15 itself. The same applies to the requirements that an institution must fulfil to be recognised as an external complaints body (sub. 2 sent. 2). The explanatory memor-

andum to the UrhDaG names § 3 (6)–(9) NetzDG as the relevant provisions.[8] In the meantime, after the reform of the NetzDG, the reference is to **§ 3 (6)–(11) of the NetzDG**, which replaced or respectively supplemented the aforementioned subsections. For more details, see → mn. 10 et seqq., 15 et seq., 17 et seqq.

### 2. Responsible body

The decision on whether an institution is recognised as an external complaints body pursuant to § 15 falls within the **competence** of the Federal Office of Justice pursuant to sub. 2 sent. 1. **8**

### 3. Procedure

Pursuant to sub. 2 sent. 1, the Federal Office of Justice must act in agreement with the German Patent and Trademark Office (**DPMA**). Therefore, the DPMA must give its consent prior to the recognition. **9**

### 4. Recognition requirements

#### a) Cumulative

The requirements for the recognition of an institution as an external complaints body result from sub. 2 sent. 2 in conjunction with § 3 (6) NetzDG. The body must fulfil all the requirements mentioned therein (→ mn. 11 et seqq.) if it wishes to be recognised as an external complaints body.[9] These requirements are **exhaustive**. For example, no specific legal form is prescribed for the external complaints body.[10] **10**

#### b) Deciding persons

First of all, the institution must ensure that the persons deciding complaints act **independently** and have the necessary **expertise** (sub. 2 sent. 2 in conjunction with § 3 (6) No. 1 NetzDG). The requirement of independence is congruent with the requirement of impartiality according to sub. 1 in conjunction with § 14 (5). Thus, the decision makers may neither be employed by the OCSSP into which the complaint body is integrated nor be in close contact with this provider in any other way, for example, as a result of a regular appointment as a lawyer.[11] The decisive persons are competent if they have in-depth knowledge of copyright law. It is not necessary, however, that they be lawyers qualified to hold judicial office.[12] After all, this is not a mandatory requirement for acquiring the necessary expertise. It is also sufficient, for example, to have completed a degree in business law at a university of applied sciences with a corresponding focus. **11**

#### c) Equipment and decision-making period

According to sub. 2 sent. 2 in conjunction with § 3 (6) No. 2 NetzDG, the institution must be **properly equipped**. In addition, it must ensure that the decision on a complaint can be made **quickly**, namely **within seven days**. Accordingly, an institution is properly equipped if it is provided with financial and personnel resources to such an extent that it can meet this requirement as well as all other requirements contained in sub. 1 in conjunction with § 14 for the procedural design in the long term. **12**

---

[8] BT-Drs. 19/27426, 145.
[9] Cf. Liesching § 3 mn. 23.
[10] Cf. Spindler/Schmitz/Liesching NetzDG § 3 mn. 43.
[11] Cf. Spindler/Schmitz/Liesching NetzDG § 3 mn. 44.
[12] See, however: Spindler/Schmitz/Liesching NetzDG § 3 mn. 45.

#### d) Rules of procedure

13 The body must also have rules of procedure that regulate the **scope and conduct** for handling complaints (sub. 2 sent. 2 in conjunction with § 3 (6) No. 3 NetzDG). However, these are only minimum requirements for the rules of procedure, in the formulation of which the external complaints body has a great deal of leeway. The further requirements that § 3 (6) No. 3 NetzDG imposes on the rules of procedure (the submission obligations of social networks as well as the possibility of a review procedure similar to the cross-appeal procedure *(Gegenvorstellungsverfahren)* with regard to decisions of the complaints body) are specifically tailored to the decision on complaints under § 3 (1) NetzDG and cannot be transferred to the complaints under §§ 14 and 15.

#### e) Multiple providers

14 The external complaints body must ultimately be carried by several OCSSPs or institutions. Such institutions can be relevant industry associations or comparable associations.[13] The complaints body must also be open to the subsequent **accession of** further OCSSPs. Its responsible bodies are in charge of **ensuring that it is properly equipped** (sub. 2 sent. 2 in conjunction with § 3 (6) No. 4 NetzDG). This requirement is intended to ensure that no individual OCSSP can indirectly influence the decisions of the complaints body through its personnel and financial resources.[14] Against this background, however, it is to be expected that large OCSSPs will tend not to join external complaints bodies. Most of them already have internal complaints procedures in place[15] and, therefore, have no incentive to bear the additional costs of an external complaints body. However, joining may be attractive for smaller OCSSPs as the establishment of an internal complaints procedure could overburden them (economically).[16] In practice, the 'Freiwillige Selbstkontrolle Multimedia-Diensteanbieter' (FSM) – the first and to date only institution of regulated self-regulation recognised under the Network Enforcement Act – only received 23 cases for decision in its first year of operation.[17]

### 5. Right to recognition

#### a) Bound decision

15 An institution that fulfils the requirements for recognition as an external complaints body as defined in § 15 is entitled to recognition. The decision on this is ultimately a bound and not a discretionary decision, as the wording of § 3 (6) NetzDG makes clear: according to this, the body '**shall**' be recognised if the requirements according to this subsection are met.[18] The decision is made in the form of an administrative act.

#### b) Ancillary clauses

16 The administrative act of recognition can be subject to ancillary clauses pursuant to § 2 (1) in conjunction with § 3 (7) sent. 3 NetzDG. Specifically, according to § 36 (2) VwVfG, a **time limit**, a **condition**, a **reservation of revocation**, an **obligation** or a **reservation of obligations** can be considered. The time limit should not be less than five years (sub. 2 sent. 2 in conjunction with § 3 (7) sent. 4 NetzDG).

---

[13] Cf. Spindler/Schmitz/Liesching NetzDG § 3 mn. 52.

[14] Cf. Spindler/Schmitz/Liesching NetzDG § 3mn. 46.

[15] Grisse 14 JIPLP (2019), 887 (898).

[16] Metzger/Pravemann ZUM 2021, 288 (296); Rauer/Bibi BB 2021, 1475 (1479).

[17] FSM, Tätigkeitsbericht als Einrichtung der Regulierten Selbstregulierung nach dem Netzwerkdurchsetzungsgesetz, 3.

[18] Liesching § 3 mn. 24.

### 6. Legal situation after recognition

#### a) Obligations of the external complaints body

A recognised external complaints body is obliged to **inform** the Federal Office of Justice without delay of any changes that affect circumstances relevant for recognition or other information that it had communicated in the application for recognition (sub. 2 sent. 2 in conjunction with § 3 (8) NetzDG). This could be, for example, changes in the financial resources available, which could have an impact on the proper equipment of the complaints body (→ mn. 12). In addition, the external complaints body must prepare an **activity report** on the previous calendar year by 31 July of each year. It must publish this report on its own website as well as send it to the Federal Office of Justice (sub. 2 sent. 2 in conjunction with § 3 (9) NetzDG). For example, in its activity report for its first year, the 'Freiwillige Selbstkontrolle Multimedia-Diensteanbieter' (FSM) provided information on the course of its complaints procedure, the equipment of its review bodies and the volume of complaints.[19] **17**

#### b) Revocation of recognition

The Federal Office of Justice may **revoke** the recognition in whole or in part (cf. § 49 VwVfG) or attach **ancillary provisions** (cf. § 36 (1) VwVfG) if the conditions for the recognition of a body as an external complaints body subsequently cease to be fulfilled (sub. 2 sent. 2 in conjunction with § 3 (10) NetzDG). This is particularly relevant if it turns out that the persons in charge lack the necessary expertise and independence or that the required expeditious decision on the complaints is not guaranteed.[20] The principle of proportionality requires a step-by-step approach in such a case. First of all, the Federal Office of Justice must use ancillary provisions (e.g., an obligation) to try to ensure that the external complaints body again fulfils the requirements for recognition. Recognition can only be revoked if this does not lead to success within a reasonable timeframe or is futile from the outset.[21] If the prerequisites for recognition were not met from the beginning, a **withdrawal** of recognition under the general provision of § 48 VwVfG can be considered even without an explicit provision in the NetzDG.[22] **18**

#### c) Prohibition of cooperation

Pursuant to sub. 2 sent. 2 in conjunction with § 3 (11) NetzDG, the Federal Office of Justice has the power to prohibit an OCSSP from cooperating with an external complaints body for a **limited time**. This presupposes that it is to be expected that as a result of the involvement of this body, it is not guaranteed that the OCSSP will comply with its obligations under the UrhDaG. The purpose of this provision is to ensure that an effective complaints procedure is available even if an external complaints body is involved. Since the decision as to whether this is the case requires an evaluative prognosis on the factual side and a margin of discretion exists on the legal consequences side,[23] it is not yet foreseeable whether and, if so, in which constellations the Federal Office of Justice will make use of this far-reaching possibility. **19**

---

[19] FSM, Tätigkeitsbericht als Einrichtung der Regulierten Selbstregulierung nach dem Netzwerkdurchsetzungsgesetz, 3.

[20] BT-Drs. 18/13013, 22.

[21] Liesching § 3 mn. 25.

[22] Liesching § 3 mn. 25.

[23] Cf. Liesching § 3 mn. 26.

### 7. Legal protection

20 Administrative proceedings are available against decisions of the Federal Office of Justice (cf. § 40 (1) sent. 1 VwGO). The right to recognition as an external complaints body can be enforced by the institution that has applied for this recognition by means of an action for issuance of an administrative act pursuant to § 42 (1) Alt. 2 VwGO. Against the revocation of a recognition decision or the imposition of ancillary provisions, the external appeal body may appeal by means of an action for annulment pursuant to § 42 (1) Alt. 1 VwGO. The same applies to an OCSSP that is temporarily prohibited by the Federal Office of Justice from cooperating with an external complaints body.

## § 16
## Out-of-court dispute resolution by private arbitration bodies

**(1) For the out-of-court settlement of disputes concerning the blocking and communication to the public of a protected work by a service provider as well as concerning rights of access (§ 19), rightholders and users may appeal to an arbitration body organised under private law.**

**(2) The provisions of the Network Enforcement Act concerning arbitration bodies organised under private law shall apply subject to the proviso that the Federal Office of Justice as the competent authority shall take the decision on the recognition of an arbitration body organised under private law in agreement with the German Patent and Trademark Office.**

## § 16
## Außergerichtliche Streitbeilegung durch private Schlichtungsstellen

**(1) Zur außergerichtlichen Beilegung von Streitigkeiten über die Blockierung und öffentliche Wiedergabe eines geschützten Werkes durch einen Diensteanbieter sowie über Auskunftsrechte (§ 19) können Rechtsinhaber und Nutzer eine privatrechtlich organisierte Schlichtungsstelle anrufen.**

**(2) Die Vorschriften des Netzwerkdurchsetzungsgesetzes über privatrechtlich organisierte Schlichtungsstellen sind mit der Maßgabe anzuwenden, dass das Bundesamt für Justiz als zuständige Behörde die Entscheidung über die Anerkennung einer privatrechtlich organisierten Schlichtungsstelle im Einvernehmen mit dem Deutschen Patent- und Markenamt trifft.**

**Bibliography:** Grisse, 'After the storm – examining the final version of Art. 17 of the new Directive (EU)', 2019/79014 JIPLP (2019) 887; Kaesling, 'Die EU-Urheberrechtsnovelle – der Untergang des Internets?', JZ 2019, 586; Wagner, 'Haftung von Plattformen für Rechtsverletzungen (Teil 2)', GRUR 2020, 447. – See also the bibliography in the Introduction.

**Content**

# I. General remarks

## 1. Objective

Just like complaints procedures, out-of-court dispute resolution procedures can also contribute to **counteracting over blocking** by OCSSPs. After all, the risk of having to defend a blocking request in arbitration proceedings could already deter rightholders from demanding questionable blocking.[1] The use of an external arbitration body is particularly suitable for this purpose. If out-of-court dispute resolution was left to the OCSSP itself, the **neutrality** of the deciding persons might not be sufficiently ensured.[2] In contrast, an external arbitration body offers an increased certainty for an independent decision.[3] 1

## 2. EU law requirements

With § 16, the legislature implements **Art. 17(9) subpara. 1 and 2 DSMD.**[4] It stipulates that the Member States shall enable the out-of-court settlement of disputes within the framework of an effective and expeditious redress procedure. The implementation of this requirement took place in an overreaching manner in two respects. First, the DSMD prescribes the establishment of out-of-court dispute resolution procedures only for users. However, the German legislature also opens access to such procedures for rightholders. Second, the DSMD only requires such procedures to be set up for disputes about blocking. In sub. 1, however, they are also extended to disputes about the rights of access under § 19. This excessive implementation is permissible as the DSMD does not have a blocking effect in this respect. 2

## 3. Origin

Contrary to a proposal in the literature to resort to existing mechanisms of out-of-court dispute resolution in consumer matters,[5] the German legislature decided to regulate the out-of-court dispute resolution procedures in the UrhDaG itself. § 16 was introduced for this purpose, and it only underwent **minor changes** during the legislative process, some of which were purely linguistic. For example, the possibility of also 3

---

[1] Kaesling/Knapp MMR 2021, 11 (14); Leistner ZGE 2020, 123 (180).
[2] Kaesling JZ 2019, 586 (589).
[3] Kaesling/Knapp MMR 2021, 11 (14); Wagner GRUR 2020, 447 (455).
[4] BT-Drs. 19/27426, 145 only refers to Article 17 subpara. 2 sent. 3 DSMD.
[5] Schwartmann/Hentsch MMR 2020, 207 (212); for an orientation towards this model, see also Wagner GRUR 2020, 447 (454).

settling disputes over the rights of access pursuant to § 19 out of court was provided for the first time in the RefE. Moreover, sub. 2 initially referred specifically to the requirements for arbitration bodies organised under private law in § 3c NetzDG. This reference was replaced in the draft bill by a more general reference to the 'provisions of the Network Enforcement Act'.

### 4. Systematics

4 The out-of-court dispute resolution procedure **independently coexists with** the (internal or external) complaint procedure under **§§ 14 and 15**, which, as a potential upstream procedure, can have a relieving effect on the downstream arbitration bodies and, further downstream, on the courts.[6] However, the unsuccessful completion of a complaint procedure is not a prerequisite for recourse to an arbitration body (or the civil courts). Otherwise, the voluntariness of participation in the complaints procedure as stipulated in § 13 (1) would be partially undermined (→ § 13 mn. 4). Art. 17 (9) subpara. 2 DSMD, which prescribes the establishment of appeal and out-of-court redress procedures without establishing a hierarchy, also does not require otherwise. Rather, the effective legal protection of users required by the DSMD requires that the three means of legal protection – complaint, arbitration and court proceedings – can be used independently of each other. The specific requirements for out-of-court dispute resolution under § 16 are also closely related to the general provision for such dispute resolution procedures in **§ 13 (2)**, according to which participation is voluntary for OCSSPs, rightholders and users (→ § 13 mn. 5). **§ 13 (4)** is also relevant, according to which the possibility of out-of-court settlement of disputes has no influence on the option to have a court decision made on the subject (→ § 13 mn. 6). Accordingly, going through an arbitration procedure is not a prerequisite for litigation in court;[7] rather, the parties involved can also turn directly to the court. In theory, the court proceedings can also be conducted in parallel to the out-of-court arbitration proceedings. The need for legal protection for the former does not already cease to exist because arbitration proceedings are pending. This procedure is not equally effective for all parties due to the voluntariness of participation. In practice, however, this may not be very attractive due to the additional time and financial effort involved.

## II. Subject matter of the arbitration proceedings (sub. 1)

5 The arbitration body can be called upon in disputes concerning the **blocking** or the **communication to the public** of protected works by the OCSSP; that is, disputes that arise because the OCSSP either satisfies a rightholder's blocking request under §§ 7 and 8 or does not do so. In addition, the arbitration body can decide on disputes arising from the assertion of **rights of access** under § 19. It is unclear from the wording of the provision whether only the rights to information under § 19 (1) and (2) are to be covered or whether a dispute about the right to research data access under § 19 (3) can also be settled by the arbitration body. The latter is supported by the fact that the entirety of § 19 is referred to in sub. 1. However, access to the arbitration body under sub. 1 is only open to rightholders and users, not to the third parties who are holders of the research data access claim under § 19 (3). If they should be able to initiate arbitration procedures as well, it would be necessary to supplement the group of parties

---

[6] Metzger/Pravemann ZUM 2021, 288 (296).
[7] Rauer/Bibi BB 2021, 1475 (1479).

in sub. 1. This should definitely be done in order to ensure an uncomplicated, out-of-court dispute resolution procedure for research data access as well. Other copyright disputes not mentioned in the provision, such as the infringement of moral rights (cf. § 13 (3); → § 13 mn. 7 et seq.), cannot be settled before the arbitration body. Instead, courts must be seized upon for such matters (cf. § 13 (4); → § 13 mn. 6).

## III. Recognition of the arbitration body (sub. 2)

### 1. Relevant provisions

The recognition as an arbitration body pursuant to sub. 2 is in principle carried out according to the requirements of the NetzDG for the recognition of arbitration bodies organised under private law. These can be transferred structurally to out-of-court dispute resolution under the UrhDaG.[8] The requirements and the procedure for recognition can be found in **§ 3c NetzDG,** which, in turn, partly refers to the provisions on the recognition of external complaints bodies in § 3 NetzDG (→ § 15 mn. 7 et seqq.). The provisions of the NetzDG are slightly modified in sub. 2 with regard to the authorities involved in the recognition procedure. **6**

### 2. Responsible body

The Federal Office of Justice is **responsible** for recognising an institution as an arbitration body organised under private law (sub. 2). **7**

### 3. Procedure

The Federal Office of Justice must take the decision on recognition under sub. 2 in agreement with the **DPMA**. Therefore, the DPMA must have given its consent prior to the recognition. **8**

### 4. Recognition requirements

#### a) Cumulative

The requirements for the recognition of an institution as an arbitration body organised under private law can be found in sub. 2 in conjunction with § 3c (2) sent. 1 NetzDG. In contrast to § 15 (2) sent. 2, sub. 2 does not explicitly stipulate that not only the procedure for recognition but also the requirements for it are governed by the NetzDG. However, the reference in sub. 2 must be understood in such a way that the requirements are to be adopted from the NetzDG, too, because these requirements are neither regulated in § 16 nor elsewhere in the UrhDaG. Therefore, an institution that wishes to be recognised as an arbitration body within the meaning of § 16 must fulfil **all the requirements set out in § 3c (2) sent. 1 NetzDG.** There are no further requirements; the catalogue is **exhaustive**. Sub. 2 is thus a reference not only to the legal consequences but also to the conditions of § 3c (2) sent.1 NetzDG. **9**

#### b) Body organised under private law

The arbitration body must be organised under private law. This is further specified by sub. 2 in conjunction with § 3c (2) sent. 1 No. 1 NetzDG to the effect that the responsible body for the arbitration body must be a **legal entity** which has its **registered** **10**

---

[8] BT-Drs. 19/27426, 145.

**office** in a Member State of the EU or in a contracting state of the EEA to which the AVMSD applies. In addition, this legal entity must be established on a permanent basis and its financing must be secured. These requirements are intended to ensure that the arbitration body is accessible and viable in the long term.[9]

**c) Persons engaged**

11 With regard to the persons engaged in arbitration, it must also be ensured that they are **independent, impartial and competent** (sub. 2 in conjunction with § 3c (2) sent. 1 No. 2 NetzDG). The terms independence and impartiality are congruent. They presuppose that the persons have no material or personal dependency on the OCSSP or the users or rightholders involved, and that they are not subject to any instructions from them (also → § 15 mn. 11).[10] The requirement of competency is intended to ensure that the persons have the necessary copyright law expertise.[11] However, it is not necessary that they are fully qualified lawyers, as this is not a mandatory requirement for the acquisition of this expertise. For example, training in business law with a corresponding focus is also conceivable (also → § 15 mn. 11).

**d) Equipment and processing**

12 Pursuant to sub. 2 in conjunction with § 3c (2) sent. 1 No. 3 NetzDG, the arbitration body must also be **properly** equipped. It must also be guaranteed that it will **quickly** process the arbitration proceedings. The law does not contain more detailed time requirements for this; in particular, the arbitration procedure does not have to be completed within one week. On a systematic interpretation, this follows from the fact that this decision-making period is specified for the external complaints procedure according to § 15 (2) sent. 1 in conjunction with § 3 (6) No. 2 NetzDG, but there is no such requirement for the arbitration procedure. An arbitration body is properly equipped if it can guarantee a speedy processing of arbitration proceedings in the long term (also → § 15 mn. 12).

**e) Arbitration rules**

13 In addition, the arbitration body must maintain arbitration rules that must contain certain minimum regulations according to sub. 2 in conjunction with § 3c (2) sent. 1 No. 4 NetzDG. First of all, a regulation on the **jurisdiction** of the arbitration body is required. In addition, the arbitration rules must specify the details of the **arbitration procedure**, for example, the communication channels through which such a procedure can be initiated. The arbitration rules must enable a simple, inexpensive, non-binding and fair procedure for users, rightholders and OCSSPs (for more details on the procedural design, see → mn. 19 et seq.). If costs are incurred for participation in the procedure, these should also be stated in the conciliation rules so that the financial burden of the procedure is foreseeable in advance for the parties involved.[12] It remains to be seen how high this burden will turn out to be in practice. The operation of the NetzDG does not provide any clues in this respect because § 3c NetzDG only recently came into force.

**f) Information**

14 Finally, it must be ensured that the **public** is permanently informed about how the arbitration body can be accessed and over which disputes it has jurisdiction. In addition,

---

[9] Cf. BT-Drs. 19/18792, 48.
[10] Cf. BT-Drs. 19/18792, 48.
[11] Cf. BT-Drs. 19/18792, 48.
[12] Cf. BT-Drs. 19/18792, 49.

information must be provided on the course of the arbitration procedure, and the arbitration rules must be communicated (sub. 2 in conjunction with § 3c (2) sent. 1 No. 5 NetzDG). This can be done, for example, on the website of the arbitration body.[13] This information is of crucial importance in helping the arbitration procedure to be effective in practice as a mechanism for dispute resolution. If knowledge of how to access the arbitration body is easily accessible, this reduces the time users have to invest in appeals and thus helps to make it more attractive to them.[14]

## 5. Right to recognition

### a) Bound decision

If the requirements for recognition as an arbitration body within the meaning of § 16 are met, the applying institution is entitled to recognition. The decision on recognition is not a discretionary but a bound decision. This follows from the wording of § 3c (2) sent. 1 NetzDG, according to which the conciliation body **'shall' be recognised** if all requirements are met. The recognition decision is made by an administrative act. **15**

### b) Ancillary provisions

Pursuant to sub. 2 in conjunction with § 3c (2) sent. 2, § 3 (7) sent. 3 NetzDG, the administrative act of recognition can be subject to ancillary provisions. A **time limit**, a **condition**, a **reservation of revocation**, an obligation or a **reservation of obligations** are conceivable (§ 36 (2) VwVfG). In principle, the time limit can be of any length. The requirement under § 3 (7) sent. 4 NetzDG that the recognition of external complaint bodies should not be for less than five years is not transferred to the recognition of arbitration bodies organised under private law in § 3c (2) sent. 2 NetzDG. General administrative law does not contain any time limits either. However, they can arise in individual cases from the affected fundamental rights, particularly from the principle of proportionality. **16**

## 6. Legal situation after recognition

### a) Duties of the arbitration body

A recognised arbitration body organised under private law must immediately **inform** the Federal Office of Justice (cf. § 121 (1) sent. 1 BGB) if circumstances relevant to its recognition or other information it provided in its application for recognition change (sub. 2 in conjunction with § 3c (2) sent. 2, § 3 (8) of the NetzDG). Furthermore, by 31 July of each year, it must prepare an **activity report** on the previous calendar year, which it publishes on its website and sends to the Federal Office of Justice (sub. 2 in conjunction with § 3c (2) sent. 2, § 3 (9) NetzDG). Illustrative examples of this from the implementation of the NetzDG do not yet exist, as § 3c NetzDG only recently came into force. **17**

### b) Revocation of recognition

Once recognition as an arbitration body within the meaning of § 16 has been granted, the Federal Office of Justice may subsequently **revoke** it in whole or in part (cf. § 49 VwVfG) or **attach ancillary provisions** to it (cf. § 36 (1) VwVfG) if the conditions for its recognition are no longer fulfilled (sub. 2 in conjunction with § 3c (2) sent. 2, § 3 (10) NetzDG). The principle of proportionality requires a step-by-step approach in such **18**

---

[13] Cf. BT-Drs. 19/18792, 49.

[14] Kaesling/Knapp MMR 2021, 11 (14).

a case. First of all, the Federal Office of Justice must use ancillary provisions (e.g., an obligation) to try to ensure that the external complaints body again fulfils the requirements for recognition. Recognition can be revoked only if this does not lead to success within a reasonable timeframe or is futile from the outset. If the prerequisites for recognition were not met from the beginning, a **withdrawal** of recognition under the general provision of § 48 VwVfG can be considered even without an explicit provision in the NetzDG.

### 7. Legal protection

19 Administrative proceedings are available against decisions of the Federal Office of Justice (cf. § 40 (1) sent. 1 VwGO). The right to recognition as an arbitration body organised under private law can be enforced by the institution that has applied for this recognition by means of an action for issuance of an administrative act pursuant to § 42 (1) Alt. 2 VwGO. The external appeal body may appeal by means of an action for annulment pursuant to § 42 (1) Alt. 1 VwGO against the revocation of a recognition decision or the imposition of ancillary provisions.

## IV. Arbitration procedure

### 1. No orientation towards the NetzDG

20 The procedure according to which the arbitration body organised under private law can be invoked is – unlike the complaint procedure described in detail in § 14 – **not regulated in the UrhDaG itself**. The reference to the NetzDG in sub. 2 suggests at first glance that the procedure should be governed by § 3c (3) NetzDG.[15] According to this, the arbitration body can only be invoked if an internal cross-appeal procedure *(Gegenvorstellungsverfahren)* pursuant to the NetzDG has been completed beforehand or if an institution of regulated self-regulation has been invoked. The transfer of these requirements to arbitration proceedings under the UrhDaG is contradicted by the fact that the explanatory memorandum to the UrhDaG merely refers to the requirements of the NetzDG for the recognition of the arbitration body organised under private law.[16] On the other hand, its requirements for the procedure before this arbitration body are not mentioned. The application of the procedure regulated in § 3c (3) NetzDG is also not specified in Art. 17 (9) DSMD: According to this provision, it is not a prerequisite for resorting to the conciliation body that another internal procedure has already been completed.[17] If the German legislature had wanted to introduce such a requirement in § 16, there would at least have been an indication of this in the explanatory memorandum to the UrhDaG.

### 2. Leeway for design

21 In the absence of statutory provisions for the arbitration procedure, the arbitration bodies organised under private law have a great deal of leeway in designing one. However, in order for arbitration procedures to achieve their objective of enabling users to enforce their rights, they must be organised in such a way that **access to them is as**

[15] See Wandtke/Hauck ZUM 2020, 671 (679 et seq.).

[16] BT-Drs. 19/27426, 145.

[17] Specht-Riemenschneider, Leitlinien zur nationalen Umsetzung des Art. 17 DSM-RL aus Verbrauchersicht, 95.

**simple as possible.**[18] In particular, this can be achieved by the parties being able to communicate with the arbitration body in text form, for example, by e-mail, and not having to be present in person.[19] For the same reason, representation by a lawyer in the proceedings should not be prescribed.[20] The parties involved should also have the possibility to communicate with the arbitration body in German.[21] The arbitration procedure should also be free of charge[22] or at least so inexpensive that it does not have a deterring effect.[23]

## § 17
## Out-of-court dispute resolution by the public arbitration body

**(1) The Federal Office of Justice shall establish a public arbitration board in agreement with the German Patent and Trademark Office.**

**(2) [1]The public arbitration body shall only be competent if an arbitration body organised under private law within the meaning of § 16 is not available. [2]§ 16 subsection 1 shall apply mutatis mutandis.**

**(3) The provisions of the Network Enforcement Act on the public arbitration body shall apply mutatis mutandis.**

## § 17
## Außergerichtliche Streitbeilegung durch die behördliche Schlichtungsstelle

**(1) Das Bundesamt für Justiz richtet im Einvernehmen mit dem Deutschen Patent- und Markenamt eine behördliche Schlichtungsstelle ein.**

**(2) [1]Die behördliche Schlichtungsstelle ist nur zuständig, wenn eine privatrechtlich organisierte Schlichtungsstelle nach § 16 nicht zur Verfügung steht. [2]§ 16 Absatz 1 ist entsprechend anzuwenden.**

**(3) Die Vorschriften des Netzwerkdurchsetzungsgesetzes über die behördliche Schlichtungsstelle sind entsprechend anzuwenden.**

**Bibliography:** Grisse, 'After the storm – examining the final version of Art. 17 of the new Directive (EU)', 2019/79014 JIPLP (2019) 887; Kaesling, 'Die EU-Urheberrechtsnovelle – der Untergang des Internets?', JZ 2019, 586; Kaesling, 'Umsetzung der Plattformverantwortlichkeit in der EU: Nationale Rechtskulturen statt digitaler Binnenmarkt?', GRUR Newsletter 02/2020, 20; Wagner, 'Haftung von Plattformen für Rechtsverletzungen (Teil 2)', GRUR 2020, 447. – See also the bibliography in the Introduction.

**Content**



[18] COM(2021) 288 final, 25; cf. Grisse 14 JIPLP (2019), 887 (899).
[19] Cf. BT-Drs. 19/18792, 49.
[20] Cf. BT-Drs. 19/18792, 49.
[21] Cf. BT-Drs. 19/18792, 49.
[22] COM(2021) 288 final, 25.
[23] Cf. BT-Drs. 19/18792, 49.

## I. General remarks

### 1. Objective

1 The fact that disputes about a blocking request can first be resolved within the framework of an out-of-court dispute resolution mechanism can counteract over blocking by the OCSSP by discouraging rightholders at the outset from expressing unjustified blocking requests.[1] In this respect, an external arbitration board does not face the same concerns with regard to the independence of its decisions as a dispute resolution by the OCSSP itself.[2] This is particularly true for state arbitration bodies that offer a high guarantee of neutrality.[3]

### 2. EU law requirements

2 Together with § 16 (→ § 16 mn. 2), § 17 serves to implement Art. 17 (9) subpara. 1 and 2 DSMD. It provides that the Member States shall regulate the possibility of out-of-court dispute resolution in an effective and expeditious redress procedure. In Germany, the implementation of this provision of the Directive was overreaching in that not only users but also rightholders were given access to the arbitration procedure. Furthermore, the German legislature went beyond this by providing for arbitration procedures not only for resolving disputes about blocking but also for disputes about the rights of access under § 19.

### 3. Origin

3 Before the start of the legislative process, it was suggested in the literature to resort to existing mechanisms for alternative dispute resolution in consumer matters.[4] However, the German legislature decided to regulate out-of-court dispute resolution in the UrhDaG itself. § 17 was introduced with this aim, and **only slight modifications** were made in the legislative process, and these were mainly linguistic. A content-related modification was made by the addition of sub. 2 in the RefE: In it, reference was made for the first time to the provisions for dispute resolution by a private arbitration body in § 16.

### 4. Systematics

4 The official arbitration procedure is an independent procedure alongside the (internal or external) complaints procedure under §§ 14 and 15. The procedures are only interconnected insofar as the complaints procedure can precede the arbitration procedure and thus relieve the arbitration bodies and, at a later stage, the courts.[5] Nothing

[1] Kaesling/Knapp MMR 2021, 11 (14); Leistner ZGE 2020, 123 (180).
[2] Kaesling/Knapp MMR 2021, 11 (14); Wagner GRUR 2020, 447 (455); for more on the concerns, see Kaesling JZ 2019, 586 (589).
[3] Cf. Kaesling GRUR Newsletter 02/2020, 20 (21).
[4] Schwartmann/Hentsch MMR 2020, 207 (212); see also Wagner GRUR 2020, 447 (454).
[5] Metzger/Pravemann ZUM 2021, 288 (296).

else follows from the case law of the BGH, which obliges platform providers to meet certain procedural requirements before deleting hate speech in order to protect users' fundamental rights.[6] The DSMD does not provide for the priority of the complaints procedure or any other internal procedure of the OCSSP over the out-of-court arbitration procedure but requires – in the sense of effective legal protection of users – an equal coexistence of all existing remedies (→ § 16 mn. 4). Therefore, priority of the complaints procedure cannot be introduced at the national level with (national) fundamental rights arguments. On the contrary, this would reduce the protection of users' fundamental rights as they would be forced to participate in the complaints procedure, contrary to the express provision in § 13 (1) and could not immediately resort to an arbitration body (or a civil court). The provisions on the public arbitration procedure are closely related to those on the arbitration procedure at an arbitration body organised under private law in § 16, which are declared applicable *mutatis mutandis* by sub. 2 sent. 2. The general provisions on out-of-court dispute resolution in § 13 (2) must also be considered, according to which the rightholders, users and OCSSP do not have to participate therein (→ § 13 mn. 5). In addition, § 13 (4) is relevant, according to which the existence of or recourse to the arbitration procedure does not affect the possibility of seeking judicial redress (→ § 13 mn. 6). Therefore, the court can always be seized. For details on the relationship between the remedies, see → § 16 mn. 4.

## II. Subject matter of the arbitration proceedings (sub. 2 sent. 2)

Within the framework of the public arbitration procedure, decisions can be made on 5 the same disputes that can also be settled by arbitration proceedings before an arbitration body organised under private law. These are disputes about the blocking or the communication to the public of protected works by the OCSSP on the one hand and disputes about the rights of access under § 19 (1), (2) (sub. 2 sent. 2 in conjunction with § 16 (1)) on the other hand. However, access to the arbitration body is not open to the holders of the research data access claim under § 19 (3). They do not fall within the group of possible parties under § 16 (1) to which sub. 2 sent. 2 refers. However, *de lege ferenda*, they should definitely be included in this group because they also need an uncomplicated, out-of-court dispute resolution procedure for research data access. On all this, see also → § 16 mn. 5.

## III. Establishment of the arbitration body (sub. 1, sub. 3)

### 1. Relevant regulations

In addition to the requirements of sub. 1, the provisions of the NetzDG on the 6 official arbitration body, which sub. 3 declares to be applicable *mutatis mutandis*, are decisive for the establishment of the public arbitration body. This refers to **§ 3f NetzDG**, which regulates the establishment of such an arbitration board for disputes with video sharing platform services. This provision, in turn, refers in part to the requirements of § 3c NetzDG for arbitration bodies organised under private law (→ § 16 mn. 6 et seqq.).

---

[6] BGH GRUR-RS 2021, 23970 mn. 83 et seqq. – Facebook.

### 2. Responsible body

7 The public arbitration body is established by the Federal Office of Justice according to sub. 1. However, the Federal Office of Justice is not only in charge of its establishment but is **also the responsible body** for the public arbitration body.[7]

### 3. Procedure

8 The Federal Office of Justice must act in agreement with the **DPMA** in setting up the arbitration body (sub. 1). Therefore, it must first obtain the consent of the DPMA before setting up the arbitration body.

### 4. Requirements for the institution

9 The requirements for the design of the public arbitration body are largely identical to those for arbitration bodies organised under private law: It must be guaranteed that the persons involved in the arbitration act **independently, impartially and with expertise** (sub. 3 in conjunction with §§ 3f (2), 3c (2) sent. 1 No. 2 NetzDG; → § 16 mn. 11). In addition, it must be ensured that the arbitration body is **properly equipped** and that it **quickly** processes arbitration proceedings (sub. 3 in conjunction with §§ 3f (2), 3c (2) sent. 1 No. 3 NetzDG; → § 16 mn. 12). Furthermore, the arbitration body must maintain **arbitration rules** that meet certain minimum requirements (sub. 3 in conjunction with §§ 3f (2), 3c (2) sent. 1 No. 4 NetzDG; → § 16 mn. 13). If it charges fees for conducting the arbitration proceedings, these must be stated in the arbitration rules (sub. 3 in conjunction with § 3f (3) NetzDG; → mn. 14). Finally, the arbitration body must ensure that the public is **informed** about its accessibility and competence as well as the course of the arbitration proceedings (sub. 3 in conjunction with §§ 3f (2), 3c (2) sent. 1 No. 5 NetzDG; → § 16 mn. 14).

### 5. Legal situation after the establishment

10 Pursuant to sub. 3 in conjunction with §§ 3f (2), 3 (9) of the NetzDG (→ § 16 mn. 17), the public arbitration body is obliged to prepare an **activity report** on the previous calendar year by 31 July of each year and to publish it on its website. The obligation to additionally transmit the activity report to the Federal Office of Justice that exists in the wording due to the reference to § 3 (9) NetzDG is waived. There is no practical need for this as the Federal Office of Justice is the responsible body for the public arbitration body.

## IV. Jurisdiction of the arbitration body (sub. 2 sent. 1)

11 Pursuant to sub. 2 sent. 1, the public arbitration body only has jurisdiction for settling disputes if an **arbitration body organised under private law is not available**. This means that recourse to it is subsidiary to recourse to private arbitration bodies.[8] On the one hand, a private arbitration body is not available if the OCSSP does not participate in the arbitration procedure at such a body. On the other hand, this is the case if no recognised arbitration body organised under private law exists (cf. § 3f (1) sent. 3 NetzDG).

[7] BT-Drs. 19/27426, 47: 'an official arbitration board at the Federal Office of Justice' (the authors' translation of the German source text).

[8] Rauer/Bibi BB 2021, 1475 (1479); Wandtke/Hauck ZUM 2020, 671 (680).

## V. Arbitration procedure

### 1. No orientation towards the NetzDG

The **UrhDaG itself does not** contain requirements for the design of the arbitration procedure before the public arbitration body, nor can they be taken from the NetzDG. While it would be conceivable according to the wording of sub. 3 to transfer the provisions on the procedure before the public arbitration body pursuant to §§ 3f (2), 3 (3) NetzDG, this would not correspond to the legislative intent. For more details, see → § 16 mn. 20. **12**

### 2. Leeway for design

In the absence of statutory provisions for the arbitration procedure, the Federal Office of Justice has a great deal of leeway in designing it. The decisive factor is that the possibility for out-of-court dispute resolution before the arbitration body is designed in such a way that **access** by users to it is **as simple as possible**. Only then can it ultimately achieve its objective of enabling users to enforce their rights.[9] On the design options → § 16 mn. 21. **13**

### 3. Fees

Pursuant to sub. 3 in conjunction with § 3f (3) NetzDG, the public arbitration body may charge fees **for conducting** the arbitration proceedings. It must state these fees in its arbitration rules (→ mn. 9). This makes the costs of recourse calculable in advance for the parties involved. **14**

---

[9] COM(2021) 288 final, 25; cf. Grisse 14 JIPLP (2019), 887 (899).

# Part 6
# Final provisions

## § 18
## Measures against abuse

(1) If an alleged rightholder repeatedly requests the service provider to block another person's work as his own work or a work in the public domain, the service provider shall exclude the alleged rightholder from the procedures under §§ 7 and 8 for a reasonable period of time.

(2) If an alleged rightholder intentionally or negligently requests the service provider to block another person's work as his own work or a work in the public domain, he shall be obliged to compensate the service provider and the user concerned for the resulting damage.

(3) If a rightholder repeatedly and incorrectly requests
1. the immediate blocking of presumably legitimate uses during the complaint procedure under § 14 subsection 4; or
2. the simple blocking according to § 8 because of a distortion of his work (§ 14 Copyright Act),

he shall be excluded from the respective proceedings for an appropriate period of time.

(4) After an abusive blocking request with regard to public domain works or works anyone is permitted to use free of charge, the service provider shall ensure to the best of its ability and in accordance with § 1 subsection 2 that these works are not blocked again.

(5) If a user repeatedly and incorrectly flags a use as permitted, the service provider shall exclude the user from the possibility of flagging permitted uses for a reasonable period of time.

(6) If a service provider repeatedly and incorrectly blocks permitted uses, it may be subject to an injunction by a registered association [*eingetragener Verein*] that has the purpose of promoting the interests of users on a non-commercial and not merely temporary basis.

# Teil 6
# Schlussbestimmungen

## § 18
## Maßnahmen gegen Missbrauch

(1) Verlangt ein vermeintlicher Rechtsinhaber von dem Diensteanbieter wiederholt die Blockierung eines fremden Werkes als eigenes Werk oder eines gemeinfreien Werkes, so hat der Diensteanbieter den vermeintlichen Rechtsinhaber für einen angemessenen Zeitraum von den Verfahren nach den §§ 7 und 8 auszuschließen.

(2) Verlangt ein vermeintlicher Rechtsinhaber vorsätzlich oder fahrlässig von dem Diensteanbieter die Blockierung eines fremden Werkes als eigenes Werk oder eines gemeinfreien Werkes, so ist er dem Diensteanbieter und dem betroffenen Nutzer zum Ersatz des daraus entstehenden Schadens verpflichtet.

(3) Verlangt ein Rechtsinhaber wiederholt fälschlicherweise
1. die sofortige Blockierung mutmaßlich erlaubter Nutzungen während des Beschwerdeverfahrens nach § 14 Absatz 4 oder
2. die einfache Blockierung nach § 8 wegen einer Entstellung seines Werkes (§ 14 des Urheberrechtsgesetzes),

so ist er für einen angemessenen Zeitraum von dem jeweiligen Verfahren auszuschließen.

(4) Der Diensteanbieter hat nach einem missbräuchlichen Blockierverlangen im Hinblick auf gemeinfreie Werke oder solche, deren unentgeltliche Nutzung durch jedermann erlaubt ist, nach Maßgabe von § 1 Absatz 2 bestmöglich sicherzustellen, dass diese Werke nicht erneut blockiert werden.

(5) Kennzeichnet ein Nutzer eine Nutzung wiederholt fälschlicherweise als erlaubt, so hat der Diensteanbieter den Nutzer für einen angemessenen Zeitraum von der Möglichkeit zur Kennzeichnung erlaubter Nutzungen diese Werke nicht erneut blockiert werden.

(6) Blockiert der Diensteanbieter wiederholt fälschlicherweise erlaubte Nutzungen, so kann er von einem eingetragenen Verein, dessen Zweck auf die nicht gewerbsmäßige und nicht nur vorübergehende Förderung der Interessen von Nutzern gerichtet ist, auf Unterlassung in Anspruch genommen werden.

**Bibliography:** See the bibliography in the Introduction.

**Content**



# I. General remarks

## 1. Objective

1 The UrhDaG aims to balance the interests of rightholders, users and OCSSPs. It is based on an elaborate system of procedural checks and balances that relies to an inconsiderable extent on procedural rights not being abused.[1] Furthermore, the automated use of filtering software can multiply the effects of abuse and thus significantly increase the impairment of the concerned rights. For this reason, there were warnings about the dangers of overclaiming in the legislative process.[2] § 18 attempts to establish a counterbalance and provides sanctions against the abuse of rights of all stakeholders involved: Subs 1–3 address abusive behaviour by (alleged) **rightholders**. Subs 1 and 2

[1] See also Hofmann GRUR 2019, 1219 (1228).

[2] Becker ZUM 2019, 636 (640 et seq.); Spindler CR 2019, 277 (286); Hofmann GRUR 2019, 1219 (1228); Specht-Riemenschneider, Leitlinien zur nationalen Umsetzung des Art. 17 DSM-RL aus Verbrauchersicht, 2020, 79.

sanction the abuse of false copyright claims:[3] Anyone who repeatedly demands the blocking of public domain subject matter may no longer participate in the blocking mechanism of §§ 7 and 8 for an appropriate period of time and owes the OCSSP and user damages if this is intentionally or negligently done. The same applies to those who pass off rights of third-party rightholders as their own and demand their blocking. Both sanctions are important because copyright trolls could otherwise undermine trust in the copyright system largely without risk.[4] Calls to sanction overclaiming with fines[5] were not followed. Under sub. 3, rightholders are excluded from the blocking mechanism for a reasonable time if they repeatedly and incorrectly press the 'red button' for immediate blocking under § 14 (4) or request simple blocking for distortion of their work. However, § 18 does not contain any sanctions for rightholders who repeatedly demand the blocking of uses exempted by copyright exceptions. Subs 4 and 6 address **OCSSPs**. According to sub. 4, OCSSPs must prevent to the best of its abilities a usurpation of copyrights from causing the same content to be blocked again. According to sub. 6, a user association can claim injunctive relief from the OCSSP if the latter repeatedly and wrongly blocks authorised uses. The legislature has not taken up demands for a claim for damages by users against OCSSPs for unlawful blocking.[6] However, damages can be based on the contract between OCSSPs and users (§§ 280 et seqq. BGB). Sub. 5 sanctions the abuse of **users** through false flagging. Anyone who repeatedly and incorrectly flags content as permitted is to be excluded from this mechanism for a reasonable time.

### 2. Enforcement of the measures against abuse

2 The issue of who can ensure that OCSSPs actually impose the non-optional sanctions ('shall… exclude') is not regulated. Individual claims by affected users and rightholders are not apparent. However, user associations can indirectly enforce omitted sanctions **against usurping rightholders** with the help of the injunctive relief in sub. 6 (→ mn. 28). If OCSSPs fail to impose the sanctions required under sub. 5 **against abusive flagging of users**, they are in breach of their obligation under § 7 (1) (→ § 7 mn. 14) because they have not ensured with reasonable means that unlawful content is not communicated to the public. Such an OCSSP cannot invoke the exemption from liability under § 1 (2) if the flagging of the non-sanctioned user enabled the infringement.

### 3. Protection against unjustified sanctions

3 The question also arises as to how affected users and rightholders can take action against unjustified sanctions. If **users** are unjustifiably excluded from the flagging mechanism pursuant to sub. 5, the OCSSP violates its duties of protection (§ 241 (2) BGB) as well as its contractual obligations to make lawful content accessible.[7] The OCSSP, therefore, is contractually obliged to make the content accessible, to restore the status quo and to refrain from unlawful blocking in the future. As a rule, without a licensing agreement, there is no contractual obligation between the **rightholder** and the OCSSP, but there is a statutory obligation if the former requests the latter to block the

[3] BT-Drs. 19/27426, 43.

[4] Cf. Becker ZUM 2019, 636 (640 et seq.); Spindler GRUR 2020, 253 (260); Kaesling/Knapp MMR 2020, 816 (819).

[5] Specht-Riemenschneider, Leitlinien zur nationalen Umsetzung des Art. 17 DSM-RL aus Verbrauchersicht, 2020, 79.

[6] Kaesling/Knapp MMR 2021, 11 (15).

[7] Cf. BGH 29.7.2021 – III ZR 179/20, NJW 2021, 3179 mn. 27 – Hassrede (hate speech).

content (→ § 7 mn. 1). Therefore, the OCSSP violates its duty of protection arising from this obligation (§ 241 (2) BGB) if it wrongfully sanctions a rightholder. In both constellations, the sanctions of the OCSSPs are subject to **judicial review**.

### 4. Hearing of the person concerned

The measures under § 18 can have a significant impact on the **fundamental rights of those affected**. For rightholders, legal protection against copyright infringement is effectively reduced, and for users, the possibility to communicate on the platform is reduced. Therefore, the OCSSP must make reasonable efforts to clarify the facts, **give notice** to the persons concerned and give them the **opportunity to respond** prior to the imposition of a sanction.[8] 4

### 5. No conclusive regulation

Even though § 18 addresses the most important constellations of abuse already recognised in the legislative process, one does not need prophetic gifts to realise that the complex regulatory mechanism of the UrhDaG can and will be abused in other ways. Therefore, OCSSPs can take additional measures against abuse based on **their terms of service** and by taking that aspect into account in specifying specific measures of **best efforts to block infringing content**[9] – as long as that does not undermine the binding provisions of the UrhDaG. In doing so, they must be guided by the objective of ensuring that as far as possible no unlawful content is made accessible on the platform without blocking lawful uses.[10] Furthermore, § 18 does not displace **other sanctions under private law**, such as § 826 BGB[11], or claims under unfair competition law. 5

### 6. EU law requirements

Art. 17 DSMD does not provide for corresponding mechanisms to prevent abuse. However, the measures against OCSSPs (subs 4, 6) and rightholders (subs 1–3) can be based on Art. 17 (7), (9) subpara. 3 DSMD.[12] The measures against user abuse can be based on the general objective of Art. 17 DSMD to strengthen the enforcement of copyrights on platforms. 6

## II. Exclusion from the blocking procedure according to §§ 7, 8 (sub. 1)

### 1. Exclusion for a reasonable time

If an alleged rightholder repeatedly demands the blocking of non-existent or expired copyrights or copyrights of third parties (**false copyright claims**), the OCSSP shall exclude him or her from the blocking mechanism under §§ 7 and 8 for a reasonable time. Of course, this does not apply if the claimant has been authorised by the copyright owner to assert the rights. The OCSSP has no discretion as to whether to impose the sanction. It must ('shall') exclude the rightholder from the blocking procedure for a 7

[8] Cf. BGH 29.7.2021 – III ZR 179/20, NJW 2021, 3179 mn. 83 et seqq. – Hassrede (hate speech).
[9] Cf. CJEU C-401/19, ECLI:EU:C:2022:297 mn. 75 – Poland/Parliament and Council.
[10] Cf. CJEU C-401/19, ECLI:EU:C:2022:297 mn. 81 – Poland/Parliament and Council; CJEU C-314/12, ECLI:EU:C:2014:192 mn. 55 et seq. – UPC Telekabel Wien; Hofmann ZUM 2019, 617 (626).
[11] Spindler WRP 2021, 1245 mn. 24; cf. MüKoBGB/Wagner, 8th edn 2020, BGB § 826 mn. 247 et seq.
[12] See also Hofmann ZUM 2020, 665 (669).

reasonable time.[13] Neither the wording of the provision nor the explanatory memorandum to the UrhDaG provide guidance on the **length** of the reasonable period.[14] Therefore, the length of the exclusion is at the discretion of the OCSSP. The sanction must be **effective** and therefore suitable to deter alleged rightholders from making false claims. At the same time, the sanction must be **proportionate**. The OCSSP must take into account, among other things, how serious the infringement was (quality/quantity), whether the person concerned is a repeat offender and has already been excluded and any damage to users (material/immaterial). In particularly serious or repeat cases, the period can be extended, and in less serious cases, it can be shortened.

### 2. Alleged rightholder

8 Under sub. 1, anyone who claims **another person's work** as his own or who claims the protection of a work in the **public domain** is subject to a measure against abuse. In the latter case, it does not matter whether the work is in the public domain because it does not meet the thresholds for protection or because the term of protection has expired. **Not included** are cases in which rightholders demand blocking even though they have either granted the concerned user a licence or otherwise authorised the use. Cases in which the rightholders demand blocking pursuant to § 8 (1) even though the use is clearly covered by a copyright exception cannot be sanctioned under sub. 1. The wording of sub. 1 also does not cover cases in which someone without the necessary authorisation asserts the rights to another person's work but discloses that he or she is not asserting his or her own rights. Here, the OCSSP can protect itself by requiring proof of the corresponding authorisation in the future.

### 3. No individual fault

9 According to the wording of the law, an objective violation of the provision is sufficient. This is supported in distinction from sub. 2, which requires intentional or negligent obstruction. Moreover, the legislature did not take up corresponding proposals for amendment in the legislative process. This makes sense because it is likely to be **difficult** for OCSSPs to **establish fault**. However, to protect rightholders, sub. 1 requires **repeated** unlawful **requests** to block. Here, the extent, interval and frequency with which a rightholder makes repeated requests for blocking can be taken into account (→ mn. 10).

### 4. Repeated blocking request

10 A rightholder might be excluded from the blocking procedure only after repeated unlawful blocking requests. If interpreted literally, the second abusive blocking request is already a repeated blocking request. However, exclusion from the blocking procedure is a significant sanction for rightholders because they cannot effectively enforce their copyrights on the platform during this period. Moreover, the purpose of the sanction is to prevent abuse of the blocking mechanism. The **principle of proportionality**, therefore, requires that 'repeated' be interpreted as the key **indicator of abuse**. No subjective requirements, such as fault, are to be required (→ mn. 9). Nevertheless, the circumstances of the unlawful blocking requests must **objectively indicate abuse**. In addition to the number of false reports, OCSSPs must consider other criteria, such as the interval between false reports and the quota of unlawful blocking requests in the total volume of

[13] BT-Drs. 19/27426, 145.
[14] With criticism: Spindler WRP 2021, 1245 mn. 26.

blocking requests. So that enforcement of copyrights is not unreasonably difficult, isolated false blocking requests must 'lapse' over time. Likewise, exclusion from the blocking procedure is disproportionate if the quota of false reports in the rightholder's total reporting volume is negligible, thus clearly indicating that the rightholder is not acting abusively. On the other hand, if complaint proceedings reveal that the alleged rightholder has purposely and in full possession of the facts usurped the rights of others, the protection of users' rights requires that sanctions be imposed even in the case of only a few unlawful requests. In blatant cases, for example, unlawful blocking requests were deliberately used to suppress inconvenient expressions of opinion, the sanction can already be imposed on the second infringement.

### 5. Single blocking request for several works or subject matter

A one-time unlawful blocking request does not trigger the rightholder's exclusion **11** from the blocking procedure under §§ 7 and 8. Because the provision uses the term 'repeatedly' (not several times), the same applies in principle if several works or subject matter have been wrongly designated for blocking in one notification procedure. However, if an alleged rightholder has obviously and to a **very considerable extent** appropriated works in the public domain or third-party works in a notification process, it must also be possible for the OCSSP to exclude such copyright trolls from further notifications on the basis of its terms of service (→ mn. 5). Otherwise, they violate their obligation of result under § 7 (2) sent. 1 (if applicable in conjunction with § 8 (2)) to make content available that is lawfully uploaded by users.

## III. Liability for damages (sub. 2)

### 1. Damages

If an **alleged rightholder** unlawfully requests the OCSSP to block another's work as **12** its own work or a work in the public domain, then rightholders is obliged to **compensate** the OCSSP and the affected users for the **damage incurred**. The provision thus sends an important signal to rightholders to exercise due diligence before requesting a blocking.[15] The OCSSP can also base its claim on the infringement of a duty of care of the legal obligation that arises from the blocking request (§§ 280 (1), 241 (2) BGB; → § 7 mn. 1). The claim for damages under sub. 2 does not require the repeated violation of the law; it also covers a **single unlawful blocking**.[16] In contrast to the measure in sub. 1, the unlawful blocking must have at least been negligent. The claim for damages is symbolically important. Still, in practice, it will hardly be of any significance because the damage caused by the violation of the law (→ mn. 16) usually cannot be substantiated or will be very small.

### 2. Unlawful blocking request

The claim for damages covers acts justifying the legal measures contained in sub. 1. **13** Pursuant to sub. 2 alt. 1, anyone who demands the blocking of **another person's work or subject matter as his or her own** is liable for damages. According to the wording of the provision, constellations are not covered in which someone openly demands the blocking of another person's work or subject matter and wrongly claims to be entitled to

[15] Leistner ZUM 2020, 505 (512).
[16] BT-Drs. 19/27426, 145.

do so. Legal persons cannot be the holder of a copyright under German law. In order to prevent the abusive assertion of works by legal persons, the obligation to pay damages will have to suffice if an alleged rightholder bases its blocking request on an exclusive licence to which it is not entitled. Anyone who demands the blocking of a work or subject matter **in the public domain** is subject to the obligation to pay damages under sub. 2 alt. 2. It is irrelevant whether the thresholds for copyright protection are not fulfilled or whether the term of protection has expired.

### 3. Intentional or negligent

14 For the concept of intent and negligence, the general principles of unjustified IP rights' warnings can be used.[17] A person who is aware of the legal situation and acts contrary to it or negligently misjudges the legal situation is at fault.[18] This is not the case if the person issuing the warning is convinced as a result of expert and legal advice that he or she is entitled to do so.[19]

### 4. Claimants

15 The **OCSSP** that received a blocking request as well as the **affected user** who uploaded the blocked content are entitled to claim damages.

### 5. Compensation for the damage incurred

16 §§ 249 et seqq. BGB apply for the further requirement and calculation of the damages. OCSSPs and users can each claim the caused and attributable damage. Substantiation of this might prove to be a difficult task.[20] For example, OCSSPs cannot claim costs for resources that occurred before the unlawful blocking request was made as the request was not a cause of those costs.[21] The same applies to the user's own time and effort to fend off the unlawful blocking. The user's immaterial damage is also not compensated. However, the costs of (external) lawyers are compensable in both cases.[22] In addition, professional YouTubers or influencers can claim compensation for the **lost profit** (§ 252 BGB) that they would have made with the blocked content. The court may decide on the amount of the lost profit at its discretion (*freie Überzeugung*) pursuant to § 287 (1) ZPO. This lowers the usual standard of proof to a preponderance of the evidence (*überwiegende Wahrscheinlichkeit*);[23] in cases of severe lack of evidence, the court may award minimum damages estimated on the basis of a 'certain probability' (*gewisse Wahrscheinlichkeit*).[24] The court may take the ordinary course of events as a basis for assessing damages and, therefore, base the estimate on the user's usual advertising income in comparable cases. The alleged rightholder then has the burden of proof of special circumstances that would have prevented the user from not realising the profit to be expected in the ordinary course of things.[25]

---

[17] Hofmann GRUR 2019, 1219 (1228); Wandtke/Hauck ZUM 2020, 671 (680).

[18] BGH 1.12.2015 – X ZR 170/12, GRUR 2016, 630 mn. 14 – Unberechtigte Schutzrechtsverwarnung II.

[19] BeckOGK/Spindler, 1.7.2022, BGB § 823 mn. 225.

[20] Spindler WRP 2021, 1245 mn. 24; Wagner GRUR 2020, 447 (452).

[21] Cf. MüKoBGB/Oetker, 9th edn 2022, BGB § 249 mn. 88 et seq.

[22] Cf. MüKoBGB/Oetker, 9th edn 2022, BGB § 249 mn. 180 et seq.

[23] BGH 14.2.2008 – I ZR 135/05, GRUR 2008, 933 mn. 19 – Schmiermittel; 9.11.2010 – VI ZR 300/08, NJW 2011, 1146 mn. 18, 22.

[24] BGH 26.7.2005 – X ZR 134/04, NJW 2005, 3348 (3349); 10.7.1979 – X ZR 23/78, GRUR 1979, 869 (870) – Oberarmschwimmringe; 22.04.1993 – I ZR 52/9, GRUR 1993, 757 (759) – Kollektion Holiday.

[25] MüKoBGB/Oetker, 9th edn 2022, BGB, § 252 mn. 40.

## IV. Exclusion of immediate and distortion-based blocking (sub. 3)

### 1. Exclusion for a reasonable time

The OCSSP must exclude a rightholder from the respective blocking mechanisms if the rightholder has repeatedly and wrongly requested immediate blocking under § 14 (4) or simple blocking under § 8 because of a distortion of his or her work. The OCSSP has no discretion but 'shall' (*ist … auszuschließen*) exclude the rightholder. The sanction does **not** require individual **fault** (→ mn. 9). The only requirement is a repeated, erroneous blocking request.[26] Furthermore, wrongful blocking requests affect the status of the trustworthy rightholder (→ § 14 mn. 14). **17**

### 2. Repeated incorrect requests for blocking

As compensation for the lack of individual fault, rightholders can only be excluded from the blocking procedures if they repeatedly incorrectly request the blocking mentioned in No. 1 or No. 2. Because these are different blocking requests, a requirement is that repeatedly incorrect blocking is requested in the **respective proceedings**. For the remaining requirements, reference can be made to the explanations in → mn. 10. **18**

### 3. Immediate blocking request (§ 14 (4)) (No. 1)

A trusted rightholder may, after examination by a natural person, request the **immediate blocking** of presumably legitimate uses during the complaint procedure under § 14 (4). The immediate blocking request is **incorrectly made** if it turns out in the subsequent complaint procedure either that the **use** was in fact **legitimate** or that the continued communication to the public during the complaint procedure did **not** cause **a danger** of significant impairment of the **economic exploitation of the work**.[27] **19**

### 4. Blocking request due to distortion (No. 2)

Rightholders may also request simple blocking pursuant to § 8 (1) during the complaint procedure on account of an infringement of their moral right due to distortion (§ 14 UrhG) (§ 13 (3)). The provision was included in the UrhDaG based on a proposal of the Committee on Legal Affairs to prevent abuse of the mechanism.[28] **20**

## V. Measures against abusive blocking (sub. 4)

### 1. Prevention of renewed abusive blocking

Spectacular cases are reported from time to time in which alleged rightholders usurp works that are in the public domain or are freely licenced.[29] This is not a rare phenomenon.[30] OCSSPs are therefore obliged by sub. 4 to use the findings from a **21**

[26] See also Spindler WRP 2021, 1245 mn. 25.
[27] BT-Drs. 19/27426, 145 et seq.; Spindler WRP 2021, 1245 mn. 25.
[28] BT-Drs. 19/29894, 94.
[29] Cf. for example Kaesling/Knapp MMR 2020, 816 (819) fn. 56 with further references.
[30] BT-Drs. 19/27426, 146.

corresponding complaint procedure to ensure to the best of their abilities after an abusive blocking request that the corresponding content is not blocked (abusively) again. A blocking request is already abusive if it was objectively unjustified because the subject matter claimed is in the public domain or the legitimate rightholder has allowed anyone to use it free of charge. The OCSSP has no discretion as to whether to take the necessary measures (English: *shall*; German: *hat … sicherzustellen*).

### 2. Public domain work or licenced free of charge or subject matter

22 Copyright-protected content is in the **public domain** if it either does not meet the protection thresholds required by the respective copyright or if the term of protection has expired. The use is permitted for anyone **free of charge**, particularly by open content licences such as the Creative Commons licences.[31]

### 3. Ensure to the best of its ability

23 Because the measures against renewed abusive blocking usually have to be integrated into the automated processes for content recognition and blocking, they are subject to the same technically induced shortcomings. In this respect, there is no obligation of result for OCSSPs, but a best-efforts obligation. OCSSPs must comply with this obligation by reference to § 1 (2), observing high standards customary in the industry within the framework of the principle of proportionality.

## VI. Exclusion from the flagging mechanism (sub. 5)

### 1. Abusive flagging

24 Users 'shall' be excluded by OCSSPs for a reasonable time from the possibility to flag uses as permitted under § 11 (1) No. 3 if they have repeatedly and incorrectly made use of this mechanism (false pre-flagging).[32] Here, too, **no individual fault is required**. The requirement is only objectively unjustified flagging. This is not restricted to the repeated flagging of the same content. The measure can be applied if the user has incorrectly flagged different content. However, the question of whether repeated incorrect flagging has occurred must also take into account the **time interval**, the **objective frequency** and the **quota of correct flagging** (also → mn. 10). Cases of incorrect flagging must 'lapse' over time. This should not be too strictly applied here because of the additional safeguard mechanisms (→ mn. 25), especially if the quota of correct and incorrect markings indicates that the user is not abusing the flagging mechanism. These criteria must also be taken into account in the reasonable length of the exclusion (also → mn. 7). Individual rightholders cannot enforce the measure in individual cases. However, if the OCSSP does not comply with its obligation under sub. 5, it does not comply with the general best efforts obligation to block unlawful content (→ mn. 2). In this case, it is no longer exempted from liability and communicates content to the public according to § 1 (1) if the flagging of the non-sanctioned user made the infringement possible.

### 2. Further safeguards

25 According to § 14 (4), trustworthy rightholders can rebut the presumption of a flagging. Abuse of this control mechanism is, in turn, sanctioned by sub. 3 No. 1.

[31] Dreier/Schulze/Dreier UrhG § 32 mn. 80 et seq.
[32] Hofmann ZUM 2020, 665 (668 et seq.); Stieper ZUM 2021, 387 (389).

Furthermore, the user is generally liable to the rightholder for the consequences of unlawful flagging and is subject to **injunctive relief** and **damages** under § 97 UrhG.[33]

## VII. Injunctive relief against OCSSPs for unauthorised blocking (sub. 6)

### 1. Injunctive relief

As a counterweight to the interests of the rightholders, which can be enforced with the help of injunctive relief and claims for damages, sub. 6 grants **registered associations** (*eingetragener Verein*) **for the promotion of users' interests** a right to injunctive relief against OCSSPs that have repeatedly and incorrectly blocked permitted uses on the basis of the UrhDaG. 26

### 2. Repeated and incorrect blocking in violation of subsection 4

The user association's right to injunctive relief exists if the OCSSP has repeatedly and incorrectly blocked permitted uses. These requirements are fulfilled if the OCSSP does not comply with its **obligation under sub. 4**. In this case, after a first incorrect blocking of a public domain work/subject matter or a work/subject matter for which use free of charge by anyone is permitted, the OCSSP has incorrectly blocked a work/subject matter a second time and thus repeatedly. It can then be obliged by the user association to make **best possible efforts** to ensure that the subject matter is not incorrectly blocked again. If the user association demonstrates that such an object has been blocked a second time after a first abusive blocking request, the OCSSP has the **secondary burden of demonstrating** (*sekundäre Darlegungslast*) that it has made best efforts to ensure that the content is not blocked again in accordance with high industry standards. 27

### 3. Repeated incorrect blocking

In addition to a violation of sub. 4, the user association can also use injunctive relief to claim that the OCSSP is not fulfilling its **obligation under § 7 (2) sent. 1**. Accordingly, the OCSSP must ensure that lawfully uploaded content will not be blocked. This is an **obligation of result** (→ § 7 mn. 21). This obligation is breached if the OCSSP repeatedly incorrectly blocks the same content or if it repeatedly incorrectly blocks different content. In that case, the OCSSP can be obliged by the user association to take organisational precautions to ensure that this incorrect blocking will not be repeated in the future. The same requirements apply here as to the inverse obligation to prevent unlawful uploads. The obligation needs to be complied with (as with sub. 4) in accordance with high industry standards of professional diligence, taking into account the principle of proportionality (§ 1 (2)). This can be accomplished, for example, by adjusting the threshold values of the filtering software so that it produces fewer false positives (→ § 7 mn. 19). There should not be a conflict of duties. The obligation not to incorrectly block lawful content ends when the obligation under § 7 (1) and § 8 (1) begins – and *vice versa*: The blocking efforts under § 7 (1) and § 8 (1) are limited by the duty under § 7 (2) sent. 1. However, insofar as the OCSSP is obliged under § 7 (2) sent. 2 in conjunction with §§ 9–11 to block the availability on the platform, the OCSSP is not in breach of the obligation under § 7 (2) sent. 1, for example, if a trusted rightholder has 28

[33] BT-Drs. 19/27426, 146; Spindler CR 2020, 50 (58); Becker ZUM 2020, 681 (690 et seq.).

made the declaration under § 14 (4). In this case, the abusive behaviour of the rightholder cannot be attributed to it.[34]

### 4. Repeated failure to impose sanctions under subs 1 and 2

29 The OCSSP may also breach its obligation under § 7 (2) by failing to **impose measures** under § 18 (1, 2) on **alleged rightholders**. If the requirements for sanctions are met, the OCSSP is obliged to impose measures against abuse (→ mn. 7). If the service provider fails to do so, it is in breach of the obligation to use best efforts to take organisational precautions to prevent incorrect blocking of lawful uses.

### 5. User association

30 Any **registered association** (*eingetragener Verein*) that has as its purpose to **promote the interests of users** of OCSSPs on a non-commercial and not merely temporary basis may claim the injunction. Although the association needs to operate non-commercially, it may act in the interest of commercial platform users.[35] In the government draft (RegE), an association was entitled to claim under § 3a UKlaG. However, the Committee on Legal Affairs proposed a clarification that the user association may not only assert (via the reference in § 2a UKlaG) the exceptions set out in § 95b UrhG but all grounds for legitimate use on which users may rely against rightholders.[36] The change that followed to the provision was not intended to change its purpose; thus, the corresponding terms of the UKlaG can be used for the interpretation of sub. 6. An activity is **non-commercial** if it is not aimed at generating income because the association is essentially financed from its own resources, in particular from membership fees, public funding and donations.[37] The activity is **not merely temporary** if it is intended to be permanent, that is, for longer than one year.[38]

## § 19
## Rights of access

**(1) The rightholder may demand information from the service provider on the use of his repertoire permitted by contract pursuant to § 4.**

**(2) The rightholder may request appropriate information from the service provider on the functioning of the procedures for blocking unauthorised uses of his repertoire pursuant to §§ 7 and 8.**

**(3) [1]The service provider shall grant authorised persons pursuant to § 60d subsection 2 of the Copyright Act access to data on the use of procedures for the automated and non-automated detection and blocking of content for the purpose of scientific research, insofar as overriding interests of the service provider worthy of protection do not conflict with**

## § 19
## Auskunftsrechte

**(1) Der Rechtsinhaber kann von dem Diensteanbieter Auskunft über die nach § 4 vertraglich erlaubte Nutzung seines Repertoires verlangen.**

**(2) Der Rechtsinhaber kann von dem Diensteanbieter angemessene Auskunft über die Funktionsweise der Verfahren zur Blockierung unerlaubter Nutzungen seines Repertoires nach den §§ 7 und 8 verlangen.**

**(3) [1]Der Diensteanbieter gewährt Berechtigten nach § 60d Absatz 2 des Urheberrechtsgesetzes zum Zweck der wissenschaftlichen Forschung Zugang zu Daten über den Einsatz von Verfahren zur automatisierten und nicht automatisierten Erkennung und Blockierung von Inhalten, soweit überwiegende schutzwürdige Interessen des Diensteanbieters nicht**

[34] BT-Drs. 19/27426, 146.
[35] Spindler WRP 2021, 1245 mn. 27.
[36] BT-Drs. 19/29894, 94.
[37] Walker UKlaG, § 4 mn. 4; Köhler/Bornkamm/Feddersen/Köhler, 39th edn 2021, UKlaG § 3a mn. 1.
[38] Grüneberg/Grüneberg, 81st edn 2022, UKlaG § 3a mn. 1.

**this. [2]The service provider shall be entitled to reimbursement of the costs thereby incurred to a reasonable amount.**

**entgegenstehen. [2]Der Diensteanbieter hat Anspruch auf Erstattung der hierdurch entstehenden Kosten in angemessener Höhe.**

**Bibliography:** Gerpott, 'Artikel 17 der neuen EU-Urheberrechtsrichtlinie: Fluch oder Segen? – Einordnung des Streits um "Upload-Filter" auf Online-Sharing-Plattformen', MMR 2019, 420; Specht-Riemenschneider, 'Studie zur Regulierung eines privilegierten Zugangs zu Daten für Wissenschaft und Forschung durch die regulatorische Verankerung von Forschungsklauseln in den Sektoren Gesundheit, Online-Wirtschaft, Energie und Mobilität', available at <https://www.jura.uni-bonn.de/fileadmin/Fachbereich_Rechtswissenschaft/Einrichtungen/Lehrstuehle/Specht/Dateien/2021-08-25-LSR.pdf> (as of 1.9.2021). – See also the bibliography in the Introduction.

**Content**



# I. General remarks

## 1. Objective

The three claims granted in § 19 are all intended to contribute to the creation of more **transparency** with regard to the services of OCSSPs.[1] This becomes particularly clear with regard to the right of access to research data pursuant to sub. 3: It is intended to guarantee research and science access to data on the use of procedures for the automated and non-automated detection and blocking of content in order to be able to examine these 1

[1] BT-Drs. 19/27426, 146; BT-Drs. 19/29894, 94 et seq.

procedures and check their lawfulness. Without such access to data, the procedures and algorithms used remain uncontrollable. Research and science are thus, in a sense, the eyes of civil society and the legislature. Accordingly, research data access also takes into account the growing social importance of OCSSPs both for creative work and for the formation of public opinion,[2] which – in the interest of civil society – are in urgent need of control. The research made possible by sub. 3 is intended to create a robust empirical basis for the public debate on a possible threat of structural over blocking by OCSSPs that would impair these fundamental rights.[3] Thus, sub. 3 also fills a potentially problematic gap left by the rightholders' right of access under sub. 2: The lack of a comparable user right to information with regard to blocking procedures has been criticised with regard to the fact that information on the functioning of these procedures may also be relevant for the protection of their fundamental rights.[4] The data access claim of research and science at least partially compensates for this missing direct claim of users. In the context of the right of access under sub. 1, information is also only an intermediate objective; with regard to contractually permitted uses, the right of access is intended to create the basis for rightholders to receive **appropriate remuneration**.[5]

### 2. EU law requirements

2 The rights of access in subs 1 and 2 implement the requirement of **Art. 17 (8) subpara. 2 DSMD**.[6] According to this, Member States must oblige OCSSPs to provide information at the request of rightholders on both the procedures for blocking their content and the use of licenced content. The right to grant access to research data, on the other hand, is not provided for in the DSMD itself. The claim is based on the protection of the users' freedom of speech and freedom of information which is statutorily guaranteed on the basis of national and EU law (Art. 11 CFR; → mn. 1) as well as on the freedom of science according to Art. 13 CFR.[7]

### 3. Origin

3 While the rights of access in subs 1 and 2 – with a slight linguistic difference – were provided for from the beginning of the legislative process, the right of access under sub. 3 was only inserted on the basis of the resolution recommendation of the Bundestag's **Committee on Legal Affairs**.[8]

## II. Right of access regarding the repertoire (sub. 1)

### 1. Capacity to sue

4 The right of access under sub. 1 is available to any **rightholder** who is also the licensor. This follows from the objective of the provision, which is intended to give the

[2] BT-Drs. 19/29894, 94 et seq.

[3] BT-Drs. 19/29894, 95.

[4] Specht-Riemenschneider, Leitlinien zur nationalen Umsetzung des Art. 17 DSM-RL aus Verbrauchersicht, 86; Spindler CR 2019, 277 (289); Würtenberger/Freischem GRUR 2019, 1140 (1161).

[5] COM(2021) 288 final, 26.

[6] BT-Drs. 19/27426, 146.

[7] Specht-Riemenschneider, Studie zur Regulierung eines privilegierten Zugangs zu Daten für Wissenschaft und Forschung durch die regulatorische Verankerung von Forschungsklauseln in den Sektoren Gesundheit, Online-Wirtschaft, Energie und Mobilität, 21 et seqq.

[8] BT-Drs. 19/29894, 94 et seq.; cf. also Specht-Riemenschneider, Stellungnahme zum Urheberdiensteanbietergesetz (UrhDaG), 32.

licensor a right of access that does not go beyond the user's duty to provide information under § 41 VGG and is intended to enable the calculation of an appropriate remuneration overall, just as § 41 VGG does.[9] Thus, the capacity to sue lies with authors granting licences, holders of exclusive rights of use granting licences as well as with the holders of related rights covered by § 21, provided they act as licensors. Holders of non-exclusive licences are not entitled to information because they cannot grant the OCSSP any further licence but can at most transfer their own licence, cf. § 34 (1) UrhG. Upon transfer of their licence, however, the repertoire used is no longer assigned to them, which is why the claim fails at this point at the latest. The same applies to the only alleged rightholder. In this case, too, the requirement of 'his repertoire' about which information could be provided is not fulfilled.

## 2. Capacity to be sued

The claim is directed against the **OCSSP as defined in § 2** that uses the protected works of the rightholder entitled to the claim. OCSSPs for sharing online content as defined in § 2 (1) are covered but start-up OCSSPs as defined in § 2 (2) and small OCSSPs as defined in § 2 (3) are not. After all, the OCSSP can only comply with the right of access if it can automatically detect which content is uploaded by its users. In principle, this requires the use of the same filtering software that is used for automated blocking, as blocking is technically not categorically different from the counting required for information. However, start-up OCSSPs and (rebuttably presumed) small OCSSPs are exempt from the use of such technology. This must also apply in a mirror image with regard to the right to information. 5

## 3. Content of the claim

Pursuant to sub. 1, the OCSSP must provide the rightholder with information on the **use** of his or her repertoire **permitted by contract pursuant to § 4**. '**Repertoire**' means the rights in works and other subject matter. Thus, the claim arises from the outset only if and to the extent that works to which the rightholder has the original copyright or related rights or the exclusive rights of use for communication to the public are communicated to the public based on a licence agreement. For statutorily permitted uses, the right of access arises from § 41 (1) sent. 1 VGG, insofar as a statutory claim to remuneration exists.[10] 6

## 4. Extent of the claim

Information must be provided about the use that the rightholder has contractually permitted. In fact, this is mainly about the transmission of the number of cases and the volume of use. According to the objective of the guarantee to provide information to calculate the appropriate remuneration, the turnover achieved with the use is also a necessary information.[11] What the rightholder additionally needs to know for this purpose depends on the respective licence agreement.[12] The claim limits of § 41 VGG apply,[13] which limit the duty to provide information in two respects. First, the information must be **necessary** to be able to claim appropriate remuneration from the OCSSP (cf. § 41 (1) sent. 1 VGG). Second, the information does not have to be 7

---

[9] Cf. BT-Drs. 19/27426, 146.
[10] Cf. Dreier/Schulze/Raue VGG § 41 mn. 2.
[11] COM(2021) 288 final, 26.
[12] Cf. BeckOK UrhR/Freudenberg, 40th edn., 1.8.2023, VGG § 41 mn. 3.
[13] BT-Drs. 19/27426, 146.

provided if it would only be possible for the OCSSP with an **unreasonably high effort** (cf. § 41 (1) sent. 2 VGG).[14] The OCSSP must make certain efforts to gather and prepare the necessary information. However, the effort involved must be in reasonable proportion to the acts of use undertaken and the resulting claim to remuneration.[15] At this point, differences may arise, particularly among OCSSPs for sharing online content, start-up OCSSPs and small OCSSPs. However, an unreasonably high effort for comprehensive information does not exclude the right of access; it limits the extent of the right of access only to that information the provision of which is reasonable according to what has been said.[16]

### 5. Competing claims and disputes

8 The statutory right to information stands independently alongside a possible **contractual right to information** of the rightholder against the OCSSP.[17] If the OCSSP has agreed in the licence agreement to provide other or more comprehensive information to the rightholder, this agreement is not affected by sub. 1. Conversely, the right to information under sub. 1 cannot be excluded in the licence agreement. Pursuant to § 22, this is mandatory law (→ § 22 mn. 1) prescribed by the DSMD in Art. 17 (8). Likewise, the right of access under sub. 1 has no effect on the right to information of the collecting societies against OCSSPs as users of those works for which the collecting societies hold the rights of use under § 41 VGG.[18] In cases of dispute, recourse can be had to out-of-court arbitration under §§ 16 and 17 in addition to the courts.[19]

## III. Right of access regarding blocking (sub. 2)

### 1. Capacity to sue

9 With regard to the information pursuant to sub. 2, the '**rightholder**' is entitled to claim under the wording of the law. Just like sub. 1, the wording of sub. 2 does not contain a restriction on the group of persons entitled to claim, but just like sub. 1, sub. 2 is to be limited teleologically to the author, the holder of neighbouring rights pursuant to § 21 and the holder of an exclusive licence. According to its objective, sub. 2 serves to prepare claims for recourse and injunctive relief against insufficient action by OCSSPs with regard to the blocking of content. However, the holder of a non-exclusive licence cannot assert such claims against the OCSSP.

### 2. Capacity to be sued

10 Every **OCSSP** that uses the protected works of the rightholder entitled to claim is capable of being sued. As in sub. 1, neither the wording nor the telos of the provision limits the circle of parties capable of being sued with regard to start-up OCSSPs or small OCSSPs in sub. 2. Only OCSSPs within the meaning of § 3 are excluded from the scope of application of the UrhDaG and, therefore are not capable of being sued for a claim under § 19 (2).

---

[14] Cf. Dreier/Schulze/Raue VGG § 41 mn. 3.
[15] Cf. BeckOK UrhR/Freudenberg, 40th edn, 1.8.2023, VGG § 41 mn. 4.
[16] Cf. BeckOK UrhR/Freudenberg, 40th edn, 1.8.2023, § 41 mn. 4.
[17] BT-Drs. 19/27426, 146.
[18] Cf. COM(2021) 288 final, 26.
[19] BT-Drs. 19/27426, 146.

### 3. Content of the claim

11 The claim is directed at the provision of information on the **functioning** of the procedures by which the OCSSP complies with its obligation to block pursuant to §§ 7 and 8.

### 4. Extent of the claim

12 The scope of the claim under sub. 2 is limited: The OCSSP must only provide **appropriate information**. Appropriate information is information which, on the one hand, is detailed enough to make the procedures used sufficiently transparent for the rightholders but, on the other hand, does not have a detrimental effect on the trade secrets of the OCSSP.[20] Appropriateness is thus also and precisely to be determined according to the objective of the provision. The information that OCSSPs must provide pursuant to sub. 2 is the result of an individual assessment based on the specific circumstances of each case.[21] This assessment must be guided by the question of what information is necessary to determine whether the OCSSP is sufficiently fulfilling its obligations under §§ 7 and 8. Due to the high effort involved, OCSSPs are not obliged to provide detailed and individual information on each protected work (cf. recital 68 DSMD), nor are they obliged to disclose the source code of the software used for blocking[22] or to describe the characteristics of this software in detail.[23] However, in order to fulfil the right of access, they can, for example, describe in abstract terms the type of means used, provide information on third-party providers whose technologies they use, indicate the average efficiency of these technologies and changes thereto (such as updates or changes concerning the use of third-party providers)[24] and provide information on training data and blocking decisions. The protection of business secrets is not a reason to generally refuse to provide the information. Rather, the information must be blacked out or shortened as regards the data that are subject to business secrecy protection. Here, the requirements of Art. 15 (4) GDPR that appropriately resolves the conflict between the right of access and the protection of business secrets can be used as a guideline. The general parameters for the use of the technologies used should also be specified.[25]

### 5. Competing claims

13 The statutory right of access on blocking procedures stands independently alongside a possible **contractual right to information** of the rightholder (recital 68 DSMD). Sub. 2 does not affect the OCSSP's obligation to provide additional or more detailed information based on a licence agreement. Conversely, it is not possible to contractually waive the statutory right of access. This is contrary to § 22 (→ § 22 mn. 1).

### 6. Criticism, necessary expansion

14 The right of access under sub. 2 is too narrow in personal and, closely related to this, in factual terms. From a personal point of view, it should be extended to **associations**

[20] BT-Drs. 19/27426, 146 with reference to recital 68 DSMD; COM(2021) 288 final, 25 et seq.
[21] Gerpott MMR 2019, 420 (425).
[22] Spindler CR 2019, 277 (289).
[23] COM(2021) 288 final, 26.
[24] See also COM(2021) 288 final, 25 et seq.
[25] Commission, Targeted consultation addressed to the participants to the stakeholder dialogue on Article 17 of the Directive on Copyright in the Digital Single Market, 19.

**under § 3a UKlaG**, and from a factual point of view to **information on the number and content of unlawful blockings**. After all, the associations under § 3a UKlaG are entitled under § 18 (6) to claim injunctive relief from the OCSSP in the event of repeated unlawful blocking of authorised uses. In practice, however, they can only do this if they can also take note of these events. This would be ensured by a corresponding extension of the right of access in the two directions mentioned.[26]

## IV. Right of access to research data (sub. 3)

### 1. Right to be granted access (sub. 3 sent. 1)

#### a) Entitlement character

15 Finally, § 19 (3) contains a derived research data access claim. It is derived because it is based on the already existing data access claim in sub. 2. Even if the wording at first glance seems to call into question the claim character of sub. 3 ('shall grant […] access to data'), sub. 3 is also intended to have a genuine claim character according to its objective.[27]

#### b) Capacity to sue

16 According to sub. 3 sent. 1, all **rightholders within the meaning of § 60d (2) UrhG** are entitled to be granted access. These are research organisations (§ 60d (2) sent. 1 UrhG), that is, universities, research institutes and other institutions that conduct scientific research and alternatively or cumulatively fulfil one of the following three conditions: They pursue non-commercial purposes (§ 60 (2) sent. 2 No. 1 UrhG), they reinvest all profits they make in scientific research (§ 60d (2) sent. 2. No. 2 UrhG) or they are active in the **public interest** within the framework of a state-recognised mandate (§ 60d (2) sent. 2 No. 3 UrhG). Therefore, commercial research organisations are not excluded at the outset from the personal scope of application.[28] However, even research organisations that fulfil the conditions of § 60d (2) sent. 2 have no capacity to sue if they cooperate with a private company that exerts a determining influence on them and obtains privileged access to the results of their scientific research (§ 60d (2) sent. 3 UrhG). Thus, whether the research organisation is entitled to claim depends largely on the design of the public–private–partnership.[29] In addition to the research organisation itself, the individual researchers who belong to it are also entitled to this right.[30] There is no restriction to a specific subject area: the research organisation can conduct research in both the humanities and the natural sciences (recital 12 DSMD).[31]

#### c) Capacity to be sued

17 According to sub. 3 sent. 1, every **OCSSP** is obligated to grant access. Here, too, there is no differentiation between OCSSPs according to § 2 (1), (2) and (3). Only OCSSPs according to § 3 UrhDaG have no capacity of being sued.

---

[26] Specht-Riemenschneider, Stellungnahme zum Urheberdiensteanbietergesetz (UrhDaG), 31 et seq.

[27] Cf. BT-Drs. 19/29894, 95.

[28] Specht-Riemenschneider, Studie zur Regulierung eines privilegierten Zugangs zu Daten für Wissenschaft und Forschung durch die regulatorische Verankerung von Forschungsklauseln in den Sektoren Gesundheit, Online-Wirtschaft, Energie und Mobilität, 63.

[29] Specht-Riemenschneider, Studie zur Regulierung eines privilegierten Zugangs zu Daten für Wissenschaft und Forschung durch die regulatorische Verankerung von Forschungsklauseln in den Sektoren Gesundheit, Online-Wirtschaft, Energie und Mobilität, 64.

[30] BT-Drs. 19/29894, 95.

[31] For more details on the term 'research organisation' cf. Dreier/Schulze/Dreier UrhG § 60d mn. 5.

**d) Eligibility requirements**

The access claim under sub. 3 sent. 1 has two prerequisites. First, access to the data must be granted **for the purpose of scientific research**. The term must be understood in the same way as that in § 60d (1) UrhG. From a systematic point of view, this follows from the fact that the term research organisation in sub. 3 sent. 1 is also based on the identical term in § 60d UrhG. Therefore, any activity that pursues the goal of gaining new knowledge in a methodical, systematic and verifiable manner is covered.[32] Second, the granting of access must **not conflict with any overriding interests of the OCSSP that are worthy of protection**. To determine whether the OCSSP's interest that is worthy of protection outweighs the public interest in research, the fundamental rights concerned must be weighed.[33] In particular, the former may prevail if the confidentiality interests of the OCSSP would be unreasonably impaired by the data access.[34] However, a mere impairment is not sufficient; it must be unreasonable and thus substantial. It can be concluded from this that the legislature generally assumes that the research data access interest prevails. Only in individual cases can the fundamental rights be weighed in favour of the OCSSP's interest in secrecy through appropriate explanations. If confidentiality interests or the OCSSP's protection of business secrets are held against the research data access claim, this interest can generally also be met through blacking out and shortening without having to lead to an exclusion of the claim. On the other hand, according to the clear wording of sub. 3, **conflicting interests of third parties** (such as their personal rights or business secrets) do not constitute a **barrier to the** right of access. In any case, it is intended that the DSMD be consistent with the GDPR (cf. recital 85 of the GDPR). In this respect, at least the GDPR restricts Art. 19 (3) by requiring blacking out and shortening if necessary. 18

**e) Content of the claim**

The OCSSP must grant the rightholder access to data on its use of procedures for the automated and non-automated detection and blocking of content. The claim thus goes further in two respects than the rightholders' right of access under sub. 2. First, the access claim concerns not only the functioning of the blocking procedures under §§ 7 and 8, but **all content recognition and blocking processes**, regardless of whether or not these procedures are carried out by the OCSSP in an automated manner. This should include, for example, not only information on the filtering technologies used and the type of content affected but also information on how the OCSSP deals with complaints about (failed) blocking and other decisions about restrictions on the communication of content to the public.[35] Second, the right under sub. 3 goes beyond the right of access under sub. 2 in that the OCSSP is not obliged to provide information but must grant access to the data. This requires that the OCSSP provides the claimant with not only a (possibly subjectively tinged) summary but also **the data itself**. Sub. 3 does not contain specifications on the format or the 19

---

[32] Specht-Riemenschneider, Studie zur Regulierung eines privilegierten Zugangs zu Daten für Wissenschaft und Forschung durch die regulatorische Verankerung von Forschungsklauseln in den Sektoren Gesundheit, Online-Wirtschaft, Energie und Mobilität, 63.

[33] Specht-Riemenschneider, Studie zur Regulierung eines privilegierten Zugangs zu Daten für Wissenschaft und Forschung durch die regulatorische Verankerung von Forschungsklauseln in den Sektoren Gesundheit, Online-Wirtschaft, Energie und Mobilität, 71.

[34] BT-Drs. 19/29894, 95.

[35] BT-Drs. 19/29894, 95.

procedure of provision. However, it is necessary to use a format common in research and science to effectively guarantee the data access claim.

#### f) Necessary extension

20 The right to be granted access to research data should be broadened in personal terms. The restriction to mainly non-commercial research, which is made by the reference to § 60d UrhG, is too far-reaching to help the claim achieve comprehensive practical validity. Instead of the institution or person conducting the research, the **purpose of the research should be taken into account**. This could certainly be defined as being oriented towards the common good, which can also include commercial research. This research purpose alone justifies access to research data, not the non-commerciality of the research. Risks to the rights of third parties can and should be countered by restrictions on the use of the data and specific requirements for accessing the data.[36]

### 2. Right to reimbursement of costs (sub. 3 sent. 2)

#### a) Capacity to sue

21 The claim for reimbursement of costs is available to any **OCSSP** that has granted data access to an entitled person pursuant to sub. 3 sent. 1.

#### b) Capacity to be sued

22 The opposing party to the claim is the **entitled party** who has received access to the research data. This is not clear from the wording of the provision, but it follows from the systematic connection with sub. 1.

#### c) Content of the claim

23 The OCSSP can demand that it be reimbursed for the costs that were **actually incurred** because it granted the authorised party access to the research data. The OCSSP may not make a profit from this; it is only permitted to cover the costs.[37] Furthermore, the OCSSP cannot pass on the costs of data collection to the beneficiary. Financing these is the sole responsibility of the OCSSP. Otherwise, there would be a risk of overly high cost-reimbursement claims, which would make research data access unattractive in practice.

#### d) Extent of the claim

24 The reimbursement of costs cannot be demanded without limit. Rather, the OCSSP must only be reimbursed the costs to a **reasonable amount**. It must be taken into account that the costs shall not be prohibitively high. Otherwise, the right to be granted access would in practice run empty.[38]

---

[36] Specht-Riemenschneider, Studie zur Regulierung eines privilegierten Zugangs zu Daten für Wissenschaft und Forschung durch die regulatorische Verankerung von Forschungsklauseln in den Sektoren Gesundheit, Online-Wirtschaft, Energie und Mobilität, 159 et seq.

[37] Cf. also Specht-Riemenschneider, Studie zur Regulierung eines privilegierten Zugangs zu Daten für Wissenschaft und Forschung durch die regulatorische Verankerung von Forschungsklauseln in den Sektoren Gesundheit, Online-Wirtschaft, Energie und Mobilität, 146 et seq.

[38] BT-Drs. 19/29894, 96; on comparable, already existing provisions: Specht-Riemenschneider, Studie zur Regulierung eines privilegierten Zugangs zu Daten für Wissenschaft und Forschung durch die regulatorische Verankerung von Forschungsklauseln in den Sektoren Gesundheit, Online-Wirtschaft, Energie und Mobilität, 77.

## § 20
## Domestic agent to receive service

**§ 5 subsection 1 of the Network Enforcement Act shall accordingly apply to the service provider's obligation to appoint a domestic agent to receive service.**

## § 20
## Inländischer Zustellungsbevollmächtigter

**Für die Verpflichtung des Diensteanbieters zur Bestellung eines inländischen Zustellungsbevollmächtigten für das gerichtliche Verfahren gilt § 5 Absatz 1 des Netzwerkdurchsetzungsgesetzes entsprechend.**

**Bibliography:** See the bibliography in the Introduction.

**Content**



## I. Objective

The OCSSP must appoint an authorised agent for service in Germany to ensure that **effective judicial enforcement** is not hindered by the necessity of service abroad. This is intended to address concerns that OCSSPs based abroad have rejected documents served in the German language in the past, for example, in Ireland, with reference to a lack of language skills.[1] § 20 largely refers to § 5 (1) NetzDG. 1

## II. EU law requirements

Art. 17 DSMD does not contain a specific obligation to designate a domestic agent for service of process. However, the requirement can be based on the general requirement for effective remedies for users **(Art. 17 (9) subpara. 2 DSMD)** as well as the general obligation under EU law to effectively protect copyright (e.g., **Art. 8 (1) InfoSoc Directive; Art. 3 Enforcement Directive**). Art. 11 (1) DSA requires a provider of intermediary services without establishment in the EU to designate a legal representative in *one* Member State and, therefore, not necessarily in Germany. But this is a minimum requirement for a non-EU-service provider and should not prevent Member States from introducing additional requirements for all service providers. 2

## III. Domestic agent for service of documents

The domestic service agent can be either a natural person or a legal entity. It must be authorised by the OCSSP and have the logistics to accept and process formal service in Germany.[2] The OCSSP only has to appoint the agent for **court proceedings**. The legislature did not take up suggestions in the legislative procedure to appoint the 3

[1] Cf. KG ZUM-RD 2019, 569 (570) on § 5 NetzDG old version.
[2] BT-Drs. 19/27426, 64.

representative as a receiving agent for all legally relevant acts under the UrhDaG. Service can be effected for **court proceedings** before German courts for all disputes about blocking or about the communication of content to the public by OCSSPs.[3] Thus, the provision covers put-back claims by users against OCSSPs on a contractual basis (→ § 5 mn. 4) (cf. § 5 (1) sent. 2 NetzDG). This also applies to service of documents initiating such proceedings, service of final court decisions and service in **enforcement or execution proceedings** (§ 5 (1) sent. 3 NetzDG). OCSSPs must **provide information** about the authorised agent in an easily recognisable and directly accessible manner on their platforms (§ 5 (1) sent. 1 NetzDG).

## § 21 Application to related rights

**(1) This Act shall apply accordingly to related rights within the meaning of the Copyright Act and their rightholders.**

**(2) Only the photographer and the performer shall be entitled to the direct remuneration pursuant to § 4.**

## § 21 Anwendung auf verwandte Schutzrechte

**(1) Dieses Gesetz ist auf verwandte Schutzrechte im Sinne des Urheberrechtsgesetzes und ihre Inhaber entsprechend anzuwenden.**

**(2) Der Direktvergütungsanspruch nach § 4 steht nur dem Lichtbildner und dem ausübenden Künstler zu.**

**Bibliography:** See the bibliography in the Introduction.

**Content**



## I. Objective

1 According to the provision, the UrhDaG is applicable *mutatis mutandis* **to all related rights** of the Copyright Act (UrhG) and, thus, extends the liability of OCSSPs to all rights protected under the UrhG. In principle, the term 'work' in the provisions §§ 1–20 can thus be expanded to include 'and related rights'. This is partly an autonomous decision of the German legislature as the extension to all related rights was not required by Art. 17 DSMD (→ mn. 2). At the suggestion of the Committee on Legal Affairs, the **direct remuneration right** in § 4 (3) was limited to **photographers** and **performing artists**, whose protection is based partly on personality rights. Because the UrhDaG is only applicable *mutatis mutandis*, the different nature of the related rights can be taken into account. For performing artists, the protection against distortion under § 13 (3) is, therefore, not based on § 14 UrhG but on the more specific § 75 UrhG.[1] Furthermore, the fact that the remuneration right cannot be waived and of its limited assignability in § 5 (2) sent. 3 should not be applied to related rights that are transferable (→ § 5 mn. 9).

---

[3] BT-Drs. 19/27426, 147.

[1] BT-Drs. 19/29894, 96.

## II. EU law requirements

Art. 17 (1) subpara. 2 DSMD only requires the Member States to extend the liability regime to the related rights listed in Art. 3 (1) and (2) InfoSoc Directive: **Performers, phonogram producers, film producers** and **broadcasting organisations**. The extension to all other related rights of the UrhG includes, for example, **photographers**. The latter is unproblematic under EU law due to the opening clause in Art. 6 (3) DSMD. Whether that also applies to the inclusion of the **press publisher's right** is not entirely clear due to the fully harmonising provision in Art. 15 DSMD. But due to the reference to Art. 3 (2) InfoSoc Directive, it is in conformity with EU law.[2] The inclusion of the **database producer** is also doubtful because the harmonising effect of the Database Directive is diminished by its inclusion. According to the explanatory memorandum to the UrhDaG, the inclusion of the database producer was intentional.[3] In the case of non-harmonised related rights, the German legislature is not subject to any restrictions (stricter → § 12 mn. 10). 2

## § 22 Mandatory provisions

**The provisions of this Act may not be derogated from by contract.**

## § 22 Zwingendes Recht

**Von den Vorschriften dieses Gesetzes kann durch Vertrag nicht abgewichen werden.**

**Bibliography:** See also bibliography in the Introduction.

**Content**



## I. Objective

According to § 22, the provisions of the UrhDaG are **non-dispositive law**. The parties affected by the law cannot waive or alter the provision bi- or trilaterally – neither in general terms and conditions nor in individual agreements. Corresponding agreements are invalid according to § 22 and not according to § 134 BGB because the provision already **restricts the legal ability** of the parties.[1] For example, according to § 5 (1), rightholders cannot require in their licence agreements with OCSSPs that the OCSSPs prohibit their users from making content available on the platform that is covered by copyright exception – or to make such acts *de facto* impossible (→ § 5 mn. 1, 4). The same applies to corresponding prohibitions that OCSSPs want to impose on their users in terms of service. In addition, OCSSPs and rightholders cannot contractually waive the right to information under § 19 (1) (→ § 19 mn. 8). 1

---

[2] Stieper ZUM 2021, 387 (393 et seq.).

[3] BT-Drs. 19/27426, 147.

[1] See MüKoBGB/Armbrüster, 9th edn 2021, BGB § 134 mn. 9.

## II. EU law requirements

2 Art. 17 (7) DSMD requires that cooperation between OCSSPs and rightholders must not result in the unavailability of content uploaded by users, even though it does not infringe copyright.

## III. International scope of application

3 § 22 is applicable in any case if German law is applicable as the **contracting statute** on the basis of the Rome I Regulation (→ Introduction mn. 13).[2] Furthermore, § 22 is to be regarded as an **overriding mandatory provision** within the meaning of Art. 9 Rome I Regulation. It not only serves to balance individual interests but also the general interest in the availability on platforms of content that is exempted by exceptions.[3]

---

[2] Cf. the overview in Dreier/Schulze/Raue Vor § 120 mn. 71 et seqq.
[3] Cf. for general information on the requirements: Dreier/Schulze/Raue Vor § 120 mn. 80.